Africa at the Crossroads:
Theorising Fundamentalisms
in the 21st Century

Edited by

Artwell Nhemachena
&
Munyaradzi Mawere

Langaa Research & Publishing CIG
Mankon, Bamenda

Publisher
Langaa RPCIG
Langaa Research & Publishing Common Initiative Group
P.O. Box 902 Mankon
Bamenda
North West Region
Cameroon
Langaagrp@gmail.com
www.langaa-rpcig.net

Distributed in and outside N. America by African Books Collective
orders@africanbookscollective.com
www.africanbookscollective.com

ISBN-10: 9956-764-08-6

ISBN-13: 978-9956-764-08-2

List of Contributors

Munyaradzi Mawere holds a PhD in Social Anthropology from the University of Cape Town (UCT) in South Africa. Professor Mawere also holds a Master's Degree in Social Anthropology from UCT, a Master's Degree in Development Studies, and Master's Degree in Philosophy and B. A. (Hons) Degree in Philosophy from the University of Zimbabwe. He is currently Professor in the Department of Culture and Heritage Studies at Great Zimbabwe University. Before joining this university, Professor Mawere was a lecturer at the University of Zimbabwe and at Universidade Pedagogica, Mozambique, where he has worked in different capacities as a Senior lecturer, Assistant Research Director, Postgraduate Co-ordinator and Associate Professor. He has an outstanding publishing record of more than one hundred and twenty pieces of work which include more than twenty-five books and over a hundred book chapters and papers in scholarly journals. Professor Mawere has published extensively on poverty and community development, knowledge studies, political anthropology, science and technology studies (STS), environment and agrarian issues, democracy and African states, coloniality, decoloniality and transformation, African philosophy and political systems, culture and heritage studies. Some of his bestselling books are: *Humans, Other Beings and the Environment: Harurwa (Edible stinkbugs) and Environmental Conservation in South-eastern Zimbabwe* (2015); *Democracy, Good Governance and Development in Africa: A Search for Sustainable Democracy and Development*, (2015); *Culture, Indigenous Knowledge and Development in Africa: Reviving Interconnections for Sustainable Development* (2014); *Harnessing Cultural Capital for Sustainability: A Pan Africanist Perspective* (2015); *Divining the Future of Africa: Healing the Wounds, Restoring Dignity and Fostering Development*, (2014); *African Cultures, Memory and Space: Living the Past Presence in Zimbabwean Heritage* (2014); *African Philosophy and Thought Systems: A Search for a Culture and Philosophy of Belonging* (2016); *Colonial Heritage, Memory and Sustainability in Africa: Challenges, Opportunities and Prospects* (2016); *Development Perspectives from the South: Troubling the Metrics of [Under-]development in Africa* (2017); and *Theorising*

Development in Africa: Towards Building an African Framework of Development (2017).

Artwell Nhemachena holds a PhD in Social Anthropology from the University of Cape Town in South Africa. Dr Nhemachena has studied Sociology and Social Anthropology. He has lectured at several universities in Zimbabwe including the University of Zimbabwe, Women's University in Africa and Great Zimbabwe University before pursuing PhD studies in South Africa. His current areas of interest include Indigenous Knowledge Systems, Environment, Democratic Governance, Social Theory from the South, Decoloniality and Transformation, African Jurisprudence, Human Security, Food Security and Food Sovereignty, Conflict and Violence, Poverty and Development, Science and Technology Studies. He has published on Democracy, Environment, Indigenous Knowledge, Decoloniality, Health, Resilience and Theory.

Nokuthula Hlabangane was awarded a PhD in Anthropology in 2012 by the University of the Witwatersrand, South Africa. Her doctoral thesis is titled "The political economy of teenage sexuality in the time of HIV/AIDS: The case of Soweto, South Africa". Her research interests include knowledge and power; how these intersect to form a potent and dangerous potent that informs various levels of life. So far, her research interests have directed her towards home – she chooses to be a student in her own community – the reasons have been both ideological and practical. Her ethics are about redress and restoration and as such she has a vested interest in decolonizing anthropology (and the academy at large) by painting pictures of strength and resilience where others have left bleak images of savagery and inferiority. Her research practices shy away from delving into cultural pluralism, a fascination with the thick description of the mundane-made-exotic. Rather, she attempts to interpret micro-practices through macro-systems. Her thinking is informed by decolonial meditations that places a responsibility for African(ist) intellectuals to see Africa from within. She also gravitates towards trans-disciplinarity in her work. Hlabangane teaches at the University of South Africa.

Oliver Mtapuri is a professor at the University of Kwa-Zulu Natal. He holds a PhD in Development studies (UKZN) and an MBA degree from the University of Zimbabwe. He is an Associate of the Institute of Chartered Secretaries and Administrators. Before joining the academe, Oliver worked for 12 years in the Government of Zimbabwe as a Labour Economist/Researcher in the Ministry of Labour and Social Welfare. Prior to joining UKZN, Oliver was a full Professor at the University of Limpopo. Oliver's areas of research interest include poverty, redistribution and inequality, community-based tourism, public employment programmes, research methodologies, financial management, climate change and project management. Recently he has taken a keen interest in the nexus between the environment and poverty and the "Anthropocene" particularly in light of the surfacing of many 'poverties' and many 'inequalities' afflicting contemporary societies. Oliver was the Editor in Chief (Founding) of the *Journal of Business and Public Dynamics for Development.*

Bankie Forster Bankie was born in Europe of African parenthood, a lawyer by training, with experience in diplomacy, the Academy and Youth matters. His research areas of interest are inter- African relations/Pan-Africanism, Afro-Arab relations, Diasporas/African integration and Sudanese studies. After 1972, he resided in a number of African countries in West, South and North East Africa. From 1984 – 6 served as Charge d'Affaires at the Ghana Embassy in Luanda, Angola with concurrent responsibility for Congo (Brazzaville), SWAPO, ANC and FRETLINE (East Timor). Residence starts in Namibia in 1991. Work starts in the Transitional Planning Team (TPT) for the new University of Namibia (UNAM), as Personal and Executive Assistant to The Vice-Chancellor Designate, which University was established by law in 1992. Thereafter, he served as Staff Development Officer for the new University, going on to the new Faculty of Law, as Researcher in the Human Rights and Documentation Centre. In 1996 joined the Secretariat of the Law Reform and Development Commission of The Ministry of Justice, serving as Researcher and acted as assistant to The Government Coordinator for Human Rights. Between 2000 and 2004, Bankie served as Head of Administration in The Centre for

Advanced Studies of African Society (CASAS) in Cape Town, South Africa. Thereafter he returned to Namibia and in 2006-8 worked in Juba, South Sudan in an administrative capacity towards the establishment and in the Kush Institution, in the Office of the President of South Sudan. He worked for five years at the National Youth Council of Namibia (NYCN) as acting Secretary to its Board and Sub-Committees, trained Youth on Pan-Africanism in the Youth Leadership Development Program (YDLP). Internationalist, since November 2015 Director of the Pan-African Institute for the Study of African Society (PAISAS) Trust, in Windhoek, Namibia.

Munesti Ruzivo holds a PhD in Religious Studies. He is currently teaching in the Department of Religious Studies, Philosophy and Classics at the University of Zimbabwe.

Tasara Muguti is registered with UNISA as a PhD candidate. He holds an M.A and B.A Hons in Economic History, Grad. C.E, Lecturer-Department of History and Development Studies, Great Zimbabwe University, Masvingo, Zimbabwe, e-mail address: muguti.tasara4@gmail.com

Nkwazi Mhango is the author of *Saa ya Ukombozi* (Tanzania Educational Publishers (TEPU), 2009), *Nyuma ya Pazia* (Langaa RPCIG, 2015) (Swahili fiction), *Souls on Sale* (Langaa RPCIG, 2015), *Born with Voice* (Langaa RPCIG, 2015), *Psalm for the Oppressed* (Langaa RPCIG, 2016) (English poetry), *Africa Reunite or Perish* (Langaa RPCIG, 2015), and *Africa's Best and Worst Presidents: How Neocolonialism and Imperialism Maintained Venal Rules in Africa* (Langaa RPCIG, 2016) (Scholarly tomes). Other five manuscripts are in the pipeline. Mhango is a staunch proponent of deconstruction theory that he has been working on based on Africanology as new ways of addressing Africa's problems. So, too, Mhango is a poet, teacher, columnist, Human Right Activist, Journalist, Peace and Conflict Scholar, and member of Writers' Association of Newfoundland and Labrador (WANL) St. John's, NL, Canada; also has contributed five chapters in various scholarly books; and an alumnus of Universities of Dar es Salaam (Tanzania) Winnipeg and Manitoba (Canada) respectively.

Fidelis Peter Thomas Duri is a lecturer in the Department of History and Development Studies at Great Zimbabwe University. He is a holder of a PhD in History from the University of the Witwatersrand in Johannesburg, South Africa. He has published a number of books and articles which focus on environmental history, socio-cultural dynamics, subaltern struggles, African border studies and politics in Zimbabwe during the colonial and post-colonial periods. He has also reviewed and edited a number of scholarly books and articles and is also a member of the editorial boards of international journals such as the *Zimbabwe Journal of Historical Studies* and the *International Journal of Developing Societies*.

Tobias Dindi Ong'aria is a Kenyan, a Jesuit, trained as a journalist. He is currently a student of Philosophy at Arrupe College, Jesuit School of Philosophy and Humanities, in Harare Zimbabwe. Some of his published works include: *Towards Peace Journalism: Assessing the Role of the Media in Ethnic Conflicts in Africa*, in Chiedza Journal of Arrupe College, Vol 17, No. 2 May 2015 and *Philosophy and Africa: Reading Kwame Appiah*, in Chiedza Journal of Arrupe College, Vol 18, No. 2 May 2016. He has also served The Editor of two issues of Chiedza Journal; *Overcoming the Dependency Syndrome in Africa* (Vol.18, No.1) and *Reviewing the Concepts of Leadership in Africa* (Volume 18, No.2).

Tafirenyika Madziyauswa was born in Bulawayo in Zimbabwe in 1972 and did part of primary school there. It was in Gweru where he completed his primary schooling. He attended Nashville and Chaplin High schools for Ordinary and Advanced level education, respectively. He holds a teaching qualification (Diploma in Education- Secondary) from the now defunct Gweru Teachers' College, a Bachelor of Arts Honours Degree in English and Communication and a Master of Arts in African Diasporean Literature, both from Midlands State University in Gweru, Zimbabwe. He has extensive teaching experience having taught English, Literature in English and History at a number of schools in Zimbabwe. I briefly taught Communication Skills (2006-2007) as a pilot project at Midlands State University, as a teaching Assistant. He has also taught English and English for Speakers of Other Languages at International Training College in Namibia from 2014 to March 2016. Currently, he is a PhD candidate at the University of Witwatersrand in Johannesburg, South Africa. His research interests include auto/biography, Caribbean and Afro-American literature, African literature especially Zimbabwean, South African, Kenyan and Nigerian literature, children literature, identity studies, ageing and older people in literature, language planning and policy and is also interested in Judith Butler's gender performativity theory.

Benias Tirivaviri holds Masters in Strategic Management, BSc Agriculture Management, former Regional Coordinator, National Association of non-governmental organization (NANGO), Masvingo, Zimbabwe. Tirivaviri has extensive experience in working with civic organisations and has strong research interests in issues that deal with human rights and democracy.

Mapetere Kudakwashe holds a PhD in instructional Leadership in History and Med History. He is the incumbent chairperson for the Department of Curriculum Studies, Great Zimbabwe University, Masvingo, Zimbabwe. Dr Mapetere has strong research interests in issues that deal with instructional leadership in History, human rights and democracy.

Table of Contents

Chapter One

Theorising Fundamentalisms and Fetishisms in the 21st Century

Artwell Nhemachena & Munyaradzi Mawere

African nations stretching from Guinea Bissau to Somalia are subject to war, coups, and large-scale demonstrations. These nations face similar economic situation, with failing agricultural markets and booming mining industries. In the 1990s, the IMF and the WTO imposed liberal reforms that battered Africa's agricultural sector. Meanwhile, after the markets were opened, global elites invested their surplus wealth into African mining commodities which displaced populations, damaged the environment, and funded militant groups. In response to rising violence in Africa, the U.S invested more in AFRICOM and justified militarisation of the continent at home by invoking outrageous fears of fundamentalist Islam (Al Jazeera, 29 May 2012).

Faith and patriotism are the two great thaumaturges of this world. Both are divine; all their actions are prodigies. Do not go to them talking of examination, choice, or discussion; they will say that you are blasphemy. They know only two words: submission and belief... (deMaistre *et al* 1996: 88).

There is no time to waste. It has been quite frustrating to see negotiators negotiating only based on their very narrow national perspectives. This is not a national issue; it's a global issue-UN Secretary General Ban Ki-Moon on climate change deliberations (Reuters, 19 October 2015)

Just like there is a Jewish fundamentalism, or an Islamic or Christian one, you also got a technological fundamentalism. It is the religion of those who believe in the absolute power of technology, a ubiquitous, instantaneous and immediate technology (Armitage 2000: 44).

Terrorist Africa or Terrorised Africa? Fundamentalism and Terrorism in the World

The crossroads around which the title of this book is premised can be dated to the era of enslavement, through to the (neo-)colonial era, when some in the Western world that fetishised material profits consequently enslaved and colonised other human beings. Blinded

1

by the zeal for and faith in material profits, they defied Godly distinctions by collapsing Africans and their resources together such that distinctions ceased to be made [by them] between human Africans and other things [including other creatures]. The paradox in all this is that those that defied God [by enslaving and colonising others] have opportunistically made efforts to transform themselves into God [by occupying positions of supremacy over other people and creatures, and by presuming that everyone else and everything else has to bow down to their epistemologies, theologies, technologies, polities, ideologies and theocratic tendencies]. For the Westerners, transforming themselves into "Godly" positions of supremacy over everything else in the planet has for long been premised on terrorising others, through enslavement and colonisation, while at the same time paradoxically defining those that were terrorised as the terrorists [in the logics of what Mamdani (2007) calls the politics of naming]. Thus, denying the God of Creation *ex nihilo* and substituting Him with creation via the Big Bang, the Westerners sought to become God by purporting to create the world via enslavement and colonial Big Bangs on Africans. In spite of their deleterious effects on Africans, enslavement and colonisation have been mischievously described by some Westerners as progressive, civilising, enlightening and developmental. In other words, the Westerners that came to Africa with Big enslavement and colonial Bangs became *de facto* gods and goddesses of the violence of the Big Bang replacing the God of creation *ex nihilo*. The underlying assumption here is that the Big Bang gods and goddesses celebrated the attendant terrorism of enslavement and (neo-)colonialism that continue to exist in various guises in the contemporary world that pretends to decry terrorism while celebrating and taking as natural planetary violence by the global north that has become *de facto* God of the Big Bang in the contemporary world.

Arrogation of the position of God has historically included naturalising the violence and terrorism of enslavement and (neo-)colonisation and via Western epistemologies trying to keep these forms of violence off the fora in the academies. Arrogation of the position of God has also included naturalisation of Western epistemologies, ontologies, religions, polities, economies, cultures in

Africa to the extent that these have tended to displace African institutions, ontologies and epistemologies. Naturalisation and arrogation of the position of God has also come in the form of the contemporary droning of the world and the consistent monopolisation of the air by the hegemonics in the world that have arrogated rights including to declare no fly zones to those, in the global south, that they seek to attack. Via other institutions including the International Criminal Court, in which the hegemonics in the world have declared their immunity, the hegemonics have become some kinds of unmoved movers (see for instance Frede *et al* 2000) of the world. The setting up of military bases including in foreign territories (Turse 2015; Al Jazeera, 29 May 2012), in which the locals are often paradoxically enjoined to demilitarise, signal fundamentalist tendencies in the world. Like God, the global hegemonics tend to move others in the world without in return being earnestly moved by them.

Libraries of African academies have therefore become shrines where often hapless and unwary Africans have paid huge amounts of hard earned money to pay respects to Western gods and goddesses that populate much of the literature that is availed. In context where even in African academies the singular Western stories continue to be evangelised (Nyamnjoh, 2015), the intellectual evangelists can best be understood as agents of epistemic and ontological terrorism bent on terrorising African students, scholars and populations in general, in the fashion of violently (neo-)colonial epistemic and ontological Big Bang. With their wits terrorised out of Africa, African scholars and students have not only become intellectually xenophile but many have become excellent at irrelevance to the continent including their localities (Nyamnjoh 2012) which they understand only as potential converts to the Western gospels of which they have become addicted to. In other words, Western epistemologies and ontologies have become fetishes for many who even gamble away the little they have in the [increasingly vain] hope that attending the epistemic shrines will get them on the way to [Western] "heavenly" kingdoms.

Through proselytisation of its epistemologies, ontologies, theologies, technologies and institutions, the West has come to have quasi-mysterious presence in many places in the world. To many that

3

do not know [and who are precluded from knowing] Western violent history in African territories and the rest of the global south, the presence of the West in many places in the world may be deemed to be "Godly". The West, and in particular the imperial powers, has become an absent presence in different parts of the world where it has presences or manifestations (Casey, 1982: 558-9). Understood in the Nietzschean thesis that God is dead, the West has effectively become the "living god" with quasi-omnipresence, omnipotence and omniscience in the world. It has become a theological and theocratic "God" about who Nesteruk (2005: 7) notes some scholars as claiming that the living God who is worthy of worship is mysteriously present in this world but He is present in His actual absence. The West has further arrogated providence in its giveness to Africa and the global south more generally and because of this arrogation of providentiality, the imposition of Western sanctions over the rest of the world has increasingly and effectively become a form of providential withdrawal of "Western grace" that the West presupposes to be indispensable. Understood in terms of Western sanctions, the arrogation of godly space is rendered graphically in Nesteruk's (2005: 17) observation that: "Thus, the withdrawal of God in this sense is a 'condition" for his authenticity and uniqueness in personal events of revelation, and, at the same time, is the affirmation of his 'presence in absence' in our midst". For Nesteruk (2005: 16) "The personal meeting with God …requires one to make an effort even in the conditions of severe abandonment by God."

The ways in which the global north plays God are underscored in The Guardian (2 February 2016) which reported that: "We are indeed playing God with our genes. But it is a good thing because God, nature or whatever we want to call the agencies that made us, often get it wrong and it's up to us to correct mistakes".

When the West abandons [or more properly sanctions] its enslavement and colonial victims [paradoxically without having paid restitution and compensation], it still requires the victims to make efforts even in these conditions of severe abandonment. Yet, when the West extends "humanitarian aid" it forgets, and seeks to create amnesia, about the exploitative conditions under which conditions for its "humanitarianism" have been created and sustained by looting from the supposed beneficiaries of the humanitarianism. In other words, it is never made clear that humanitarian aid does not originate from some mysterious manna but comes from global exploitation of those that are subsequently described as beneficiaries of the aid. To presume as is conventionally done that the West simply and mysteriously has plenty to donate to the entire world is to presume that the West is "God" possessed with omnipotence to magically turn in humanitarian aid without exploiting others the very same way God magically provided the Egyptians manna from heaven. Put differently, by not disclosing that humanitarian aid originates from [surplus] exploiting the supposed beneficiaries, there is the playing of God here. This speaks to fetishisation of the West and the humanitarian aid that it purportedly extends to Africa and the rest of the global south.

From the "worshipping" of capitalism [and ceding sovereignty to Western markets] which African countries are exhorted to attract as investments (Bond, 2003), to surviving in practices of global apartheid, one witnesses fundamentalisms, in the secular and religious senses. Forced by the Bretton hood institutions to worship the neoliberal markets, Africans are forced into market fundamentalism that has had ruinous effects on African families, humanity, personhood, marriages, cultures, and polities. Market fundamentalism, like new atheisms (McAnulla, 2014), mirrors features of religious fundamentalism in that it evinces intolerant and absolutist views that have been evangelised by IMF and World Bank and their agents right round the world.

When the then British Prime Minister, Margaret Thatcher asserted that there is no alternative to neoliberalism in the 1980s, (BBC News, 7 March 2013), this can best be understood as fundamentalism. Similarly, when capitalists justify pursuing profit and self-interest, even if ruthlessly by quoting Adam Smith's [providential] invisible hand of the market argument (Bishop 1995), there is need to understand this as a form of fundamentalism similar to religious fundamentalism or even worse. Indeed, some scholars have understood the invisible hand as referring to the providential hand of "God" or the hand of Jupiter (Aydinonat 2008: 72; Poole 2004). Underscored in the very existence of market fundamentalism is the fact that while Western powers are often quick to stage wars on religions in the global south, deemed to be fundamentalist, such as Islam, the same Western powers create and sustain various forms of fundamentalisms such as global [secular] fundamentalism (Cristini 2013: 159), (neo-)liberal market fundamentalism, globalisation fundamentalism, and technological fundamentalism that are favourable to the Western projects of global dominance.

Defining fundamentalism, Conkle (1996) notes that religious fundamentalism is a type of religion that regards its sacred texts as a source of truth that is absolute, plain and unchallengeable. Conkle (1996: 339) proceeds to note that secular thinking can also take on fundamentalistic characteristics and so the public role of this "secular" fundamentalism should also be viewed with scepticism. While the term fundamentalism, in religious contexts, has been linked to radical movements abroad that are perceived to be not only irrational, but also violent – murderous actions by people claiming to be following the will of God, this book views fundamentalism as broader than conventional religious renditions often associated with the term. When people kill others because of beliefs in [Western] ideologies such as democracy, human rights, liberalism, humanitarianism, all these instances need to be construed as forms of fundamentalism. When capitalists motivated by beliefs in the sanctity of profit and riches kill or put in place mortifying structures such as the resilient colonial ones, this should also be construed as fundamentalism that breeds what scholars like Paul farmer (2005) understand as structural violence on the impoverished. When IMF and World Bank motivated, as they were, by beliefs in the sanctity of the neoliberal market and invisible hands of the market, coerced African governments to implement neoliberal "free" market reforms, this should be understood as forms of fundamentalism for which the Africans have been sadly sacrificed.

While in religious fundamentalism, adherents believe that they are receiving instruction directly from God or Allah to kill, in secular fundamentalism, adherents believe that they are directly receiving instruction, to kill or starve others, from a superior secular force such as the global institutions and some Western powers, individual governments and other institutions such as the International

6

Monetary Fund and the World Bank that visit austerity and punitive measures on the global south. For Conkle (1996: 340-1), both secular and religious fundamentalists are absolutists or people who believe they are appointed carriers of a sacred gospel and feel so sure they are right that they have no compunction about killing heretics or doing anything else to advance their cause. Fundamentalism is more than textual interpretation, it also reflects unquestioning faith, this faith needs no reasoned explanations, and it needs not be defended against challenges that proceed from contrary premises.

Fundamentalism is evident not only when humanity adopts religious beliefs as well as scientism uncritically but also when they adopt ideologies of (neo-)liberalism and pluralism uncritically. Although ideas of (neo-)liberalism and pluralism have been understood by some scholars to be antidotes for fundamentalism, the challenge is that Africa has lived through rapacious and ravaging (neo-)liberal market fundamentalism that belies assertions of liberalism and pluralism as antidotes to fundamentalism. (Neo-)liberalism and pretences of inclusive pluralism are in fact often used by the hegemonic in the world to frog-march states and government in the periphery into the one world government that is feared by many, in which the only unchallenged sovereign becomes the dominant state in the global north. Besides, inclusivity and pluralism are nothing unique to Western liberalism since these were at the heart of African hospitality to Western travellers, missionaries and hunters from prior to colonisation of Africa. In other words, African precolonial liberal, inclusive and pluralistic attitudes and dispositions were taken advantage of by incoming Western colonisers who sought to infiltrate the continent, dispossess its peoples, exploit the Africans and jettison African institutions often also turning one African against the other as preludes to create spaces for colonial infiltration. In Africa where logics of liberalism are best understood in terms of hospitality and tolerance which (neo)colonists have sadly abused, to coerce Africa to be liberal is amounts to enforcement of hospitality by those that have historically and monumentally abused that African hospitality – it in fact amounts to absence of democracy for those that have been abused.

The problem with much of the discourses on fundamentalism is that they exclude the [arguably more fundamental] economic dimension of fundamentalism, in their focus on religious fundamentalism. Much scholarship on fundamentalism takes on the guise of ethereality in that there is evident fight by scholars from dealing with the materialities and economics of fundamentalisms. The fact that there is an interaction between Islamic fundamentalism, politics and poverty (Akinola 2015) is largely ignored in the focus on the religious aspects. Similarly, the fact that there are connections between religions and materialities, (Meyer *et al*, 2012), which explain why material insecurities spill into religious insecurities are ignored. Thus, the connections between global market and economic fundamentalism, which hold that everything can become a commodity to be traded (Shiva 2002 cited in Coleman et al 2013) and religious fundamentalisms, are marginalised in the discourses and praxis of curbing fundamentalisms. For these reasons, noted are, ways in which economic deterioration and dispossession assist in generating fundamentalist dispositions and the possibilities of mobilisation of broad sectors of the population by fundamentalists (Eisenstadt, 1999: 142). More recently, Pope Francis has been noted by The Guardian (28 November 2014) as stating thus: "What is required is a concerted commitment on the part of all, based on mutual trust, which can pave the way to lasting peace, and enable resources to be directed, not to weaponry, but to the other noble battles worthy of man: the fight against hunger and sickness, the promotion of sustainable development and the protection of creation, and the relief of the many forms of poverty and marginalisation…"

Whether or not these "humanitarian" measures suffice without the total reversal of colonialism is subject to further scholarly discussions in this book but what is clear from the foregoing is that fundamentalism in the global south is not necessarily a cause of authoritarianism, terrorism, dogmatism or insularity rather it is a result of enslavement and (neo-)colonial dogmatism, terrorism, disinheritance, insularity and authoritarianism. Western epistemologies have sadly historically confused causes and effects as their colonial *modus operandi*. Purported African "barbarism" and "savagery" were presented as causes of colonisation when in fact it is colonisation that effected untold barbarism and savagery including plunder, exploitation, deceit, murder, immorality, unlawfulness, loss of social ties etc. Equally, African underdevelopment was presented as the cause of Western civilisation and development missions when in fact it is colonial "civilisation" and "development" that effected underdevelopment in Africa. Similarly, religions in the global south are presented as causes of fundamentalism when in fact fundamentalism is an effect of (neo-)colonial plunder, impoverishment, suppression and exploitation of people of the global south many of whom have lost faith in the Western gospels of development and place their faith in God [who has been paradoxically cancelled out by Western secularism] as they know Him unadulterated by Western ideologies.

The issue here is that while tolerance, liberalism and pluralism are touted as antonyms and antidotes to fundamentalisms (Griffin 2003: 1632, 1631); those in Africa that have been historically tolerant and liberal to others have been exploited and taken advantage of in enslavement and colonial history. In fact, openness, tolerance and liberalism have been preached by colonisers whose fundamentalist instincts saw them plundering and exploiting those that openly and liberally welcomed them in Africa. In the contemporary era, Africa is exhorted by Westerners to remain open including to the virus of exploitation, as an antidote to fundamentalism. African bodies are exhorted to be open, and therefore tolerant, including to infestation and infection by viruses that result from limitless liberal freedoms. Furthermore, and as argued in some chapters in this book, Africans are exhorted to be tolerant, liberal and open to consumption of toxic genetically modified organisms (GMOs) that are paradoxically rejected in some of their countries of origin. Still on Africa, the continent is expected to be open, tolerant and liberal to biomedical and other experiments in which Western corporations and institutions [that shy away from experimenting with their own Western folks] travel to Africa to execute experiment on the people of the continent.

Lastly, Africa is expected to be open, liberal and tolerant to Western immigration [even to the extent of including Westerners and former settlers as indigenous people] even as Western nations are busy shipping back and erecting walls against migrants from the global south. In all these instances, it is the African body, the African marriages, families, African nations and African institutions more generally that are expected to be [indiscriminately and often to the point of indecency] open, tolerant, liberal to penetration by the Western other who paradoxically retains the fundamentals and fundamentalisms of politics, economics, culture, law, life, technology, religions, nationalism, epistemologies etc. This openness has created transnational subjectivities, using African minds as raw materials, that are relied upon by those that benefit from global and Eurocentric fundamentalisms to discredit the local and the national and continental fundamentals of being. Thus, openness creates transnational subjectivities that in turn paradoxically buttress global fundamentalism even though such openness is touted as an antidote to fundamentalisms. One wonders why Africa alone should be open, in unequal terms, to its Western counterparts.

The challenge here is about how to accord African fundamentals of [human] being in the world [and prevent them from falling into zones of nonbeing] if liberalism, openness and tolerance are taken or pushed to excess. In fact, colonialism, which pushed Africans into zones of nonbeing, is about excess in which colonial settlers, motivated by excess, sought liberal access to resources and territories beyond their own. Colonialism is not merely about domination, hegemony authoritarianism, dogmatism: it is *a fortiori* about excess beyond one's own and thus (neo-)colonial fundamentalism is accessive and excessive in that it involves practices beyond one's territories and one's legitimate ambit. This means that fundamentalism is not merely about dogmatism, authoritarianism, insularity but it is also about creating multiplicities, including by blasting the peripheral others into smithereens. (Neo-)colonial fundamentalism is about creating and keeping the multiplicities [often conceived in derogatory terms as tribes, ethnicities, etc.] in the peripheries that were created during the colonial era. To be recognised as multiplicities and pluralities is not necessarily antonymic to fundamentalism particularly in a context where colonialism itself relied for centuries on creating and keeping African multiplicities and pluralities as forms of divide and rule. In fact such multiplicities and pluralities buttress (neo-)colonial fundamentalism and the fundamentalism of contemporary global apartheid that cannot fathom Pan Africanism and African unity, for example.

The fact that fundamentalisms necessarily splinter and divide is evident in market fundamentalism that divide Africans as they are enjoined to compete in the (neo-)liberal "free" market. In any case, the fact that the (neo-)liberal "free" market is fundamentalistic underscores that the Western "freedom" itself is not necessarily liberating but is fundamentalistic in so far as it allows the West to be dogmatic and to dictate to the rest of the world, while hiding under the cloak of the invisible hands of the "free" market. Similarly while Western liberal democracy purports to bring pluralistic freedom, it in fact buttresses Western [dogmatic and insular] fundamentalism and for this reason the fact that the West postures to be the champion and patriarchy of democracy even as it fails to recognise [possibilities of] other forms of democracy, is telling. The point here is that freedom as purveyed in conventional parlance is a sleight of hand that is meant not necessarily to oppose fundamentalisms but to hide fundamentalisms originating from the hegemonics and global patriarchs in the world. Providing numerous and multiple false crutches and false alternatives to Africans has for long been an inveterate strategy of (neo-)colonial minds that hide their fundamentalisms in coatings of freedom, emancipation, decolonisation etc.

If liberalism, tolerance and pluralism are not necessarily antidotes to fundamentalism, it follows that critiques of scientific fundamentalism that considers the world of science as absolute, (Oyen *et al* 2012) are not necessarily an antidote to fundamentalism. One of the lethal types of fundamentalism is Eurocentric fundamentalism which is used as the norm and hegemonic common sense to define what is democracy, what is terrorism, what is economy, what are human rights, what is environment and who is a fundamentalist (Grosfoguel 2014: 126), and the most lethal part of this fundamentalism is that Eurocentrists have inveterate proclivities to define to excess and beyond their legitimate territories and boundaries. They are quick to terrorise everyone else with

Eurocentric definitions that are deemed to be *a priori* and "fundamentally" universal. In this sense, while cultures of the global south are often deemed to be traditional, patriarchal and patrimonial, Western cultures and traditions of planetary dominance, dogmatism, and patriarchy are conveniently shielded from critique via veils of pseudo-liberalism. Thus, while Westerners are so much critical of the Islamic veils, the Westerners themselves adorn numerous veils that are meant to hide their plunder, exploitation, fundamentalism and disinheritance of peoples of the global south. Western veils, that hide their fundamentalism, are much broader than Islamic fundamentalism's facial veils: thus Western humanitarianism can be understood as a veil for plunder and resilient (neo-)colonisation; Western liberalism can similarly be construed as a veil for fundamentalism and dogmatism by those that do the defining of what is liberalism; Western ideologies of liberalism, equality and democracy are thus veils for western hegemony including fundamentalism.

In fact, there are numerous hegemonic veils that are designed to hide the rapacious fundamentalistic global apartheid whose script has been woven more tightly with growing opposition to apartheid at African national levels. In this vein, Dunaway *et al* (2016) cite Ansley (1997: 592) who notes, about global apartheid, thus: "This world bifurcation is supposedly grounded in white supremacy which is defined to be political, economic and cultural system in which whites overwhelmingly control power and markets…and the relations of white dominance and non-white subordination are daily re-enacted across a broad array of institutions and social settings.

Similarly underscoring aspects of fundamentalistic global apartheid, Mamdani (2010: 53-54) argues that: "…the new global regime of R2P bifurcates the international system between sovereign states whose citizens have political rights, and the *de facto* trusteeship territories whose populations are seen as wards in need of external protection… Looked at closely and critically, what we are witnessing is not a global but a partial, transition. The transition from the old system of sovereignty to a new humanitarian order is confined to those states defined as "failed" or "rogue" states… The result is a bifurcated system whereby state sovereignty obtains in large parts of the world but it is suspended in more and more countries in Africa and the Middle East…To the extent the global humanitarian order claims to stand for rights, these are residual rights of the human and not the full range of rights of the citizen".

This global apartheid is an institutional system on minority rule whose attributes include differential access to basic human rights, wealth and power structures, by race and place, structural racism, embedded in global economic processes, political institutions and cultural assumptions; and international practice of double standards that assume inferior rights to be appropriate for certain "others" defined by location, origin, race or gender (Salin Booker and William Minter 2001: 11 cited by Harrison 2004). This global apartheid explains the resilience of colonial type experimentations (Maghari *et al* 2011; Sunday Express 19 January 2014; Bratch 2015; Sanya 2014) on Africans and peoples of the global south more generally. Thus, there are Western experiments, on Africans, with genetically modified [food] organisms which result in reduction in the average age, in birth defects, mutagenesis, miscarriages, depression and suicide, disorders of the central nervous system and other neuropathologies, leukaemia and other types of cancers, skin problems, asthma, allergies and other respiratory and lung related problems, male sterility and impotence, hormonal disruption, diminished childhood development, multiple sclerosis, death (The Guardian (11 September 2015). Recently [in 2016], the Chicago Tribune (25 November 2016) reported that: "Now all eyes are on South Africa, where researchers will begin inoculating thousands of volunteers Monday in the latest-and, some say, most promising-effort to develop a vaccine that prevents the disease…in 2007, South Africa was one site of a second phase of testing for an HIV vaccine developed by pharmaceutical giant Merck. The study was called off soon after it began, however, when early results from other locations showed that the vaccine seemed to be making people more susceptible to HI than a placebo".

These types of experiments result from Western scientific fundamentalism that regards Africans as indistinct from animals that are targeted for experiments. Making this contention clear, Conkle (1996: 359) points out that: "Due especially to its heavy reliance on science, comprehensive secular fundamentalism also supports naturalism…Thus along with the rest of nature, human beings are explainable through the methods of the natural sciences. Human institutions and practices, the modes of experience of men, the goals and values of individuals and groups, are all natural, and no less so than the wheeling of galaxies and the evolution of species." This type of fundamentalism that fails to separate Africans from animals is sadly gaining traction in a contemporary world where some Western scholars are writing in favour of "becoming animals"; arguing that people of the global south are animists that do not distinguish between themselves and animals etc. It is sadly a kind of fundamentalism that along with assumptions that Africans were indistinct from technology or machines, buttressed colonialism and enslavement. As Rutsky (1999) argues, becoming a "slave to technology" makes one "less than human".

Contemporary arguments by some scholars for a kind of "liberalism", "tolerance" and "plurality" extended to include animals and the rest of nature as humans or to collapse together humans and animals/nature might be legitimised and sold on the premise that they counter fundamentalism. However, these actually amount to old colonial portrayals of Africans as animals and as pieces of technology to be exploited. In other words, the worry here is that liberalism, tolerance and pluralism if taken to extremes often recoil as forms of fundamentalism that prey on diversity and multiplicity. In short, extremist forms of liberalism and tolerance are no different from extremism in other forms of fundamentalisms. In this sense, liberalism and tolerance should be understood properly as matters of continua, they are matters of degrees, and these different degrees need to be recognised if liberals are not to turn into fundamentalists. Thus liberal democracy is a matter of degrees, rights are similarly matters of degrees, freedom is a matter of degrees and none is absolutely democratic, free, and liberal. The problem is that Western liberalism has descended into absolutism and dogmatism to the extent that it does not tolerate different forms and degrees of liberalism and democracy that issue from different places and from different epochs. Remember that extremists read their sacred scripts strictly and intolerantly!

The fundamentalism of liberalism is underscored by Haphong (2015) who argues that United States of America's Imperialism has promoted wars of austerity and pillage as projects of "democracy" and "counter-terrorism" and to further these, it defines the world's people as "terrorists" or unable to govern themselves without help from the "benevolent" west. For Haphong (2015), colonialism's racist paradigm of the innate "inferiority" of the colonised remains an imperial staple diet.

To push Africa towards extremist liberalism is in fact to push the continent and its peoples into the hypothetical Hobbesian state of nature without modes of governance and without forbearances. This is a chaotic state in which there is no semblance of government and where citizens are without a common power to keep them in awe (Wolfenden, 2010). In this state everyone is against everyone else because there is no governing body or as in the case of much of Africa the governing bodies have been pushed into legitimation crises. While precolonial Africa had governments and states, colonial Hobbesian assumptions served as justification for colonisation and so, logically, a descent into the hypothetical Hobbesian state of nature does not help in contemporary African efforts towards decoloniality, as it in effect prepares ground for recolonisation and the emergence of the new empire in the form of a one world government with the West preponderating over the entire world as the only sovereign. In a context where the Western push on Africa towards extremist liberalism happens alongside a resurgence of animism and animalisation debates (Nhemachena, 2016) the outlines of a descent into the hypothetical Hobbesian state of nature become clear. Though discourses on animism paint it as African and as providing lines of flight away from Western modernity, scholars like Smith (2011) underscore the fact that monikers such as "brute", "cockroach", "lice", vermin", "dog", "beast" are constantly in use to refer to and to dehumanise other humans thereby making atrocities possible.

In this sense missions and evangelisations of extreme liberalisms are in fact replicas of *missions civilisatrices*: their dark side is that they are *missions barbare* or missions to create barbarians [that lack understanding of limits or boundaries of freedom and restraint] in the guise of promoting civilisation. If civility is about restraint, and restraint entails cognisance of limits or boundaries, then extremist liberalism does not only presuppose lack of restraint but also lack of civility and lack of understanding of limits or boundaries or borders between civility and its opposite. Extremist liberalism can therefore be understood to be as atavistic as other forms of extremist fundamentalism. To advocate extremist liberalism can be construed as another way of describing the supposed beneficiaries of such extremism as barbaric, savage and without restraint but it is a way that global hegemonics have taken care to conceal using linguistic acrobatics. Thus, one of the effective and contemporary ways to create barbarians and savages or to describe others as savages and barbarians is to endear them to extremist liberalism that knows no restraints, boundaries and borders. While liberalism is held to define human rights, democracy and freedom, extremist liberalism without restrain, borders and boundaries is in fact subhuman particularly in contexts where the ability to exercise restraint defines humanity.

Unfortunately, there is coalescence or assemblages of various forms of fundamentalisms in the West: from Eurocentric fundamentalism to global fundamentalism to technological fundamentalism, market fundamentalism, and religious fundamentalism and so on. There is also fetishisation of empire, fetishisation of technology biopower and a celebration of the melding of humanity with the machine in the production of new revolutionary organisms (Newman 2010: 127). Terrorised by Western epistemologies that claim the death of God even as humanity is simultaneously threatened about the impending judgment of God, technological fundamentalists tend, according to Futrell (2004), to believe that the imminent apocalypse can be averted through technological accomplishments to enable them to redeem man's fall from grace once again redeeming his place in God's kingdom. For this reason, human intelligence, personality, autonomy are being projected onto machines (Arregui 2011: 55) as a prelude to an era described as posthuman. Thus, such technological fundamentalism and instrumentalism dangerously feed complacency and blind acceptance of technological advances without analytical reflection (Shime 2013: 94).

Unfortunately, Westerners design [including some posthuman robotics] technological means believed to enable human beings to evade the judgment of God but the same Westerners do not design technologies for Africans to use to evade the judgment and fundamentalism of the Westerners. In fact, since the era of the enslavement to (neo-)colonialism, Westerners have designed technologies to catch Africans so as to exploit them, to disinherit them, and to use them against their fellows Africans causing divisions that in religious spiritual parlance would be attributed to demons of division. Thus while some in the West seek to evade God's judgement, they paradoxically cannot fathom Africans escaping or evading the grip and judgement of the West that has put in place networks of institutions to entrap Africans within Western matrices of power. In this sense, the "humanitarianism" and other forms of [often phantom] aid, the Eurocentric extensions of liberal rights, freedoms, democracies and so on can best be understood as endearments for purposes of fishing out of Africa and creating transnational [read "global"] subjectivities. The idea of transnational subjectivities is best captured by Dobson (2007) who argues that there has been the displacement of the self under transnationalism. For Dobson, the contemporary subject is asked to view itself as an actor within a global system and no longer simply as a being imbued with agency within a local or national setting. For purposes of this present book, it is necessary to note here that these transnational subjectivities do not necessarily translate to democracy, freedom, liberty and democracy because they [unwarily] collapse back into the master-frame-nets of global fundamentalism as well as those of Eurocentric [Big Bang] fundamentalism. Eurocentric democracy, freedom, rights, liberties are therefore designed for the masters and not for African localities, nationalities, continentalities or individuals in the global south. The global south always risks running back into booby master frames of fundamentalisms even as they paradoxically think they are running to global freedom and liberty. In short, it can be argued that Western donations of freedoms, liberties and democracy always recoil as bondage within the master frames of global and Eurocentric fundamentalisms.

Therefore, in contemporary decolonial movements and discourses, it is necessary to separate local, national agents of global imperial and Western fundamentalism from the masters of those fundamentalisms if decoloniality is to be meaningful and go beyond local struggles. As Frantz Fanon (1963: 15-18) notes about Africans [leaders] in a (neo-)colonial context "...the order is given to reduce the inhabitants of the annexed country to the level of superior monkeys in order to justify the settlers' treatment of them as beasts of burden...Everything will be done to wipe out their traditions, to substitute our language for theirs and to destroy their culture without giving them ours...The different tribes fight between themselves since they cannot face the real enemy-and you can count on colonial policy to keep up the rivalries; the man who raises his knife against his brother thinks that he has destroyed once and for all the detested image of their common degradation..."

In struggles for decoloniality and against various forms of fundamentalisms, Africans need not just resort to fighting between themselves: they need to face the real enemy that is the source [and not merely agent] of the fundamentalisms. For this reason local, national and continental hegemonics can be understood merely as shadows or tails of master global and Eurocentric fundamentalists: *zombified* by the masters, they play [(un)wittingly] the role of buffers. Anxious to deflect blows of genuine liberation and genuine decoloniality, the masters always shift [including their own] blame to those that they have *zombified*. Of course in a world where postmodernist theorists propound erosion of distinctions and dedifferentiation, where they claim surrealism and hype reality and so forth, these theoretical efforts should be understood as tools to cloud the real sources of African tribulations so as to sustain fundamentalisms (Nhemachena, 2016). The postmodernist efforts to argue against existence of reality must be understood as means to cloud the real enemies so that Africans continue to fight one another instead of facing the common real enemies. Similarly the postmodernist theoretical propositions against fundamentals and metatheories should be understood as efforts to cloud common enemies that fortress or prop-up fundamentals of African impoverishment and disinheritance. In fact, postmodernism along with extremist liberalisms are effectively anti-politics machines, to make politics [and of course economics] impossible in the global south. They are not necessarily meant to be antifundamentalist or anti-foundationalist, as indeed they prop-up the colonial status quo of Western economic, political, religious and other fundamentalisms. This is why African governments and states are from time to time accused by Westerners of breaching the [Western] fundamentals of economics, politics, religions, environments etc.: fundamentalisms appear to be permitted in the world but it depends on whose fundamentals and fundamentalisms are at stake.

Chapter Outlines

Chapter Two is entitled "Humanitarian" Fundamentalism: Interrogating "Global" Process of Fishing in African Troubled Waters. In this chapter, Munyaradzi Mawere and Artwell Nhemachena argue that although some of the evils and catastrophes that haunt Africa today are traceable to the invisible machinations of the global north, ironically most of the "humanitarian" aid that Africa receives comes from outside the continent, mainly the same global north that once colonised Africa. It is arguable that much "humanitarianism" from the north is meant to perpetuate the gospel of *the white men's burden*, facilitate the fiddle of the global north as planetary good Samaritans, even if they paradoxically cultivate dependency syndrome on the continent. These fiddles by some capitalists from the global north, that play both sheep and wolf, have generated consternations among many formerly colonised countries of Africa that have become unease with the –isms from the north. Consequently, humanitarianism from the north has not been wholesomely acceptable on the continent where both politicians and some academics have increasingly become critical of it. Against this backdrop, the chapter interrogates humanitarianism arguing that it has, overtime, become an aspect of "global" *civil religion* [in which the global north plays God]particularly visible in places where such humanitarianism has become a pretext for invasions of other sovereign countries. Thus, the chapter interrogates the planetary supremacist position that more often than not, the global north has arrogated to itself arguably to a point where it uses humanitarianism to fish [from Africa and the global south more generally] for global discipleship. Underscoring the parallels logics between fishermen and humanitarianism, the authors draw attention to the fact that some forms of humanitarian aid [such as cheap genetically modified food organisms] are known to be toxic yet the West encourages Africa to consume the GMO food, much as a "fisherman" uses baits to hook-up fish.

In chapter three, Nokuthula Hlabangane, focuses on the coloniality of research in Africa and she uses the case study of HIV/AIDS in South Africa. She argues that the Rhodes Must Fall student movement is in danger of being understood narrowly as merely a demand for the transformation of the physical spaces of the university institution to reflect the demographics of the country. Hlabangane argues that it is abidingly important to also ask why the cry for Rhodes to fall began and why it continues to gain momentum in South Africa. What exactly does this cry mean? How can it be interpreted faithfully? For her, embedded in the movement is a demand to overhaul and re-imagine the negotiated post-1994 settlement in all its nuances. For instance, it is noted that students say that after Rhodes, they will raise the ever-present yet side-stepped question of land redistribution and restitution in South Africa. Hlabangane notes sentiments that underscore the inextricable relationship between the personal and the political – how ostensibly unrelated issues, are, in fact, upon deeper and thus just analyses, related. For the author, the burgeoning tendency to paint actors in the South African socio-political space in undifferentiated terms such as "student movement" masks important continuity of the past in the present. For her, it remains important to ask which students? How and why do they not fit into the dominant post-apartheid narrative?

In chapter four, Oliver Mtapuri looks critically at poverty and fundamentalism in Africa. Thus, his chapter four interrogates poverty from a perspective which argues that the conscious and deliberate perpetuation of poverty is a form of fundamentalism with its associated principles and values. He argues that, in the world, there are people who are parasitic and are incessantly feeding off and on the sweat of the 'povertised' of society. The chapter explores how poverty prevents the fulfilment and enjoyment of human rights and results in the deferral and postponement, abandonment and foregoing of the destination of people as happiness, freedom, self- and collective affirmation, and self-actualisation. The chapter further explains why poverty, as a form of fundamentalism, affects many Africans relative to other groups from different continents. His chapter also examines how the measurement of poverty speaks to the 'fundamentalisation' of poverty. The author argues that this is partly evident in the manner in which poverty statistics are derived and interpreted to express the primacy of the exclusivity of the rich and a system of neoliberalism in which the 'trickle-down effect' – a hollow hypothesis - that should benefit the so-called poor has yet to materialise for inclusivity. Mtapuri argues that povertisation as a form of fundamentalism emerges when spaces to productively produce food have been appropriated; when markets and trade have been appropriated; as have places which are supposed to be called home, have also been appropriated; when mineral resources, the land, the sea, earth and its diversity, knowledge production and indeed, everything of value has been appropriated.

Munetsi Ruzivo's chapter five is entitled 'Questioning the Cult of the State: Evangelicals on the Zimbabwean National Pledge 2014-2016'. In this chapter, the author critically examines the emergence of the cult of the state in Zimbabwe's recent past. His discussion of the emergence of the cult draws from the recent announcement by the Zimbabwean Minister of Education, Dr Lazarus Dokora, to the Zimbabwean nation that all pupils in both primary and secondary schools will in the future be required to recite the National Pledge. Ruzivo argues that while the Evangelical Fellowship of Zimbabwe was critical of the cultic announcement by the minister, the Evangelical Fellowship of Zimbabwe paradoxically also deals with matters of belief. Thus, in both cases, there is imposition of beliefs on school pupils by the government as well as by Evangelical Fellowship of Zimbabwe. For this reason, Ruzivo argues that it is questionable why the Evangelical Fellowship of Zimbabwe wants to maintain religious organisational monopoly to impose religious beliefs on pupils. Ruzivo's chapter investigates circumstances surrounding the introduction of the National Pledge by the

21

Zimbabwean government in all secondary and primary schools. His chapter further explores arguments proffered by government officials and their supporters on the need for the National Pledge. Thirdly, the chapter argues that in secular state no form of religion should influence government policies. The chapter interrogates the position of both government and Evangelicals on the teaching of religious propaganda of either civil or religious nature. The author proceeds to argues that although civil religion tends to thrive in secular state and may appear to be not exclusive and intolerant to other varieties or forms of religions, in Zimbabwe, it may be as intolerant and fundamentalist as evangelical groupings.

Artwell Nhemachena and Bankie F Bankie present chapter six which is entitled 'Foot Soldiers of the New Empire or Horizontal Saviours? Interrogating Civil Society Organisations and Fundamentalisms in Twenty-First Century Africa'. In this chapter, the authors interrogate assumptions in some parts of the world that some civil society organisations have assumed the roles of missionaries of the [new] empire or the old empire that has [with African independence] simply morphed into an invisible absent present [quasi-theological] leviathan. The authors wonder about the empire of which the civil society organisations have become. However, noting the resilience of (neo-)colonialism, the authors argue that empire is still alive even though the old empire has long been pronounced dead and has already received countless scholarly obituaries particularly after the declarations of independence of African states. The authors proceed to draw on debates on (neo-)colonialism and (neo-)imperialism in order to surface the existence of an invisible [global] government that other scholars have noted as directed by a kind of "global" [*invisible and powerful*] 'secret masonic society' that deploys financial muscles to direct world affairs, including [surreptitious] wars in peripheral states. Drawing on scholarly works that indicate that civil society organisations are funded from capitalism's coffers, Nhemachena and Bankie underline their anxiety to know if civil society organisations are not connected to the powerful masonic secret society that controls the global finances from which civil society is often funded. They then pose the question as to whether civil society organisations do not in fact

22

deliver people in their various 'constituencies' into the fold of the empire dominated by the secret societies. The authors conclude that often civil society organisations play the role of new missionaries delivering Africans, and people of the global south more generally, into the fold of empire. Some of the techniques used to deliver Africans into the fold of empire include the age old tactics of generating frightening statistics about poverty, suffering, corruption, ethnic hatred, "tribal" wars, and other forms of violence that frighten the wits out of Africans so that they run to the quasi-theological empire, and not necessarily to God as they know Him.

Tobias Dindi Ong'aria's chapter seven is entitled 'Dismantling Fundamentalisms in Science: Trailing Feyerabend's Epistemological Anarchism and the Place of African Science'. Ong'aria presents his insightful chapter as an attempt at possibilities of redeeming African science into the discourse in philosophy of science, from a perspective of Paul Feyerabend's everything goes, into a possible existence in a cosmopolitan milieu. He asks critical questions such as; can Feyerabend's epistemological anarchism offer a prospect for African Science? If yes, how far can it be taken? And if African Science is to be relooked at, are there any 'dogmas', as Feyerabend criticises in Western Science, that ought to be tolerated? Ong'aria explores Feyerabend's criticism of method in Western Science and then he explores African Science, or what could rightly be termed so, and how Feyerabend's contribution could offer prospects to it. His chapter also examines what needs to be upheld in method, despite Feyerabend's criticism, if African Science is to flourish again. Ong'aria concludes that although 'anything goes' could be a promising idea, an extreme adherence to it has negative implications for African Science.

Interrogating patriotic history in Zimbabwe in chapter eight, Tafirenyika Madziyauswa argues that such patriotic history constitutes fetishisation of knowledge. He argues that the recent Zimbabwean crisis culminated in emergence of new forms of discourses meant to sustain the so-called 'Third Chimurenga'. For Madziyauswa, the crisis resulted in the emergence of a new form of religion fronted by prominent academics and manifesting as the fetishisation of knowledge. He argues that, during the crisis in

Zimbabwe, the ruling party, that is, the Zimbabwe African National Union-Patriotic Front (ZANU PF) engaged academics to disseminate a set of ideas that sought to make the ruling elites the chief narrators or gatekeepers of Zimbabwe's past. This chapter, therefore, discusses how the discourse that emerged with the advent of the "Third Chimurenga" is inclusionary and exclusionary as well as monolithic and bigoted or dogmatic. In this chapter, the author argues that patriotic history is used to legitimise intolerance to any version of the past not officialised by the dominant class. He links this to the logics of religious fundamentalism which also entails dogmatism and bigotry.

Nkwazi Nkuzi Mhango presents chapter nine which is entitled 'History, Culture, Religion and (Under-)development in Africa'. He argues that development has been doctored, romanticised, essentialised and monopolised by the West, which superimposes its *diktat* on others as it ignores its unfair trajectory that enabled it to achieve such level of *development*. He further argues that development is not supposed to be monopolised or superimposed on others. For Mhango, development is not supposed to be narrow, tyrannical and prejudiced. One of the critical questions that inform the author's chapter is where is the autonomy, for countries whose development is defined by others? In this chapter, Mhango addresses the history of Africa showing that it is based on cultural and religious imperialism and religion that have worked as the agents of [under] development from the time colonialism and slavery were introduced to Africa up until now.

Fidelis P. T. Duri's chapter ten interfaces the past and the present as a means to interrogate traditional leadership, politics and materialism in Zimbabwe since the precolonial period. Duri argues that although African indigenous political philosophy in pre-colonial Zimbabwe viewed traditional leaders (chiefs, headmen/women and village heads) as selfless and altruistic community leaders, these leaders have always been opportunistic. Duri therefore dispels concerns in 21st century Zimbabwe that many traditional leaders, particularly the chiefs, have abrogated their traditional mandate and have overtime become political opportunists for purposes of accumulating material wealth. His chapter contends that this trend of opportunism has firm roots in pre-colonial times, persisted during the colonial era, and became entrenched after independence. Duri concludes that since the pre-colonial period, there has always been a nexus between political elevation and monopolistic tendencies such as unfettered access to material resources and accumulation of personal/ individual wealth by the aristocracy.

Chapter eleven is authored by Tasara Muguti, Benias Tirivaviri and Kudakwashe Mapetere. Focusing on Zimbabwe's recent constitution making process, the authors argue that Zimbabwe has not yet reached a stage in which a truly people driven and democratic constitution can be crafted. They make this argument on the basis of a critical appraisal of the way in which the constitutional making process was carried out. Indeed, the major political protagonists were always trying to dominate and manipulate the process at every stage for political expediency which in the end resulted in a 'constitution without constitutionalism'. The authors further argue that the views that were advanced by the people at the outreach meetings ended up being hijacked by the dominant political parties. They conclude that there was too much politicisation of the constitutional making process to the extent that citizens were cowed into submission through manipulation, intimidation and in extreme cases even violence perpetrated by the dominant political parties

References

Akinola, O. 2015. Boko Haram Insurgency in Nigeria: Between Islamic Fundamentalism, Politics and Poverty, in *Journal: African Security* 8 (1): 1-29.

Al Jazeera., 29 May 2012. The Militarisation of Poverty in Africa, https://www.globalpolicy.org/empire/51672-the-militarisation-of-poverty-in-africa.html.

Armitage, J. 2000. From Modernism to Hypermodernism and Beyond: An Interview with Paul Virilio, in Armitage J., ed, *Paul Virilio: From Modernism to Hypermodernism and Beyond*, SAGE Publications: London.

Arregui, A. G. 2011. Too "high" Tech: Metonymical Fallacies and Fetishism in the Perception of Technology, *Journal of Contemporary Anthropology* II (1): 47-62.

Aydinonat, N. E. 2008. *The Invisible Hand Economics: How Economists Explain Unintended Social Consequences.* Routledge: London and New York.

BBC News, 7 March 2013. Economy: There is No Alternative (TINA) is Back www.bbc.com/news/uk-politics 21703018

Bishop J D., 1995, Adam Smith's Invisible Hand Argument, *Journal of Business Ethics* 14 (3): 165-180.

Bond, P. 2003. *Against Global Apartheid: South Africa Meets the World Bank, IMF and International Finance.* Zed Books Ltd: London and New York.

Bracht, M. 2015. *Genocide in German South West Africa and the Herero Reparations Movement.* Thesis, University of South Carolina Scholar Commons.

Casey, E. S. 1982. Presence and Absence: Scope and Limits, in *The Review of Metaphysics*, 35 (3): 557-576.

Chicago Tribune, 25 November 2016. New HIV Vaccine Trial, The First in Years, To Begin. www.chicagotribune.com/news/nationworld/ct-hiv-vaccine-20161125-story.html.

Coleman, D. W. *et al.*, 2013. Fifty Key Thinkers on Globalisation. Routledge: London and New York.

Conkle, D. O. 1996. Secular Fundamentalism, Religious Fundamentalism and the Search for Truth in Contemporary America. Digital Repository, *Maurer School of Law*: Indiana University http://www.repository.law.indiana.edu/facpub.

Cristini, H. 2013. Does Muslim and Secular Fundamentalism Suffer from the Same Pharmakon? *The Asian Conference on Ethics, Religion and Philosophy, Official Conference Proceedings* iafor.org/archives/offprints/acerp2013-offprint.

Daily Observer, 9 September 2014, Ebola, AIDS Manufactured by Western Pharmaceuticals, USDOD? www.liberian observer.com/security/ebola-aids-manufactured-western-pharmaceuticals-us-dod.

De Maistre, J. M. *et al.*, 1996, *Against Rousseau: On the State of Nature and on the Sovereignty of the People*. McGill-Queen's University Press: London.

Dobson, K. 2007. Transnational Subjectivities: Roy Miki's Surrender and Global Displacements, in *Studies in Canadian Literature*, http://journals.lib.unb.ca/index:php/SCL/article/view/10572

Dunaway, A. W. *et al.*, 2016, Challenging the Global Apartheid Model: A World-Systems Analysis, *Journal of World-Systems Research* 22 (1): 16-22.

Eisenstadt, S. N., 1999, *Fundamentalism, Sectarianism, and Revolution: the Jacobin Dimension of Modernity*. Cambridge University Press: Cambridge.

Fanon, F. 1963. *The Wretched of the Earth*. Grove Press: New York

Farmer, P. 1999. Pathologies of Power: Rethinking Health and Human Rights, in *American Journal of Public Health* 89 (10): 1486-1496.

Frede, M. *et al.*, 2000. *Aristotle's Metaphysics Lambda: Symbosium Aristotelicum*, Clarendon Press: Oxford.

Futrell, D. J. 2004. Technological Fundamentalism? The Use of Unmanned Aerial Vehicle in the Conduct of War. MSc Dissertation Virginia Polytechnic Institute and State University

Global Research, 28 October 2015. The Arab Spring: Made in the USA www.globalresearch.ca/the-arab-spring-made-in-theusa/5484950.

Griffin, L. C. 2003. Fundamentalism from the Perspective of Liberal Tolerance, Scholarly Works. Paper 720, https://scholars.law.unilv.edu/facpub/720.

Grosfoguel, R. 2014. A Critical View of Wallerstein's Utopistics from Dussel's Transmodernity: From Monoepistemic Global/Imperial Designs to Pluri-Epistemic Solutions, in Reifer T., ed, *Global Crises and the Challenge of the 21st Century: Antisystemic Movements and the Transformation of the World System*. Routledge: New York.

Haphong, D. 2015. What is Neo-liberalism? A Revolutionary Analysis of the Final Stage of Imperialism, in Global Research www.globalresearch.ca/what-is-neo-liberalism-a-revolutionary-analysis-of-the-final-stage-of-imperialism/5433448

Harrison, F. V. 2004. Global Apartheid, Environmental Degradation, and Women's Activism for Sustainable Well-Being: A Conceptual and Theoretical Overview, in *urban Anthropology* vol 33 (1).

Harrison, P. 2004. *The Invisible Hand and the Order of Nature*. Harris Manchester College: Oxford.

Kohler, G. 1995. The Three Meanings of Global Apartheid: Empirical, Normative and Existential, in *Alternatives: Global, Local, Political* vol 20, No 3: 403-413.

Lewis, C. 30 June 2014. (The Centre for Public Integrity) False Pretences. http://www.publicintegrity.org/2008/01/23/5641/false-pretencies.

Maghari, B. M. *et al.*, 2011. Genetically Modified Foods and Social Concerns. *Avicenna J Med Biotechnol* 3 (3): 109-117.

Mamdani, M. 2007. The Politics of Naming: Genocide, Civil War, Insurgency, in London Review of Books vol 9 (5): 5-8.

Mamdani, M. 2010. Responsibility to Protect or Right to Punish? *Journal of Intervention and State building* 4 (1): 53-67.

McAnulla, S. 2014. Secular Fundamentalists? Characterising the New Atheists Approach to Secularism, Religion and Politics, in *British Politics* 9 (2): 124-145.

Meyer, B. *et al.*, 2012. Introduction: Materiality Religion-How Things Matter, In: Houtman D *et al.*, Eds, Things, Religion and the Question of Materiality, Fordham University Press: 1-24.

Nesteruk, A. V. 2005. The Universe Transcended God's 'Presence in Absence' in Science and Theology, in *European Journal of Science and Theology* 1 (2): 7-19.

Newman, S. 2010. *The Politics of Postanarchism,* Edinburgh University Press: Edinburgh.

Nhemachena, A. 2016b. Animism, Coloniality and Humanism: Reversing the Empire's Framing of Africa, In: Mawere, M. and Nhemachena, A., Eds, *Theory, Knowledge, Development and Politics: What Role for the Academy in the Sustainability of Africa?* Langaa RPCIG: Bamenda.

Nyamnjoh, F. B. 2012. Potted Plants in Greenhouses: A Critical Reflection on the Resilience of Colonial Education in Africa, in *Journal of Asian and African Studies* 47 (2): 129-154.

Nyamnjoh, F. B. 2015. Beyond an Evangelising Public Anthropology: Science, Theory and Commitment, in *Journal of Contemporary African Studies* vol 33 (1): 48-63.

Ohihon, I. B. 2012. Fundamentalism, Security Crisis and Tolerance in Global Context: the Nigerian Experience, in *The Politics and Religion Journal* Issue 1: 89-111.

Poole, E. 2004. The Invisible Hand Conspiracy: The Case for a Capitalist Theology. In *Faith Business* vol 8 (4): 24-27.

Rausch, C. C. 2015. Fundamentalism and Terrorism, in *Journal of Terrorism Research* 6 (2). DOI: http://doi.org/10.15664/jtr.1153.

Reuters, 19 October 2015, South Africa Likens Draft Climate Deal to Apartheid, www.reuters.com/article/un-climate-change-summit-talks-iduskCNOSD1U920151019.

Richmond, A. H. 1994. *Global Apartheid: Refugees, Racism, and the New World Order.* Oxford University Press: Toronto.

Rogers, M. B. *et al.*, 2007. The Role of Religious Fundamentalism in Terrorist Violence: A Social Psychological Analysis, *Int Rev Psychiatry* 19 (3): 253-262.

Rutsky. R. L. 1999. Technological Fetishism and the Techno-Cultural Unconscious, in High Techne: Art and Technology from the Machine Aesthetic to the Posthuman. Minneapolis University of Minnesota Press p 129-165.

Shime, T. J. 2013. Computer Savvy but Technologically Illiterate: Rethinking Technological Literacy, in Clough M P *et al.*, eds, *The Nature of Technology: Implications for Learning and Teaching.* Sense Publishers: Rotterdam/Boston.

Smith, D. L. 2011. *Less than Human: Why We Demean, Enslave, and Exterminate Others*, St Martin's Press.

Sunday Express, 19 January 2014. The Women Made to Boil Heads of their Own People in Germany's First Holocaust. www.express.co.uk/news/world-war-1/454733/The-women-made-to-boil-heads-of-their-own-people-in-Germany's-first-holocaust.

The Guardian, 2 February 2016. Genetic Editing is Like Playing God-and What's Wrong with That?

The Guardian, 28 November 2014. Fight Fundamentalism by Tackling Poverty, Urges Pope Francis, https://www.theguardian.com/world/2014/nov/28/tackle-poverty-to-combat-fundamentalism-urges-pope-francis.

The Guardian, 24 July 2010. Technology Fetishism is Skin Deep. http://www.theguardian.com/commentisfree/2010/jul/24/technology-fetishism.

The Guardian, 11 September 2015. Effects of GMO in Argentina. Guardian-ng/opinion/effects-of-gmo-in-argentina/

Turse, N. 2015. Tomorrow's Battlefield: US Proxy Wars and Secret Ops in Africa. Haymarket Books: Chicago.

Wolfenden, K. J. 2010. Hobbes' Leviathan and Views on the Origins of Civil Government: Conservatism and Covenant, in *Journal of Social Sciences, Arts and Humanities* 2 (12): 1-2.

Chapter Two

"Humanitarian" Fundamentalism: Interrogating "Global" Processes of Fishing in African Troubled Waters

Munyaradzi Mawere & Artwell Nhemachena

"The great challenge for the humanitarian ethic and its operating system in the twenty-first century is to decolonise. There is no doubt that humanitarian action functions in neo-colonial ways. Still largely in the hands of the governments and NGOs of the former or current imperial powers ..., much humanitarian policy and practice must relinquish some of their power and hand it over to humanitarian movements in Africa, Asia, the Middle East, and Latin American" (Slini, 2006: 169-170).

"Colonialism and imperialism have not paid their scores when they withdrew their flags and their police forces from our territories. For, centuries the capitalists have behaved in the underdeveloped world like nothing more than war criminals...So when we hear the head of a European state declare with his hands on his heart that he must come to the aid of the poor underdeveloped peoples, we do not tremble with gratitude"(Fanon, 1963: 101-2).

"At the very outset of Western colonial expansion in the eighteenth and nineteenth centuries, leading Western powers...claimed to protect 'vulnerable groups"(Mamdani, 2010: 65).

"The great challenge for the humanitarian ethic and its operating system in the twenty-first century is to decolonise. There is no doubt that humanitarian action functions in neo-colonial ways. Still largely in the hands of the governments and NGOs of the former or current imperial powers ..., much humanitarian policy and practice must relinquish some of their power and hand it over to humanitarian movements in Africa, Asia, the Middle East, and Latin American" (Slini, 2006: 169-170).

"Colonialism and imperialism have not paid their scores when they withdrew their flags and their police forces from our territories. For, centuries the capitalists have behaved in the underdeveloped world like nothing more than war criminals...So when we hear the head of a European state declare with his hands on his heart that he must come to the aid of the poor underdeveloped peoples, we do not tremble with gratitude (Fanon, 1963: 101-2).

At the very outset of Western colonial expansion in the eighteenth and nineteenth centuries, leading Western powers…claimed to protect 'vulnerable groups"(Mamdani, 2010: 65).

Introduction

"Humanitarianism" is one of the "–isms" that has and continues to hit hard on Africa, making it a buzz word especially since the dawn of colonialism when African communities increasingly suffered different adversities from both "nature" and the anthropogenic evils that emanated from war atrocities, unequal encounters with people of other communities, and other forms of subjugation. More specifically, reasons for "humanitarian" interventions in Africa have been attributed but not limited to "natural" disasters, civil and political unrest, genocidal warfare, xenophobia, HIV/AIDS epidemic, afrophobia, poor living conditions, and abject poverty, among others.

While some of the evils and catastrophes that haunt Africa today are traceable to the invisible machinations of the global north, ironically most of the "humanitarian" aid that Africa receives comes from outside the continent, mainly the same global north that once colonised Africa, as foreign aid. It is arguable that much "humanitarianism" from the north is meant to perpetuate the gospel of *the white men's burden*, facilitate the fiddle of the global north as planetary good Samaritans, even if they sometimes paradoxically cultivate dependency syndrome on the continent. These fiddles by some capitalists from the global north, that play both sheep and wolf, have generated consternations among many formerly colonised countries of Africa that have become unease with the –isms from the north. Consequently, humanitarianism from the north has not been wholesomely acceptable on the continent where both politicians and academics have increasingly become critical of it. Against this backdrop, this chapter interrogates humanitarianism arguing that it has, overtime, become an aspect of global *civil religion* particularly visible in places where such humanitarianism has become a pretext for invasions of other sovereign countries. Thus, the chapter interrogates the planetary supremacist position that more often than not, the global north has arrogated to itself arguably to a point where it uses humanitarianism to fish for global discipleship.

The chapter is concerned with debates on global apartheid and how it plays out with discourses on humanitarianism. It is concerned with ways in which imperial powers and their proxies continue to dictate to Africa on the pretext that Africans are poor and therefore cannot be choosy beggars even if in a world where the Africans have been disinherited by those that continue to arrogate power to dictate over the continent. The paradox that those that loot from the global south (Bond, 2006) return with claims of humanitarianism such that they have come to be considered by some to be God (Foley, 22 October 2008); the fact that Africans are made by those that continue to loot the continent to shoulder the crises and burdens of Western capitalism that also denies them sovereignty (Bond, 2003: 20), negates claims that human rights are universal and inclusive of Africans so inhumanely treated by global capital and by some Western institutions (Nolan, 2015). When the West, that did not only impose colonialism and enslavement, continues to trivialise the humanity of Africans by force-feeding them with toxic (neo-)colonial, cultural, social, economic and political policies such as the Economic Structural Adjustment Programmes imposed by the Washington Consensus (Bond, 2003; Wekwete, 1999: 7; Shillington, 2005: 476; Orvis *et al*, 2015: 539), notions of humanitarianism become more than suspect: its presence in Africa begs the question that if asked, the so-called humanitarians themselves cannot answer satisfactorily.

The suspicions against global Western humanitarianisms are underscored by thinkers such as Good *et al*, (2008: 168) who argue citing Zolo (2003) thus: "Their pragmatic operation seeks to generalise human rights, but often ends up legitimising a banal force that gives rise to a kind of humanitarian fundamentalism". Similarly, Mertus *et al* (2006: 165) pose a critical question:

If fundamentalism is best understood as a very contemporary and innovative reaction to the challenge of modernism by making a radical appeal to exaggerated tradition, religious texts, strict rules, and moral absolutes, are these NGO documents the expression of a new humanitarian fundamentalism?

These humanitarian fundamentalisms are underpinned by the global apartheid, dating back to the eras of enslavement and colonialism, and for this reason, there is resilience of apartheid which antiapartheid fighters have not been quick to notice as existing in some "international institutions" and at different levels including the "global". Thus, Dalby, (2008) points out citing Thomas Shelling, that we live in a world that is one fifth rich and four fifths poor; for Dalby, the rich are segregated into rich countries and the poor into poor countries; the rich are predominantly lighter skinned and the poor darker skinned, most of the poor live in homelands that are physically remote, often separated by oceans and great distances from the rich. Migration on any scale is impermissible.

For Ansley, (1997: 592) cited in Dunaway *et al* (2016: 17):

> This world bifurcation is supposedly grounded in white supremacy which is defined to be political, economic and cultural systems in which whites overwhelmingly control power and material resources…and the relations of white dominance and non-white subordination are daily re-enacted across a broad array of institutions and social settings.

This world bifurcation is also problematised by Salih Booker and William Minter, 2001: 11) cited in Harrison, (2004: 4) who argue that: "…an institutional system of minority rule whose attributes include: differential access to basic human rights, wealth and power structured by race and place, structural racism, embedded in global economic processes, political institutions and cultural assumption; and the international practice of double standards that assume inferior rights to be appropriate for certain "others" defined by location, origin, race or gender".

When Africans are forced to consume genetically modified food (GMO) that is rejected by those that manufacture it and resisted in other places in the world, this raises questions about global apartheid and not just humanitarianism and human rights. When Africans are forced to implement economic policies that are detrimental to their populations, this raises questions not just about subsequent

34

humanitarianisms but about the underlying global apartheid that allows some to dictate to others including at a global level. When Africans are forced to sign climate deals that disproportionately weigh against them, this raises questions about global apartheid that require all states and institutions including the United Nations to tackle without prejudice to the rights to sovereignty by all peoples and states in the world (see for instance, Mamdani 2010: 54; Natural Society, 24 May 2013; Doyle, 19 October 2015). As Mamdani (2010: 54) states: "The international humanitarian order...is not a system that acknowledges citizenship. Instead, it turns citizens into wards...To the extent the global humanitarian order claims to stand for rights; these are residual rights of the human and not the full range of rights of the citizen".

Fishing in Troubled African Waters: Retracing the Strangulations and Tribulations

Although humanitarianism is defined in terms of providing relief and assistance to victims and addressing sources of distress (Hoffman, 2015; Belloni, 2007; Barnett *et al*, 2008; Chambard, 2016); humanitarianism arguably also serves to justify colonisation and enslavement of Africans and other people of the global south. In the global south, colonial epidemics such as typhoid fever, malaria, locusts, droughts, rinder pests and famine (Jan Bart, 2004: 224; Iliffe, 1990), provided colonists with opportunities not only to convert Africans but to also experiment on and give colonised peoples toxic education and poisoned food almost to the points of extinction in such places as Australia and North America (Churchill, 2004; Jan Bart, 2004). Thus, medical systems were used not only to heal Africans but to control them within the imperial yoke (Rankin, 2015); for this reason, medical humanitarianism was one of the most important tools of empire in the sense that it provided opportunities to justify colonialism while also blaming Africans as responsible for their own illnesses (Seth, 2009: 374; Everill *et al*, 2013). In the contemporary era, Africans who have been made to believe that global pharmaceutical corporations are merely humanitarian [rather than profit maximisation] in nature are still subject to medical and

35

other experiments that serve to perpetuate the imperial system (The New York Times, 3 July 2007; Nhemachena *et al*, 2016; Warikandwa *et al*, forthcoming).

So, while some consider humanitarian imperatives to be fundamental, to come first, that is the right to receive humanitarian assistance and to offer it as it is enshrined in the humanitarian charter with human rights law, humanitarian law and refugee law (Slini, 2006: 163), humanitarianism has an intractable dark side in Africa. Just like in the colonial era, humanitarian interventions in contemporary Africa are preceded by dramatic and exaggerated presentations of problems, even if phantomatic, such that Western humanitarian organisations get foothold into the continent's internal affairs (The Guardian, 26 October 2008: BBC News, 1 February 2006; Nhemachena, 2016a), particularly in a world touted by Western scholars as postmodern enough to efface distinctions between the African inside and its outside (Nhemachena, 2016b). Sometimes muddled, superficial, incomplete, confused, stereotypical pictures and images of Africa are presented (Dolinar *et al*, 2013) so as to frighten Africans into submission to (neo-)imperial "humanitarian" machinations.

Although Africa remains the richest continent bestowed with diverse natural resources in the world (Adeniji 2015; Mawere 2014; Mawere 2017), it remains the most alienated in terms of ownership and exploitation of those resources. While there is a growing body of scholarship explaining Africa's troubles in terms of the continent being "resource cursed", as if it is inherently the resources of Africa that are a problem; other scholars have pointed out the problem of mounting Euro-modern consumerism that has not only side-lined productiveness on the continent but it also resulted in Africans sacrificing their morality, dignity, cultures, societies, humanity and God (Nyamnjoh, 2005: 295). Consumerism that is emphasised on a continent where Africans are not only divested of ownership of resources but where there is acute poverty has resulted in fierce competition, commodification of sex, immorality, cultural decadence including exhibitionism (Nyamnjoh, 2005: 297, 299); it has also resulted in diseases afflicting both the individual physical bodies as well as the socio-cultural bodies.

African bodies suffer afflictions including countless inexplicable ones that require vigilance about their diets, their environments, the medicines and the technologies that they consume. The challenge here is that humanitarianism continues to issue from those that not only make profits from exploiting Africans but from those that in the past have donated food, clothing, epistemologies that have proven to be toxic to the continent. Humanitarianism continues to issue from those that continue to dump millions of metric tonnes of toxic e-waste to Africa putting to risk the lives of millions of Africans who are simply described as poor and without choice but given to surviving on mining rubbish dumps of the toxic e-waste (The Guardian, 14 December 2013; The Guardian, 23 September 2009; Independent, 18 February 2009; The Guardian, 16 May 2012).In other words, it is questionable why "humanitarianists" evangelise so much freedom in a continent where colonial and other forms of exploitation have ensured that the only viable freedom that people have is to mine rubbish dumps of toxic e-waste that is shipped daily from the former colonisers. While this might appear to be a graphic description of the scavengers of physical rubbish dumps accruing from "donations", the problem of mining rubbish dumps on the African continent is far more widespread particularly when one takes into cognisance the donations of old, irrelevant and toxic publications (Nyamnjoh, 2012), that are a regular feature of African libraries which would be described as having no choice, thanks to poverty in Africa but to mine the intellectual rubbish dumps coming in as Western donations. The key question here is whether it is human to donate and pretend to be humanitarian by giving away only that which one no longer likes or no longer has use for; conversely, the question is about whether those to whom "donations" are made are ever asked to catalogue their priorities not merely in terms of the "donations" but also in terms of their legitimate demands in a world where many on the African continent have been forcefully disinherited.

Erroneously describing Africans as poor and without choice [as has become conventional in some scholarship] is in fact a product of the intellectual toxic waste that fails to acknowledge the fact that to be disinherited, as Africans are, is not synonymous with being simply poor (Nhemachena, 2016a). Thus, humanitarianism that operates from the foundational premise of Africans simply being poor is in fact a false start; it fails right from the point of diagnosis to correctly represent the source of African strangulations and tribulations. The point here is that in the evangelisation of global humanitarianism, the gospel of poverty has become a dogma, to the point of fundamentalism, which is intended to replace alternative explanations of African tribulations, including disinheritance by those that preach humanitarianism. It is therefore humanitarianism itself that is averse to the alternative narratives of those that it deems to be in need of its salvation. In other words, it is humanitarianism that by silencing the narratives of the other dehumanises them to the point of what Fanon (1963) calls 'petrification'. To the extent that such humanitarianism dehumanises and animalises the other, colonially disinherited but simplistically pasted with tags of poverty, it repeats the old colonial experiences denigrating the beings of the others. Because the African others are in this humanitarianism game force-fed with what they would otherwise reject under normal circumstances, it is a humanitarianism that, while it pretends to care for the body and being of the other, denigrates the body of the other. Particularly in a postmodern dispensation, denigration and destruction of the body and being of the other can appear in the guise of caring for it; destruction can appear in the guise of humanitarianism and this in fact has been the practice of colonialism, as it is of the hunting practices of baiting animals that are first of all subjected to scotched earth system of removing all other alternative sources of food.

The colonial practices precisely involved disinheriting other people that were colonised as a way to leave them with no viable alternatives to edge out of the emerging imperial matrix. Imperial practices of disinheriting Africans were meant to make it impossible for Africans to refuse to take the imperial baits; the practices left Africans with no viable options-bite the bait or starve have been the choices for centuries now. Thus, when Africans are seen mining rubbish e-waste dumps for survival, it is not that they naturally [not by fiat of God] have no option but that their viable options have been taken away from them over the centuries of (neo-)colonialism.

Therefore, to argue, as will be seen below, that Africans should eat [contentious] donations of genetically modified foods, simply because they are poor and they can't choose, is to miss the more fundamental question which is: "Who has taken away Africans' choices in a world where others retain theirs, in the guise of respect for human rights?"

To uncritically evangelise the gospel of "African poverty", without taking into cognisance the history of disinheritance of Africans is to repeat the colonial practices of ignoring the history of Africans; it repeats the colonial gospel that Africans have not had history, have been pre-historical; it repeats the colonial practice of depicting Africans out of contexts and then caricaturing them. History, which may well be informative for those Africans that are rejecting genetically modified food donations, is replete with (neo-)imperial malfeasance and mischief on the beings and bodies of Africans as well as other peoples in the global south.

While consumerism and humanitarianism would consider access and availability as crucial, there are also questions of taste and safety that need to be considered. The question is not merely that there is no choice but also whether it is safe. Absence of choice therefore should not necessarily result in recklessness whereby Africans eat poisonous food simply because they have no choice and that it is the only kind of food that has been made accessible and available. From sexual practices to food consumption and skin bleaching, matters of safety and taste count: not only accessibility and availability matters in such cases. Matters of safety and taste are evident in instances where African women who consumed *depo provera* and norplant contraceptives (see Levitt 2015) were later diagnosed with cancer, sterility and loss of sex drive. Equally, when native Americans consumed clothing brought by early colonists, they discovered that they suffered diseases [from the poisoned clothing] that were introduced to which they had no immunity (Churchill 2004; Jan Bart, 2014: 235). Similarly, when African liberation fighters in Zimbabwe, South Africa, Namibia and Angola thought they were consuming the food, they often discovered that they were consuming Apartheid and colonial regimes' fatal chemical and biological agents deliberately laced in tinned foods, clothing, fabrics, drinks, cigarettes, medical supplies, corn, tinned beef, orange juice and sweets (Gould *et al*, 2002: 2, 26, 27). A closer look at the debates about "humanitarian donations" of genetically modified foods is reminiscent of these experiences.

The "Humanitarianism" of Genetically Modified Food and Herbicides Donations

Although Slini (2006: 163) argues that: "The humanitarian charter…is rooted firmly in human rights law, humanitarian law, and refugee law, which gives explicitly legal status to its humanitarian values of restraint and protection in 'calamity or armed conflict'", there is a growing body of scholars that is warning for instance that some genetically modified foods that sadly often constitute donations in Africa are dangerous to health and life. Rutz (2012), notes for instance, that Soya bean products are feminising and they have large amounts of estrogen-female hormones which suppress masculinity and stimulate one's female side physically and mentally. Rutz (2012) proceeds to point out loudly, thus:

> Soya is feminising, and commonly leads to a decrease in the size of the penis, sexual confusion and homosexuality. That's why most of the medical (not socio-spiritual) blame for today's rise in homosexuality must fall upon the rise in soya formula and other soy products…Homosexuals often argue that their homosexuality is inborn because 'I can't remember a time when I wasn't homosexual.

In a global apartheid context where some of the proponents of genetically modified foods shy away from them (Global Research, 5 November 2016), these effects would ordinarily be expected to get more pronounced among the world's poor and disinherited, some of who are already suffering *inter alia* increasing levels of impotence and sterility. Further exposing the dark side of some genetically modified foodstuff, The Guardian, (11 September 2015) states the fatal effects as including: "Birth defects, mutagenesis, miscarriages, depression and suicide, disorders of the central nervous system and other neurological pathologies…cancers, chlorane and other skin

40

problems, asthma, allergies… sterility and impotence, hormonal disruption and other hormonal disorders, diminished childhood development, multiple sclerosis, and death". In spite of these effects, it is noted by Natural Society (2015) that:

> Syngenta covers up how their pesticide, Altrazine, was causing frogs to change genders and have serious fertility issues…Monsanto lies about the true effects of their herbicide glyphosate on fertility…University of California, Berkeley, developmental endocrinologist …and his colleagues report that Altrazine at all levels found in the environment demasculinises tadpoles, and turns them into hermaphrodites-creatures with both male and female sexual characteristics. The herbicide also lowers levels of the male hormone testestorone in sexually mature male frogs…

In spite of the dangerous effects of genetically modified organisms and the fact that the Zambian President [after sending scientists around the world] called it [GMO food) "poison", Liberty Voice, (22 January 2014) reports that there are some who encouraged developing countries to accept the GMOs. Liberty Voice states thus:

Gates has requested that everyone think with an open mind about the fact that the modified seeds are a need of the hour and cannot be ignored without comprehensive and conclusive study of their side effects… Gates is of the opinion that GMOs are a particularly important subject for poor countries where governments find it very difficult to feed everyone.

But former Zambian President, Levi Mwanawasa [and the Zimbabwean Minister of Agriculture Dr Joseph Made have] described GMOs shipment to Africa as efforts by the donors to use Africans as guinea pigs in the global experiments with genetic engineering (The Daily News, 13 February 2016; BBC News, 29 October 2002).

Thus, while The Guardian, (24 June 2013) states that: "…Owen Paterson, the UK's Environment Minister is claiming that genetically modified (GM) crops are necessary to help address hunger in developing countries, and that it was immoral for Britain not to help developing countries to take up GM", this statement is problematic.

It is problematic in that whereas he encouraged developing countries to accept GMOs, The Economist, (19 September 2002) reports that British supermarkets, such as Tesco, audit their suppliers and they have samples of food tested for traces of DNA that would indicate some ingredients have been genetically modified. Also, The New York Times (24 October 2015), reports that countries in the European Union have banned the cultivation of genetically modified crops within their borders. The questions that boggle the African fair minded are: "If already banned elsewhere – for example in the European Union – why then are GMOs forced on Africans? Is this because those that force Africa to take up GMOs believe that Africans are subhuman?" So, while the BBC News, (29 October 2002) and The Telegraph, 30 October 2002) note that officials of the World Food Programme as well as officials of the World Health Organisation encouraged Africans to consume GMOs, these GMO crops are paradoxically resisted even in their countries of origin in the Western countries. One witnesses consensus between World Food Programme, World Health Organisation and Monsanto officials in the following statements: "World Food Programme spokesman, Richard Lee told the BBC that it would be very difficult to meet the needs of the Zambian people" (BBC News, 29 October 2002);"The [Zambian] decision is a blow against the use of GM technology in southern Africa and came despite lobbying by the World Health Organisation for African nations to embrace genetic engineering to increase crop yields" (The Telegraph, 30 October 2002) and "…Monsanto spokesman for Africa, has accused groups such as Greenpeace of perpetuating starvation by helping to persuade African governments to reject GM foods" (The Telegraph, 30 October 2002).

Apart from the World Health Organisation, the World Food Programme and Monsanto pressurising African countries to accept GMOs, the United States Agency for International Development also argued through its head, Andrew Natsios, that those who rejected GMOs were putting millions at risk in a 'despicable way' (Zerbe, 2004: 594). Whereas some in the United States Department argued that African "beggars can't be choosers" (Weiss, 2002 cited in Zerbe, 2004: 600); others such as The US ambassador to the World

Food Programme, Tony Hall, argued that Zambia's decision to reject US food aid was a crime against humanity [interpreted in this chapter to mean a crime against Western experimenters on Africans] (Zerbe, 2004: 600). Yet paradoxically, even in the U.S.A itself, Archer Daniels Midland, the largest, US exporter of Soya and maize, requires its providers to segregate GM and non-GM crops (Reuters, 1999 cited in Zerbe, 2004: 601).

As hinted above, to force-feed the so-called "poor" of the world with contentious genetically modified food amounts to fascism masquerading as humanitarianism and human rights. It amounts to Westernersdictating to other people in the world [much as there have been dictations of economic policies, politics, social-cultural, environmental and legal issues] what should get into their stomachs. So, much as the UN Secretary General, Ban Ki-Moon has been reported as dictating on Africans governments in climate change meetings (Doyle., 19 October 2015); there is also dictation by Western powers of what Africans have to eat. Dictation to Africans by Western organisations and institutions that have no accountability and that cannot be legally held to account by [the disinherited and impoverished] Africans concerned does not remove the risks extant in consuming the contentious food, it simply add to the risks.

In other words, we loudly argue that global organisations and institutions must stop dictating to Africans whether directly or indirectly via African leaders, if the humanitarianism that they purport to champion is to mean anything more than opportunities for the global north to meddle in[trips and trap] African affairs. Further, we advance that humanitarian organisations' ethical guidelines should include full commitment to defend freedom of choice and protection of all humans' rights, drawing careful attention to all acts and events that violate the rights of peoples and their communities. We in fact deplore the arbitrary and unwarranted dictation of GMOs' consumption in Africa by the global north which is being instituted in the false name of global humanitarianism. We add that global humanitarianism that builds on and develops on the basis of colonial expropriations and that continues to pass legislations to protect and prioritise the interests of multinational corporations [such as Monsanto] (see for instance New York Times, 29 February

2016) over [African] people cannot be worth its name on the continent. Humanitarianism that continues colonial type experimentations on African people is not only vacuous but nefarious: experiments have been carried out for centuries on African cultures, farming, industries and polities, that otherwise provided sufficiently for precolonial Africans (Mhango, 2016) to the extent that they did not rely on aid, donations or loans. Since colonialism, Africa has lost sustainability as it became tripped and trapped by imperial corporations that still demand pounds of flesh from their centuries old victims, now defined misleadingly as simply "poor" African international beggars who cannot choose.

Apart from being a gospel designed to mislead sincere African scholars, using "poverty" as a foundational category to understand Africa necessarily serves to deny African sovereignty and autonomy thereby constituting them as international beggars. Defined as poor, even if they have incomparable resources, which they exploited and processed in the precolonial era before they were disinherited, they are excluded from major world bodies such as the United Nations in which former imperial powers still dominate by virtue of what they looted and are still looting from the continent. Similarly defined as "poor" and inconsequential, they are denied major votes and veto powers in international institutions such as the International Monetary Fund and World Bank that paradoxically derive their powers from exploiting Africa, whose Africans continue to be trampled upon. Defined misleadingly as simply "poor", Africans are considered to constitute the world's greatest criminals [but who lack viable and effective courts to try in their jurisdictions] for whom the [Western] International Criminal Court has been set up. Considered simplistically as poor, Africans are deemed to constitute in Frantz Fanon's (1963) terms, the 'wretched of the earth' or in other terms; the scam of the earth manifesting useless existence that global policies of eugenics and that Malthusian misanthropic policies of human culling [purportedly in the interest of the African environment, including "climate change"] would suit.

The logic and practice of human culling that undergirds opponents to genetically modified organisms are not hard to see even in other realms of past and contemporary life. Imperial capitalism has survived by mortally sacrificing peoples of the African continent [and the global south more generally] since the enslavement and colonial eras. Similarly, imperial capitalism has survived more recently growing anti-imperialism of the 1960s and 1970s (Harvey, 2006: 149, 152; see also Satgar, 2014: 6) by administering paralysing [neoliberal] shocks into the economies and societies of colonially disinherited Africa and the global south more generally. We can add to these the ways in which (neo-)imperialism promotes wars of austerity, counterterrorism, democracy, and in the name of humanitarianism (Haphong, 2015), which wars paradoxically kill those that they are said to protect. Whether or not labelled as collateral casualties of "otherwise humanitarian wars"; Africans [and peoples of the global south] are killed in the name of global humanitarianism whether it is through direct military combat or through donations of toxic food or medical aid that are used in the ritual flagellation of the global south in the interest of the Western [misanthropic] transformation of the world order.

Much as during colonialism when colonists legitimised their presence by pretending to protect what they called vulnerable people (Mamdani, 2010), the contemporary global order is being transformed [arguably towards greater global apartheid] using the guise of the humanitarianism of the UN 'International Responsibility to Protect' (see for instance Mamdani, 2010; Glanville, 2012). This doctrine, which states that in the event that states fail to protect their populations, bystander states in the international community can act instead, is fundamentally flawed. It is flawed in that it assumes that foreign states are necessarily bystanders when in fact Africa suffers not only because of their internal states but also because of overt and covert interference by foreign states, corporations and institutions that are sadly beyond their legal municipal jurisdictions. Further, in a global context whereas Roderick (2007) reminds scholars, we are now undergoing a new revolution in military affairs from platformcentric warfare to networkcentric warfare, it is necessarily to be particularly wary of covert and overt form of warfare. In this sense, covert warfare, that manifests as humanitarian interventions require particularly close attention. Roderick (2007), points to networked military forces in which intelligent software agents are being engineered so as to produce "agentised battlespaces". Thus, in the age of for instance the social media, it becomes difficult to locate failures of states as originating from within or from outside their jurisdictions. In other words, the very international or foreign states that [covertly, via networked agents] foment problems in selected states can paradoxically subsequently move in claiming 'responsibility to protect' populations.

Force-feeding Africans with contentious and controversial genetically modified organisms [and ideologies] that threaten their health and lives is one way emergencies and disasters can be created within states by outsider states, which contrary to the doctrine of the responsibility to protect, are not necessarily bystander states waiting to help. Imperative to note is the fact that in a world where the global media and publishing houses are monopolised by Western corporations, truths and falsehoods are not necessarily always apparent, particularly the truths of the disinherited in the global south. In a context where for the benefit of corporations and empire, evils such as enslavement and colonisation have for long been camouflaged and made to look beautiful, appealing, digestible, tempting and enticing (see for instance, Hill, 2006), it is important to note that destruction can appear as humanitarianism. In fact, the essence of the postmodern era within which genetically modified organisms are made and popularised is an epoch that claims de-differentiation including between truth and falsehoods; good and evil; delicacies and poison; human and animal, and so on. Force-feeding Africans with genetically modified organism does not only challenge their state sovereignty and citizenship rights as argued by Mamdani, (2010: 53); it also challenges the lives and wellbeing of the generality of Africans who via the responsibility to Protect are misleadingly made to believe that it is only their states that be omission or commission threaten their wellbeing and lives. Further, force-feeding Africans with GMOs [illegally] presupposes that they are indistinct from animals on which experiments have for centuries been done. In other words, humanitarianism that experiments on Africans paradoxically denies Africans humanity.

The fact that ordinary Africans are not made aware via their own indigenous languages about the controversies between scientists around genetically modified organisms is lamentable. There are still assumptions in scholarship, in spite of scholarly arguments for decoloniality of knowledge, that Africans do not have their [presumably safer] science or alternative knowledge that can be used in seasons of food shortages on the continent. Arguments by some officials from donor countries that Africans are "poor beggars who cannot choose" are sadly tinged with erroneous assumptions that Africans have nothing to contribute and they cannot innovate. In other words, such arguments assume that Africans are not citizens but they are "wards or trustees" to be merely protected, in Mamdani's (2010) sense. Besides, the fact that 800 scientists who are against genetically modified organisms have presented a letter to governments and organisations including the UN Commission on Sustainable Development, the UN Convention of Biodiversity, The World Trade Organisation and to the U.S Congress but it doesn't seem like anyone is listening (Natural Society, 24 May 2013), indicate absence of consensus over safety of the GMOs. Similarly, the fact that 110 Nobel laureates of science [in support of GMOs] have written a letter to Greenpeace, the United Nations and the world's governments calling upon Greenpeace to cease its campaigns against genetically modified organisms and biotechnology agriculture (Daily Maverick, 2 August 2016), underscores the controversial nature of the genetically modified organisms and the credibility of the Nobel awards that the 110 Nobel laureates received.

Yet, in spite of all these controversies, the U.S attempted to coerce African governments to accept GMO food even if the same food has been banned in the United States of America. Thus, in relation to these attempts by U.S to force Africans to accept the genetically modified food that it was donating, Zerbe (2004: 601) writes:

> Rather than the inability to source non-GM food aid, the decision to provide only genetically modified maize to southern Africa reflected the unwillingness of USAID to engage in any discussion of the safety and desirability to GMOs in the region.

Having discussed these issues, we now present some relevant pictures that shed more light on genetically modified organisms and other forms of "humanitarian aid".

Picture 1: Genetically Modified supercow:
https://www.pinterest.com/pin/550635491911200874/

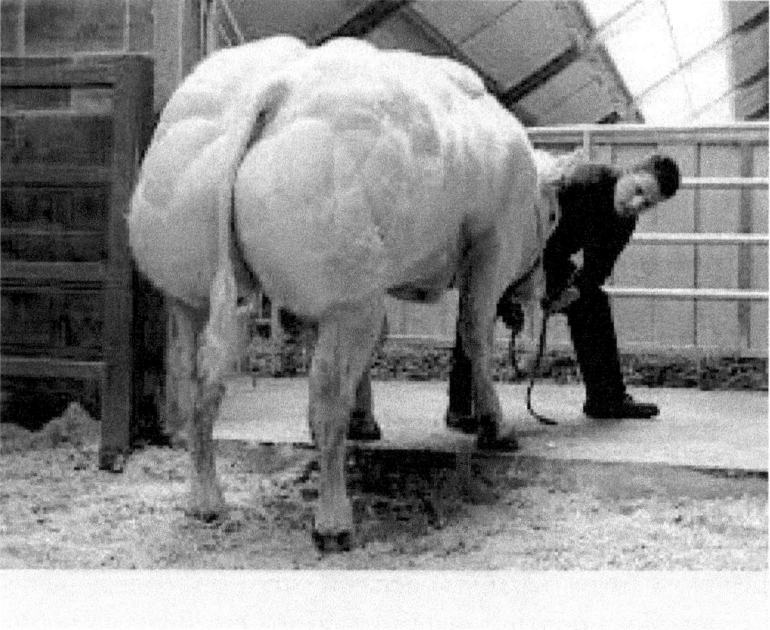

Picture 2: Brazil Admits Monsanto's Rounding up is Causing Cancer after Approving GMO Crops, 19 April 2015; in Natural Society. Naturalsociety.com/brazil-gave-green-liight-to-3-new-gm-crops-but-calls-glyphosate-cancerous/

Picture 3: GMO Birth Defects:
https://www.pinterest.com/snoonroof2012/monsanto-birth-defects/

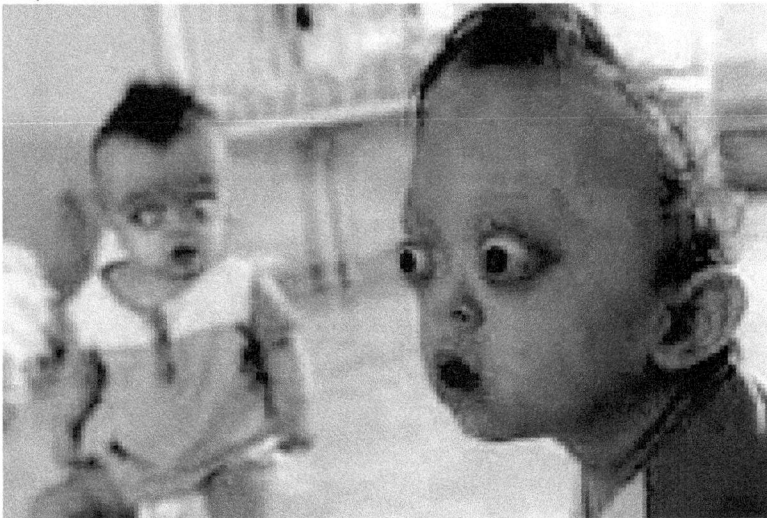

Picture 4: Seattle organic restaurants at www.seattleorganicrestaurants.com/vegan-wjole-food/gene-of-genetically-modified-foods-can-be-transfered-into-human-blood-DNA.PhP

Picture 5:

https://www.pinterest.com/pin/550635491911200874

Picture 6:

https://www.pinterest.com/pin/550635491911200874

Africa's Electronic Graveyards Where the West Dumps Old PCs, Laptops, Microwaves, Fridges and Phones: Source: Mail Online, 23 April 2015

Picture 7: 90 containers sent back to UK after Brazilian authorities said they were full of waste: The Guardian, 23 September 2009, Toxic Waste Illegally Shipped to Brazil as Recycling

Picture 8: The Guardian 7 May 2012, Europe's Second hand Clothes Bring Mixed Blessings to Africa

Conclusion

This chapter has unravelled the controversies associated with humanitarian aid to Africa, particularly the aid that comes from the global north or more specifically from the imperial powers. It has been argued in this chapter that the imperial powers, just like their towering ghost neo-colonialism, remain fast holding and hanging on the fringes of Africa while trying to control the heart strokes of the latter through nefarious mechanisms which include campaigns for Africa to force feed its people with GMOs and dangerous skin substances. On the basis of such observations as those enunciated in this chapter, we conclude with Frantz Fanon (1963: 101-2) thus:

Colonialism and imperialism have not paid their scores when they withdrew their flags and their police forces from our territories. For, centuries the capitalists have behaved in the underdeveloped world like nothing more than war criminals…So when we hear the head of a European state declare with his hands on his heart that he must come to the aid of the poor underdeveloped peoples, we do not tremble with gratitude.

References

Adeniji, D. M. 2015. *Humanitarianism and State Security in Africa*, Garamond Projects Ltd: Abuja.

All Africa, 18 December 2013. Zambia: Why Zambia Must Reject GM Crops. Allafrica.com/stories/201312190550.html.

Barnett M *et al.*, 2008, *Humanitarianism in Question: Politics, Power, Ethics.* Cornell University Press: Ithana & London.

BBC News., 1 February 2006. Can Aid do More Harm than Good, news.bbc.co.uk/2/hi/Africa/4185550.stm.

BBC News., 29 October 2002, Famine-Hit Zambia rejects GM Food Aid. News.bbc.co.uk/2/hi/Africa/2371675.stm.

Bond, P. 2003. *Against Global Apartheid: South Africa Meets the World Bank, IMF and International Finance,* Zed Books: London and New York.

Bond, P. 2006. *Looting Africa: The Economies of Exploitation*, Zed Books: London.

Branczik, A. 2004. Humanitarian Aid and Development Assistance www.beyondintractability.org/essay/humanitarian-aid.

Burnard, T. 2001. Slave Naming Patterns: Onomastics and the Taxonomy of Race in Eighteenth-Century Jamaica, in *The Journal of Interdisciplinary History* vol 31, No 3: 325-346.

Chambard, E. 2016. The Politics and Problems of Humanitarian Aid, Journal of Foreign Affairs. Keckjournal.com/2016/03/the-politics-and-problems-of-humanitarian-aid/.

Chipaike, R. 2012. The Libyan Crisis: The Militarisation of the New Scramble and More, *International Journal of Humanities and Social Sciences* vol 2, No 8: 43-48.

Churchill, W. 2004. Genocide by any Other Name: North American Indian Residential Schools in Context, In: Jones, A. Ed, *Genocide, War Crimes and the West: History and Complicity*, Zed Books: New York: 78-115.

Codevilla, A. M. 2014. *To Make and Keep Peace Among Ourselves and with all Nations*, Stanford. Hoover Institution Press: California.

Daily Maverick. 2 August 2016. 110 Nobel Laureates Warn Greenpeace of "Crime Against Humanity" on GMOs https://www.dailymaverick.co.za/opinion/sta/2016-08-02-110-nobel-laureates-warn-greenpeace-of-crime-against-humanity-on-gmos/.

Daily News. 13 February 2016. Made Rejects GM Food, https://www.dailynews.co.zw/articles/2016/02/13/made-rejects-gmo-food.

Dalby, S. 2008. Globalisation or Global Apartheid? Boundaries and Knowledge in Postmodern Times, *Journal Geopolitics* 3 (1): 132-150.

Dolinar, M. *et al.* 2013. The Use of Stereotypical Images of Africa in Fundraising Campaigns, *European Scientific Journal,* 9 (11):20-40.

Doyle, A., 19 October 2015, South Africa likens Draft Climate Deal to Apartheid, in Reuters www.reuters.com/article/un-climate-change-summit-talks-idusk-NoSD.IU920151019.

Du Preez, A. 2009. *Gendered Bodies and New Technologies: Rethinking Embodiment in a Cyber-era,* Cambridge Scholars Publishing: New Castle Upon Tyne.

Dunaway, A. W. *et al.,* 2016. Challenging the Global Apartheid Model: A World-Systems Analysis, *Journal of World-Systems Research* 22 (1): 16-22.

Everill, B. *et al.* 2013. *The History and Practice of Humanitarian Intervention and Aid in Africa,* Palgrave MacMillan: Basingstoke.

Fanon, F. 1963. *The Wretched of the Earth,* Grove Press: New York.

Fermor, C. 2012. NATO's Decision to Intervene in Libya (2011): Realist Principles or Humanitarian Norms? *Journal of Politics and International Studies* vol 8: 323-361.

Ferris, E. 2005. Faith-Based and Secular Humanitarian Organisations, in International Review of the Red Cross vol 87, No 858.

Foley, C. 22 October 2008. Humanitarian Harzard in The Guardian https://www.theguardian.com/commentsifre/2008/octo/22/i nternationalaidanddevelopment.afghanistan

Glanville, L. 2012. The Responsibility to Protect beyond Borders, in Human Rights Law Review 1-32.

Global Research, 5 November 2016. Obama Signs 'Monsanto Protection Act' Written by Monsanto-Sponsored Senator. www.globalreasearch.ca/obama-signs-monsanto-sponsored-senator/5555283.

Good, M. J. D. *et al.,* 2008. *Postcolonial Disorders,* University of California Press: Berkeley, Los Angeles, London

Gould, C. *et al.,* 2002. Project Coast: Apartheid's Chemical and Biological Warfare Programme, *United Nations Institute for Disarmament Research,* Geneva: Centre for Conflict Resolution, Cape Town.

Haphong, D. 2015. What is Neoliberalism? A Revolutionary Analysis of the Final Stage of Imperialism, In: *Global Research* www.globalresearch.ca/what-is-neo-liberalism-a-revolutionary-analysis-of-the-final-stage-of-imperialism/5433448.

Harrison, F. V. 2004. Global Apartheid, Environmental Degradation, and Women's Activism for Sustainable Well-Being: A

Conceptual and Theoretical Overview, in Urban Anthropology vol 33 (1).

Harvey, D. 2006. Neo-liberalism as Creative Destruction, Geogr Ann, 88 B (2): 145-158.

Hill C O., 2006. *The Roots and Flowers of Evil in Baudelaire, Nietzsche, and Hitler,* Illinois Open Court: Chicago and La Salle.

Huffman, P. J. 2016. Humanitarianism in Treatment: Analysing the World Humanitarian Summit, in the Future of United Nations Development System, Briefing 41.

Illife, J. 1987. *The African Poor: A History,* Cambridge University Press.

Illife, J. 1990. *Famine in Zimbabwe, 1890-1960.* Mambo Press: Gweru

Independent, 18 February 2009, Dumped in Africa: Britain’ toxic waste.
www.independent.co.uk/news/world/africa/dumped-in-africa-britain8217s-toxic-waste-1624869.html

Jan-Bart, G. 2004. Imperial Germany and the Herero of Southern Africa: Genocide and the Quest for Recompense, In: Jones, A. Ed, *Genocide, War and the West: History and Complicity,* Zed Books: New York.

Kalonaityte, V. *et al.,* 2005. The Power of Translation: Preserving Legitimacy and Self-Value Through the Justified Exclusion of the Other.

Kieler, J. 2007. *Resistance Fighter: A Personal History of the Danish Resistance Movement 1940-1945,* Gefen Publishing House: Jerusalem.

Levitt, J. I. 2015. *Black Women and International Law: Deliberate Interactions, Movements and Actions,* Cambridge University Press: New York.

Liberty Voice, 22 January 2014. Bill Gates Ruffles Feathers, Defends Genetically Modified Organisms.
Guardianlv.com/2014/01/bill-gates-ruffles-feathers-defends-genetically-modified-organisms/.

Mail and Guardian, 31 March 2016, An African First! Liberia Outsources Entire Education System to a Private American Firm. Why all Should Pay Attention. Mgafrica.com/article/2016-03-31-liberia-plans-to-outsource-its-entire-education-system-to-a-private-company-why-is-this-a-very-big-deal-and-africa-should-pay-attention.

Mamdani, M. 2010. Responsibility to Protect or Right to Punish? *Journal of Intervention and State building* 4 (1): 53-67.

Master, C. 2005. Bodies of Technology: Cyborg Soldiers and Militarised Masculinities. *International Feminists Journal of Politics*, 7 (1): 112-132.

Mawere, M. 2014. *Culture, indigenous knowledge and development in Africa reviving interconnections for sustainable development,* Langaa Publishers: Bamenda.

Mawere, M. 2017. *Theorising Development in Africa: Towards Building and African Framework of Development,* Langaa Publishers: Bamenda.

Mazrui, A. A. 2003. Towards Re-Africanising African Universities: Who Killed Intellectualism in the Post-colonial Era? *Alternatives: Turkish Journal of International Relations* vol 2, No 3 & 4: 135-163.

Mertus, J. *et al.*, 2006. Human Rights and Conflict: Exploring the Links Between Rights, Law and Natural Society, 2015, New Study: Pesticides a Major Cause of Infertility, Male Erectile Dysfunction: naturalsociety.com/new-study-pesticides-a-major-cause-of-infertility-male-erectile-dysfunction.

Natural Society, 24 May 2013, 800 Scientists Demand Global GMO "Experiment" End, naturalsoceity.com/800-scientists-global0gmo-experiment-stop/

New York Times, 29 February 2016. Chemical Safety Bill Could Help Protect Monsanto Against Legal Claims. www.nytimes.com/2016/03/01/business/monsanto-could-benefit-from-a-chemical-safety-bill.html?_r=0.

Newsweek, 4 November 2016. Uganda Court Orders Closure of 63 Schools Backed by Mark Zuckerberg and Bill Gates. Europe.newsweek.com/Uganda-court-orders-closure-of-63-schools-backed-mark-zuckerberg-and-bill-gates-516953?rm=eu.

Nhemachena, A. 2016. (Post-)development and the Social Production of Ignorance: Farming Ignorance in 21st Century Africa, In Mawere, M. Ed, *Development Perspectives from the South: Troubling the Metrics of [Under]development in Africa,* Langaa RPCIG: Bamenda p 77-118.

Nhemachena, A. 2016. Animism, Coloniality and Humanism: Reversing the Empire's Framing of Africa, In: Mawere, M. *et al.*, Eds, *Theory, Knowledge, Development and Politics: What Role for the Academy in the Sustainability of Africa?* Langaa RPCIG: Bamenda, pp. 13-54.

Nhemachena, A. 2016. The Notion of the "Field" and the Practices of Researching and Writing Africa: Towards Decolonial Praxis, *Presented at the International Conference on Social Anthropology,* University of Venda: South Africa.

Niiler, E. 2013. Robots are Getting Closer to Having Human like Abilities and Senses, *The Washington Post*, 5 August 2013.

Nolan, M. 2015. Teaching the History of Human Rights and Humanitarian Interventions in *Radical Teacher: A Socialist Journal on the Theory and Practice of Teaching*, No 103

Nyamnjoh, F. B. 2005, Fishing in Trouble Waters: Disquettes and Thiofs in Dakar, *Africa* 75 (3): 295-324

Nyamnjoh, F. B. 2012. Potted Plants in Greenhouses: A Critical Reflection on the Resilience of Colonial Education in Africa, *Journal of Asian and African Studies*, 47 (2): 129-154

Orvis, S. *et al.*, 2015. *Introducing Comparative Politics: Concepts and Cases in Context*, SAGE: California

Rankin, J. 2015. *Healing the African Body: British Medicine in West Africa, 1800-1860*, University of Missouri Press.

Roderick I., 2007, (Out of) Control Demons: Software Agents, Complexity Theory and the Revolution in Military Affairs, *Theory and Event* vol 10, Issue 2.

Rutz, J. 2012. The Shocking Effects of Soy on Both Sexes www.ourinterestingworld.com/health/shocking-effectes-of-soy

SABC News, 22 June 2016. 15:46, Men Sexual Health a Crisis in South Africa.
www.sabc.co.za/news/a/eb93b2004b3a3abe97afbf830b7eb7b6/men-sexual-health-a-crisis-in-sa-20160622.

Satgar, V. 2014. The Crises of Global Capitalism and the Solidarity Economy Alternative, In Same, Ed, *The Solidarity Economy Alternative: Emerging Theory and Practice*, University of Kwazulu Natal Press: Pietermaritzburg.

Seltin, J. 2009. Production of the Post-human: Political Economies of Bodies and Technology, *Parrhesia* No 8: 43-59.

Seth, S. 2009. Putting Knowledge in its Place: Science, Colonialism, and the Postcolonial, *Postcolonial Studies* 12 (4): 373-388.

Shillington K., 2005, *Encyclopaedia of African History Vol 1*. Fitzroy Dearborn Publishers: New York.

Steinmetz, G. 2005. The First Genocide of the 20th Century and its Postcolonial After-lives: German and the Namibian Ovaherero, in the *Journal of the International Institute*, vol 12, issue 2.

The Economist., 19 September 2002. Better Dead than GM-Fed? www.economist.com/node/1337197.

The Guardian, 11 September 2015, Effects of GMO in Argentina. Guardian.ng/opinion/effects-of-gmo-in-argentina/.

The Guardian., 14 December 2013, Toxic 'e-Waste' Dumped in Poor nations, Says United nations. http://www.theguardian .com/global-development/2013/dec/14/toxic-ewaste-illegal-dumping-developing-countries.

The Guardian., 23 September 2009. Toxic Waste Illegally Shipped to Brazil as Recycling, Says Environment Agency. https://www.theguardian.com/environemtn/2009/sep/23/bra zil-recycling-illegal-waste.

The Guardian., 24 June 2013. GM Crops Won't Help African Farmer http://www.thguardian.com/global-development/poverty-matters/2013/jun/24/gm-crops-african-farmers.

The Guardian., 26 October 2008. Human Rights and Wrongs, http://www.theguardian.con/commentisfree/2008/october/26 /humanrights-internationalaidanddevelopment.

The Guardian., 7 May 2012. Europe's Second Hand Clothes Brings Mixed Blessings to Africa. https:///www.theguardian.com/world/2012/may/07/europes-secondhand-clothes-africa

The Herald., 12 October 2015. Mudede and the Black Woman's Burden www.herald.co.zw/mudede-and-the-black-woman's-burden/.

The New York Times., 24 October 2015. With GMO Policies, Europe Turns Against Science.

www.nytimes.com/2015/10/25/opinion/sunday/with-gmo-policies-europe-turns-against-science.html/r=0.

The New York Times. 31 July 2007. Why Africa Fears Western Medicine. www.nytimes.com/2007/07/31/opinion/31 washington.html?_r=o.

The Telegraph., 30 October 2002, Starving Zambia Rejects America's GM Maize, www.telegraph.co.uk/news/worldnews/africanand indianocean/zambia/1411713/starving-zambia-rejects-americas-gm-maize-html.

Thill, M. 2011. *Caryl Phillips' Cambridge-the Ambiguity of a Slave's Identity Through (Re)naming.* Grin Verlag: Norderstedt.

Thomas, J. P. 27 November 2016. Are GMO Foods, Vaccines, and Big Pharma Producing an Infertile Generation? Health Impact News https://healthimpactnews.co/2014/are-gmo-foods-toxic-chemicals-and -big-pharma-producing-an-infertile-generation/

Wekwete, K. 1999. Background Paper Prepared for the Africa Regional Workshop on

Wilson, C. B. 1999. Sensors in Medicine, in *BMJ* 13, 319: 1288.

Zerbe, N. 2004. Feeding the Famine? American Food Aid and the GMO Debate in Southern Africa, in *Food Policy* 29: 593-608 www.sciencedirect.com.

Zizek, S. 2013. *Demanding the Impossible,* Polity Press: Cambridge.

Chapter Three

On the Coloniality of Research in Africa: The Case of HIV/AIDS in South Africa

Nokuthula Hlabangane

Introduction: Epistemic Justice and Fundamentalisms

The continuing resounding student "Rhodes Must Fall" cry is in danger of being understood narrowly as merely a demand for the transformation of the physical spaces of the university institution to reflect the demographics of the country. It is abidingly important to also ask why the cry for Rhodes to fall began and why it continues to gain momentum in South Africa. What exactly does this cry mean? How can it be interpreted faithfully? Embedded in the movement is a demand to overhaul and re-imagine the negotiated post-1994 settlement in all its nuances. For instance, students say that after Rhodes, they will raise the ever-present yet side-stepped question of land. The now famous adage by Chigumadzi, (2016), the "hair issue is the land issue" underscores the inextricable relationship between the personal and the political – how ostensibly unrelated issues, are, in fact, upon deeper and thus just analyses, are related. The burgeoning tendency to paint actors in the South African socio-political space in undifferentiated terms such as "student movement" masks important continuity of the past in the present. It remains important to ask which students? How and why do they not fit into the dominant post-apartheid narrative?

Ndlovu-Gatsheni, (2016:55) traces the long-standing dissent by the "de-tribalised", urban "underclass" of whom both the most affected by the AIDS epidemic and those crying for Rhodes to fall are a part. He argues that they are a class who are pauperized by a society that has inequality as its core. Failure to see these webs of significance is yet another violence visited upon this underclass who are the sacrificial lambs for the post-1994 'improvised nation'. Therefore, a more sophisticated, nuanced reading of the Rhodes

61

Must Fall movement that offers a critical understanding of the underlying politics that propel it is warranted. This, perforce, entails reading this movement as part and parcel of a struggle for humanity that is centuries-long and is wide-ranging. This chapter argues, therefore, that a narrow, simplistic reading of the students' movement as an isolated incident is an act of bad faith. It follows from a long-standing tradition to simplify what are essentially complex issues in a quest to make them accessible and amenable to equally simplistic remedies. This cynical posture is a political tool that is employed to hollow out complex issues such that the webs of significance in which they are mired are obscured and thus culpability is placed at the present and the constitutive absent present is absolved of responsibility (see Nhemachena, 2016).

Magubane in Ndlovu-Gatsheni (2016), condemns the voluminous and detailed descriptions of social change that are devoid of any sustained theoretical argument. He argues that this tendency contributes little or nothing to understanding developments in South Africa. Importantly, "...they do worse than merely fail. Together they manage to obfuscate the complexities of the social movement in Southern Africa and *deny* in their premises its historical originality" (my emphasis). Maldonado- Torres, (2012), laments the tendency to offer reductionist analyses to complex issues such as the crisis engulfing the university today. He attributes this to the theoretical tendency that underplays the impact of racialization and coloniality on the nature and complexion of the university. Such theorization rather dissociates the political from the economic when in fact, there is a symbiotic relationship between the two. In fact, as Hira, (2012) argues colonization has five arms; the geographic, political, economic, cultural and social. Taken together, they constitute the resilient colonial matrix of power (Grosfoguel, 2008) such that focusing on one, leaves the others intact and thus amounts to tinkering at the edges and failing to go to the core of the question.

The tendency to focus on the trees while ignoring the forest is a colonial bias whose genesis can be traced back to Descartes' methodic doubt and a quest for certainty:

I shall now close my eyes, I shall stop my ears, I shall call away all my senses, and thus holding conversation only with myself and considering my own nature. I shall try, little, by little, to reach a better knowledge of and a more familiar acquaintanceship with myself (Tuana, 1992: 36).

This tendency to call away parts of oneself in a quest for certainty pervades all phenomena that are apprehended through the prisms of Euro-modern rationality. This Cartesian tendency is not only about severing the body from the mind but generally is the mode that relies on a cumulative process of gathering "data" piecemeal in order to reach an acquaintance with a proscribed issue. In other words, credible understanding of phenomena, through this method, is reached by 1) separating issues into compartments that seemingly do not have a relationship, 2) studying them in situ and not subjecting them to a rigorous historical analysis, 3) it relies on the here and now, postulating that the devil is in the detail without fully appraising what the detail may actually hide and 4) it postulates a "here and there" analysis of the world, strategically being obliviousto the dialectical relationship between the two areas of praxis and finally, 5) the foregoing is also implicated in the uncritical rendition of "us" and "them", separated by place and time.These dualisms are based on Euro- modern ontologies and they obscure more than they reveal.

It is important to attribute this method that favours fragmentation back to the time, place and people whose construct it is. Rene Descartes was thinking as a white man in imperial Europe. The act to separate the body and the mind was a singular act whose motive and impact were to separate imperial Europe from what was happening in the colonies. The colonial relationship was played down and an illusion of separateness was institutionalized. Dussel, (2014) argues that had Descartes, the propagator of Cartesian thinking which became the bedrock of Western science, acknowledged the relationship between the body and the mind, he would have been forced to put a price on slavery. By systematically minimising this relationship, slavery could be morally justified as the enslaved were thought of as bodies without a soul and, like the beast of burden, they could be exploited with impunity. Therefore, Western science as a product of Cartesian thinking that hides the locus of enunciation as well as the enunciator is systematically, strategically and wilfully blind to sociality and power dynamics. It hides the beneficiaries of the world order espoused by the science and naturalises the suffering of those who are imagined through its prisms. In this way, Western science privileges the enunciated and hides the enunciator. This is a strategic lever of power that needs to be unmasked. It is wilfully ignorant of the suffering perpetuated by the modernity/coloniality dialectic as it thrives on a reductionist model of the world.Maldonado-Torres, (2007) characterises the Cartesian methodic doubt as the very relationship between colonizer and colonized provided anew model to understand the relationship between the soul or mind and the body; and likewise, modern articulations of the mind/body are used as modelsto conceive of the colonizer/colonized. Harding, (1998) argues that even when western science is functioning at its best, with internal checks and balances, retains its cultural distinctiveness as Eurocentric. Knowledge is thus not neutral. To argue the contrary is, in its turn, a fundamentalism, borne out of the myth perpetuated that knowledge, especially Western knowledge, is a-contextual (and thus universal), a-political and is thus a common good.

Euro-mdern science as it is practiced today is a construct underpinned by an imperial ethos (Maldonado-Torres, 2007) and the failure to understand it as such constitutes a fundamentalism.It is a continuing will to ignorance shown by Descartes.Here, the "West" is understood not so much as a geographical location, but as a project to colonize and subjugate. Understanding what constitutes scientific and thus unbiased and irrefutable knowledge has become so normative that its roots, history and implications have ceased to be seen as valid questions. Rather, as Dussel, (2014) argues, has become "the order of things". Questions, when asked, revolve around whether this framework has been applied correctly or not. It is seldom that the very fundamental questions about the philosophy that underpins this knowledge system are asked. This article seeks to show how such thinking characterized understanding of the HIV/AIDS epidemic. I argue that HIV/AIDS understandings in Africa followed the Euro-modernist script that privileges the individual as the site of analysis – the speaking individual – whose utterances can approximate "data", read and understood in and of itself and constitutes an "answer" to a stated "question" by a researcher doing "fieldwork, "collecting data" on an operationalized issue whose contours have been decided upon by a "knowledgeable" researcher armed with "tools" to decipher the "factors" that give rise to a phenomenon and will lead to "findings" that will then inform policy. This chapter argues that subjecting understanding of the HIV/AIDS epidemic in Africa followed the template propounded by Descartes and as such constitutes epistemic injustice. I argue that the HIV/AIDS epidemic is a contemporary site that epistemic violence was visited upon a people and how such violence went unremarked upon as such processes have become "the order of things". It is not a coincidence that the Rhodes Must Fall Movement started at university where the very fundamentals of the institution are colonial, Eurocentric, racist, capitalist, sexist and militaristic (Grosfoguel, 2008). Academia was at the forefront of understanding and accounting for the HIV/AIDS epidemic. Every other institution followed its cue. As a result, dissenting voices were muted and demonized (see Fassin, 2007).In other words, I posit that the university and its uncritical adherence to the scientific method is a site that institutionalises imperial violence on the black world. It functions in the same vein as imagined by Descartes which effectively amounted to a systematic erasure of centuries-old violence visited on black bodies.

In a nutshell, the scientific method precluded the very important consideration that violence can be embodied and may thus not be registered through the scientific method that relies on "empirical evidence". Navaro-Yashin, (2003) in "'Life Is Dead Here' Sensing the Political in 'no Man's Land' speaks of abjection as a condition of the most disadvantaged in society. This abjection may play out in ways that are not amenable to representation by the scientific method. Yet again, the idea of a speaking individual whose word is taken as "empirical evidence" does not cater for instances "when words fail". From this point of view, performance in an interview situation is taken as credible representation for inherently complex issues which span boundaries of time and space. The speaking individual who can represent their reality as proscribed by the setting of the interview is taken from the westerncentric notion of an independent individual, removed from community and history. This is contrary to, for instance, the African philosophy that posits an inbuilt relationship between the living (the speaking individual in the interview setting), the living dead (whose hardships and triumphs live on in the living) and the unborn (who rely on the living to advocate on their behalf). In other words, according to African philosophy, the speaking individual speaks not in the present, but bears the responsibility of all the others who live through him. The interview occasion flattens this out. It does not do justice to represent the speaking individual holistically. It asks of him to pattern herself in the frame determined elsewhere, drawing from particular notions of being which may not justly represent him or her. It shells him out while at the same time attributing to him the utterances he makes in an orchestrated situation which is not of his making. In other words, as Gordon, (2005: 3) argues: "[Blacks] want to be human in the face of a structure that denies their humanity".

Fassin (2007) asks: what is a just society – to which he answers that it is one that remembers? I argue that the interview is an occasion for forgetting. So, the speaking individual is really merely a proxy for legitimizing a system wired to misrepresent him. The speaking individual is, in an interview, given ephemeral power which is then used in ways that he has no control over and may, in fact, be detrimental to him. Herein lies the imperial ethos in the scientific ethos. "The imperial attitude promotes a fundamentally genocidal attitude in respect to colonized and racialized people. Through it, colonial and racial subjects are marked as dispensable" (Maldonado-Torres, 2007: 27). In other words, the interview setting with the limitations of relying on a speaking individual and takes as not valid the unsayable and the unsaid precludes the possibility for historical conversations which would put the vulnerabilities fomenting the patterning of HIV/AIDS in context. The interview setting is such that the participant should die in order to fit into its framework. The speaking individual can only make sense if he plays into a pre-determined framework with a research question and objectives. Nhemachena, Mlambo and Kaundjua (2016) understand this as mimicry that lacks any originality. In other words, the speaking individual in the interview session is involved in no more than a performance in a setting orchestrated and controlled outside of her control. The idea of "participation" captures this well as does that of an "informant" whose involvement is orchestrated and externally-controlled.

Ignorance, Coloniality and Fundamentalisms

Ignorance is a major weapon of conquest. It is amply-demonstrated by Descartes methodic doubt which was informed by the prevailing politics in imperial Europe. As such, the tendency to separate issues and mask the relationships between them is part of that arsenal that Magubane cited in Ndlovu-Gatsheni,(2016) above argues does more than not explain, it obfuscates thereby giving an illusion of understanding when it set out to mask in the first place. I argue therefore that there is an intractable relationship between the current Rhodes Must Fall movement and the alienating nature of how the question of the AIDS epidemic was framed within the university. This is not surprising as the Euro-modern scientific apparatus at the heart of which is coloniality – 'an intricate matrix of power, knowledge and being' underpinned by the modernity/coloniality dialectic (Grosfoguel, 2008; Maldonado-Torres, 2007) informs both. The idea of coloniality captures the illusive space in which the colonial administration has uprooted and left the colonial space but its effects remain (Maldonado-Torres, 2007). It allows analysis that factors in "present absences" which Nhemachena, (2016: 5) characterizes in the Derridean sense of hauntology in which the imperial ethos of violence is present but is not accounted for. By privileging the "here and now", the scientific method precludes appraisal and understanding of a broader horizon, it hides presences which are ostensibly absent. He argues that "…focusing exclusively on the "here and now" produces ignorance…of the broader metaphysical and cosmological aspects bearing on life". As such, "the ways in which the broader global, imperial capitalist spectral absence presences account for violence in the local. Thus, focusing on the "here and now" also aids Africans in missing the culpability of the global imperial structural, systemic, symbolic and material violence that concretises, coalesces and materialises in the local"(Nhemachena, 2016: 6). In this vein, then, coloniality and ignorance go together as they buttress each other. Nhemachena,(2016:9) argues that "[t]he ways in which those in absence presence permeate African subjectivities are hardly considered in studies of violence. The criminal law, based as it is on Western epistemologies that privilege the present focuses on whether or not subjective intent or *mens rea* was present at the time of the offence". The same can be said for the study of HIV/AIDS. The individual behaviour, which can be singled out through western objectivist epistemologies privileging the said and seen, was found culpable for HIV infection. The circle was progressively opened up to include meso-influences found in society and later macro-factors such as structural issues. So, while it may be scientifically true that the human immune-deficiency virus is transmitted through specific behaviours, it is abundantly ignorant to attribute the patterning of vulnerability to behaviours by individuals. This does not explain the particular patterning of vulnerability which is disproportionately among the poor and marginalised in society and in the world in general.

Wilton's, (1997) notion of "engendering African AIDS" captures the very ignorance of the many contributory factors that go beyond so-called "African culture" that ostensibly informs the disproportionate vulnerability to HIV/AIDS infection. African culture is apparently expressed through specific traditions and mores that include widow-inheritance, the virgin cleaning myth and Leclerc-Madlala's, (1997) infect one, infect all. This relentless exoticisation of African sexuality (for lack of a better characterisation) speaks to the colonial understanding of the colonized as close to nature, that is, driven by bodily dictates with little, if any, consideration. In other words, the colonized and racialized are more animal than human. Maldonado-Torres, (2007) argues that, fundamentally, the Cartesian methodic doubt was about the scepticism about the very humanity of the colonial Other. He argues that skepticism becomes the means to reachcertainty and provide a solid foundation to the self. In other words, by painting the barbaric colonized and racialized subject in

68

ways that do not give him history and subjectivity, such as is the case with invoking the notion of African AIDS, their very humanity comes into question. Fundamentally, still, he argues that this form of scepticism defines the attitude that sustains the *ego conquiro* – the Imperial Man who, through various devices, conquers others. In other words, the speaking individual who severs himself from history by speaking of the "here and now" and who speaks Prospero's reason in Caliban's voice is partaking in his own conquest. By speaking in ways already prescribed for him, the speaking individual is denying his own ways of knowing and being in service of his continued emaciation – her absenting while present. Focusing on the "here and now" is an important tool in the colonial strategy of cultivating ignorance.HIV/AIDS was therefore, a more contemporary site of Othering, where the very humanity of the racialized and colonized Other is brought into doubt. In other words, the way HIV/AIDS was understood draws from a colonial fundamentalism that there is an intractable and fundamental line between Europe and its Other (de Sousa Santos, 2007). So, while the colonial powers have vacated the colonial spaces, their ways of apprehending African experiences remain. These are characterised by ignorance and a colonial ethos of erasure, all of which remain fundamentalisms through which African experiences are registered. Moreover, "…violence of absence involves (spectral) presences that dislocate, relocate and mask their violence in such a way that their violence often gets misattributed to the ontologically present that happens to be located in areas haunted by the (spectral) presences" (Nhemachena, 2016: 3). This way, the complicity of structural factors, some of which emanate from centuries-long of colonial capitalist exploitation, in the specific patterning of HIV/AIDS in the world, is minimised. This observation is true for the Rhodes Must Fall movement in South Africa.

Africa as the "field" is Part of the Colonial Matrix of Power

The Rhodes Must Fall Movement is an all-encompassing movement that entails the questioning of all and every facet of coloniality. Maldonado-Torres, (2007: 243) paints a picture of how pervasive coloniality is; "It is maintained alive in books, in the criteria for academic performance, in cultural patterns, in common sense, in the self-image of peoples, in aspirations of self, and so many otheraspects of our modern experience. In a way, as modern subjects, we breathe coloniality all the time and everyday".

The Rhodes Must Fall Movement speaks to all the above facets of the university system. Moreover, the Rhodes Must Fall Movement seeks to bring to light and oppose the hidden curriculum of the university whose objective is to generate "colonial subjects with immense abilities to parrot and mimic the colonial authorities" (Nhemachena*et al*, 2016: 24). From this point of view, "[c]olonialism and coloniality have not denied African people the space for mimetic action and participation; rather they have denied African subjects the spaces for African poesies. In fact mimetic action was a requirement of colonial epistemologies particularly in so far as colonial education sought to assimilate African subjects by infiltrating and afflicting their subjectivities". Those who choose to understand the Movement in reductionist ways complain that the physical removal of Cecil John Rhodes' statues does not amount to much as the systems which entrenchthe colonial power of Rhodes and in which this power is entrenched remains. This is a valid point but one that misses the all-encompassing nature of the call for Rhodes to Fall. As such, the Rhodes Must Fall Movement is a call for both structural and individual permutations of the colonizing tendencies embodied by the persona of Rhodes. In this sense, Rhodes is a deeply historical, global and structural fact(or) that permeates individual values and ways of being-in the-world. In this section, I focus on coloniality of research and argue, following Nhemachena *et al,* (2016: 22) that, in the first instance, relating to "research" "Africa has suffered at the hands of "discoverers", "explorers", "expeditions" and "collectors" who fed the insatiable imperial museums and libraries with African artefacts and knowledge". As if this is not enough, these global tendencies are replicated at the level of individual Africans who become mimetic players in colonial games that denigrate *a priori* the epistemological, ontological, material, spiritual, social, cultural and economic foundations of Africans (ibid). This background only scratches the surface.

The coloniality of research in Africa is intricately linked to the idea of Africa as undeveloped and is thus in need of such development which invariably has to come from the West, given its developmental status. Therefore, research, is tied to notions of Africa as a "field" where "raw data" will be "gathered" and "collected"for processing into knowledge using Eurocentric frameworks. Africa as a "field" has, for centuries, been considered to be a "magnificent natural laboratory" where animals and human beings can be examined in the laboratories of their natural environments (Tilley, 2011: 1-2 cited in Nhemachena *et al*, 2016: 16). Certainly, centuries-long of research in Africa has not resulted in a better quality of African lives. In fact, the more Africa has been researched, the poorer it has become (Nhemachena*et al*, 2016). In the process of being researched and defined in terms of the proceeds of such research, Africans have lost their ways of knowing and ways of being-in-the-world such that they have suffered a social if not a physical death of mis-appropriation, mis-recognition and mis-representation. Nhemachena *et al*, (2016: 22) attributes this to research being more about erasing, distorting, deterritorialising and jettisoning the epistemologies of the indigenous researched peoples. Research has a far-reaching history and implications for the freedom of Africa. To be sure, "The colonisation of Africa was thus imbricated with field research, colonial practices and theories of research fed into the imperial machine, enriching imperial and colonial administrators whose effectiveness depended on the availability of reliable information". Coloniality in research legitimises epistemological colonisation in which African subjectivity is treated as inferior and constituted by a series of "deficits" and a catalogue of "lacks" (Ndlovu-Gatsheni, 2012: 49 cited in Nhemachena, 2016:16). The (un)intended consequence of research has been the "de-valorisation and annihilation of African creativity; agency and value systems; cultural estrangement; self-hatred and profound sense of inferiority (Nyamnjoh, 2004: 160 cited in Nhemachena, 2016: 17).Participating in research does not, despite all the assumptions that have congealed about its benefits, result in the emancipation of the

71

individual.Nhemachena*et al*, (2016) attributes the resilience of such coloniality of global epistemic power to the persistence of the colonial label of Africa as a field for discovery, a laboratory for research experiments, a mine for collecting data rather than a continent with inherent knowledge yearning for epistemic independence and majority status. They argue, therefore, that Africa continues to be afflicted by the virus of discoverers and the curse of hunter-gatherers of data and has become a matter-of-fact whose genesis, implications and *raison d'etre* continue to escape scrutiny. It has become a fundamentalism to rather focus on the elements that make up research such as issues of methodology and the like. The fundamentals, which include the spirit that gave rise to "research" in Africa and the geo-politics embedded therein, are left unattended.Considerations of African knowledge as "raw data" from the "field" is in fact a continuation of colonial caricaturing of African people as little more than "beasts", as "wild", "savage", "impure", "barbaric" and "requiring civilisation", "domestication" and "uplifting" by the imperial powers (Nhemachena, 2016: 23).

The speaking individual and the devil that is the detail

So, while the speaking individual may be given primacy of place in the interview setting, the question remains whether his speaking has the ability to translate into speech (Gordon, 2014). Put differently, in asking whether the subaltern can speak, Spivak, (1988) was highlighting the regimes that preclude them from being heard. I argue that research as we know it is one such a regime. The speaking individual is intricately linked to "the field", that place where "raw data" is harvested and taken elsewhere to be processed. I argue that "the field" is a place of violence reminiscent of the plantation where slaves harvested cotton and sugar that were used not for their profit but that of the master. The slaves were no better that the extensions of implements used to work the field. The embeddedness of the speaking individual in the field connotes an erasure of the very essence of the speaking individual. The field is a place where "work" is done, using "tools" conceived and conceptualised elsewhere by an actor who has occidental authority to carry out this work. The question is, who benefits from this work? I argue that neither the speaking individual nor "the field" is left any better by this work. In the first instance, the work amounts to a misrepresentation such that the speaking does not amount to speech. Centuries-long of this work has left Africa bereft and alienated from itself. Further, the misrecognition resulting from the very concepts that inform "fieldwork" result in hateful solutions that tend to blame the victim for his plight while also offering no real solutions for this plight. The motive, as Magubane, (cited in Ndlovu-Gatsheni, 2016), argues was never to truly understand and thus, offer real solutions. Characterised by a wilful ignorance of the price of slavery, detailed fieldwork proceeds can only amount to "make as if" and not really confront root causes that render others slaves and thus susceptible to epidemics such as HIV/AIDS.

Informed by the adage that the devil is in the detail, the voluminous descriptions that detail this devil are the devil itself. By delving deep into detail, as is the case with fieldwork, theorisation inevitably suffers as each "field" is understood in isolation from the other. While there may be some perfunctory comparative analysis of these fields, rarely does this analysis point to the root causes of alienation and abject dehumanisation wrought by centuries-old of colonization and exploitation. Instead, the proceeds of "the field" are taken and filtered through theories whose starting point is the misanthropic scepticism (Maldonado-Torres, 2007) of those who inhabit it. So, in reality, the speaking individual is subjected to double jeopardy; that of being dis-membered (wa Thiong'o, 2009) and subjected to theories that misrecognise this dis-memberment. The detail becomes the end in itself and as such, obscures that many and age-old processes, which by hook and crook, meant that the local in which the detail can be mined is in an intractable life and death tango with the global. Discounting this fundamental truth flirts with fundamentalisms whose*raison d'etre* is to obscure and obfuscate. Lamenting and condemning the pious nature of the proceeds that came from fieldwork in Brazil at the height of the HIV/AIDS pandemic, Farmer, (2002) argues that statistics are taken to represent the essence of a people. These pious proceeds were relentless in blaming the individuals for their plight to the complete oblivion of the determining role of structural factors. The detail became a fundamentalism that made it impossible to arrive at the core issues. Instead, the detail ignored or did not put into the rightful perspective the traces that together amalgamate into a picture that places complicity for the skewed patterning of HIV/AIDS vulnerability.

The detail presents the speaking individual as the repository of all wisdom. The detail fails to engage with the philosophy that begot the notion that the devil is in the detail. It is through this philosophy that colonists "conflated Africans with animals while conflating themselves with the human and super humans. Indeed, they conflated themselves with African territories in efforts to dedifferentiate themselves from Africans as precursor to robbing them" (Nhemachena, 2016:10).It is this philosophy that dictates that issues are atomised, a-historicised and understood in the "here and now" while also framing them in the "here and there". Nhemachena, (2016:11) advances a profound thesis on present absences which, among others, make Africans carry the burdens, including curses, of the (neo)colonial imperialism. He argues that: "The challenge is that empire preaches and celebrates globalisation, including erosion of distinctions and identities, while at the same time it denies its complicity, in terms of the implicate order metaphysics underpinning globalisation, in planetary violence. Thus, empire wants to eat its proverbial cake and have it; it wants to claim erosion of distinctions while paradoxically distinguishing itself from the violence in Africa for which only African leaders are deemed accountable even if empire has spooky and pokey presence in the continent's predicament". HIV/AIDS was understood in local terms. Gory details of a distinct African sexuality gave credence to the fundamentalism that the devil is in the detail. However, the devil is the present absence of colonial powers that cause problems in colonies for which they can offer no credible solutions (Cesaire, 1952). The logics of empire are such that hateful solutions are masqueraded as benevolent, saving Africans from themselvesand from problems emanating from the "here and now". African scholars are, thus, enjoined to facilitate African people to tell their own stories in their own ways. However, stories without historical context remain just that, stories. Such stories translate into knowledge when they are restored back to the webs of significance that give them substance. Such knowledge is not pre-packaged in particular ways that give them validity. They can be told in various ways that do not sever the self from the whole, the body from the soul, thinking from feeling and speaking from silence, the said from the unsaid and the unsayable, the here and the now, the living and the dead and the us and the them.

Curing their Ills with our Superior Knowledge

Megan Vaughan (1991) makes an important contribution with her thesis of "curing their ills with our superior knowledge". It is as important to ask what it is that causes these ills, in the first place. I argue that these ills are a result of a global, systematic and deeply-historical process of colonisation, the effects of which will continue to be felt for some time to come. Colinality ensures this continuation of the colonial agenda where formal colonialism has ended. I would like to expand on the question of knowledge systems imported from elsewhere and imposed on a supposedly knowledge-less society. Such an imperial attitude pervades all aspects of the modern existence where one way of knowing and being is thought to be above others and is, thus, justified in displacing the ostensibly lesser knowledges. Grosfoguel, (2016) characterises this as "one deciding for the many". In fact, Grosfoguel, (2016) argues that racism is essentially about thinking that other people's knowledges are inferior precisely because they are inferior people. Maldonado-Torres, (2007) argues that the opposite of Descartes' maxim "I think, therefore, I am" is "I do not think, therefore I do not exist".The racist, violent erasure inherent in this way of thinking is self-apparent. Institutions from religion, education, politics, culture, law, economy, technology and health are used to perpetrate violence on others that are summarily presumed to have absence of similar [own] institutions(Nhemachena, 2016: 18).It is this very understanding that is encapsulated in the Rhodes Must Fall movement. It is the ethos that informs the high-handed "curing their ills with our superior knowledge" attitude that saw hordes of researchers coming from the Global North, armed with their superior knowledge, to study "African AIDS". To be sure, this missionary tendency is one that is cloaked in benevolence and is thus not problematized. The recipient communities, if anything, are expected to show gratitude for the interest shown in their wellbeing. It is the proverbial "I know what is good for you and you should be grateful that I even care" attitude characteristic of unequal relations.

Nhemachena (2016) attributes the violence ravaging Africa to the absence of cultural, familial, social, economic, political and spiritual foundations that anchor society. These foundations were destroyed by colonial interference. "Claiming absence while creating the absence is one (neo)colonial duplicitous strategy that is useful for perpetuating the violence of absence in Africa that has historically been sadly considered devoid of human occupation and ownership" (ibid: 16). As such, the enthusiasm shown by the international community to study HIV/AIDS in Africa should be viewed as part of an ongoing colonial relationship in which one is the master and the other the slave; one the subject and the other, the object. This object/subject relationship replicates itself at the level of research where one is the field and the other, the fieldworker. "It presupposes absence of African [representational and therefore identifiable] human essence in a similar way that legitimised the violence of enslavement and colonial holocausts" (Nhemachena, 2016: 16). Assuming absence of knowledge and wisdom co-exists with the presence of absent presences that continue to systematically leech off African knowledges and its systems of co-existence and sustainability. It is the same logics that legitimised colonial expropriations and lootings (ibid). The logic is to legitimise destroying the institutions of others in the hope of creating absence, exposure and eventually vulnerability to external manipulation, Nhemachena*et al,* (2016) continue. So, the unholy trinity of absent-presence, ravaging African systems and a disregard for African structures and systems in the vain belief that such structures do not exist or are inferior is an important part of the colonial tools of mis-representation and as a logical sequel, misappropriation. Left on their knees, Africans then become candidates for benevolence from un-entangled patron. The hidden entanglements between the subject and the object are yet another tool of the colonial logics of conquest.

Therefore, "curing their ills with our superior knowledge" is a master signifier for a number of colonial relations.

When Black Lives are not seen Through Colonial Lenses

The sexual nature of HIV/AIDS led to its medicalization.This came with the whole medical framework whose site of intervention is the body. This gave rise to the individualisation of HIV risk as a behavioural issue. These include the tendency to artificially extricate sexual behaviour, for instance, from the relations of power and meaning that animate it. Here, the focus of analysis becomes individual sexual behaviour rather than the systems of relations that underlie and shape it. Biomedicine is, by definition, concerned with individual diagnosis and prognosis. The conceptualization of the etiology of HIV and AIDS and its management has favoured these biomedical propensities. These concerns apply to the social sciences in one way or another.Wallestein, (cited in Ndlovu-Gatsheni, 2016) asserts that nineteenth century social science presumptions which were previously considered to possess a 'liberating of the spirit, serve today as the central intellectual barrier to useful analysis of the social world'. Chabal, (cited in Ndlovu-Gatsheni, 2016) echoing Wallestein's insights from his world system analysis, asserts that the social sciences have proven to be both historically and conceptually out of date to the extent as to be 'obstacles to the understanding of what is going on in our societies and what we can do about it. The opening up to interdisciplinary insights did not do justice to the question of context and power. Rather, analyses revolved at micro and meso-levels of the individual and immediate community, respectively. The theory and method influenced the analysis that Fassin, (2007); Stillwagon, (2006); Patton, (2003); Farmer, (2001); Treichler, (1999) and Wilton, (1997) argue masks crucial factors that shape individual behaviour as well as the overall patterns of the alleged behaviour. The historical and global factors are discussed above. Below, I focus on the specific case of South Africa, a seat of both the Rhodes Must Fall Movement and the HIV/AIDS epidemic.

Following Hunter, (2010); Fassin, (2007); Stillwagon, (2006); Terreblanche, (2002) and Farmer, (2001), amongst others, I argue that it cannot be a matter of little sociological importance that in South Africa, with our violent past-continued in the present, social ills such as high rates of teenage pregnancy, the sexual brutalisation of women and children and HIV vulnerability manifest without compromise along racial lines. Income, education levels and other symbolic/material privileges following apartheid planning are distributed in favour of whites.Apartheid was simultaneously structural, material and symbolic, pervading all facets of life. The Rhodes Must Fall outcry moves from this premise but raises far-ranging issues about the philosophy of the theories and methods that are employed to understand black people's lives. I have argued that the fundamentalism that the devil is in the detail is the problem that obscures and obfuscates. Gordon, (2014: 83) argues that even as 'man' is discovered through scientific means, he is in the process, made. For this reason, the detail should be held suspect.

Several scholars have produced works that foreground "the time of HIV/AIDS". They include Hunter, (2010); Peters *et al*, (2010); Posel *et al*, 2007; Treichler, (1999); Lindenbaum, (1993) and others. *Inter alia*, the ideas contained in these works posit that HIV/AIDS has exposed the fault-lines of human organization from the global to the local, that HIV/AIDS has made unprecedented demands on theoretical and methodological issues both in the "hard" and "soft" sciences and that HIV/AIDS is an epidemic of signification whose implications are wide-ranging and ubiquitous. The "time of AIDS" here denotes the overarching significance of HIV in everyday considerations for those affected and those living with the virus. The advent of the epidemic has also revived colonial constructions of what I call black sexuality for lack of a better word. Focusing on micro- and meso- levels of analysis has not only obscured the global issues that bear on local experience but also the very important need to question ways of knowing and seeing. Beyond the theoretical and methodological limitations through which "African AIDS" was understood, this paper raises the signification that formed the bedrock through which AIDS in Africa was interpreted.

The contention of whether sexuality can be dismissed as a private issue, residing in the person and thus outside of important social considerations or is a preoccupation that is implicated in other spheres of social life is an important one precisely because of its implications in the framing and analysis of sexuality. I argue that society and sexuality cannot be conceived of as separate and thus independent realms of analysis. Sexuality does not exist as a separate realm of human interaction; it is interconnected with other spheres of social life. From this point of view, sexuality is a classic example of the feminist assertion that the personal is political (Hanisch, 1969). I argue, following Gayle Rubin, (1984) that, sexual acts carry "excess of significance" that permeate cultural, political and economic spaces. This is in the same vein that Weeks, (2002: 34) asserts: "as sex goes, so goes society". This point is also made by Hunter, (2010:36) that to understand sex we need to simultaneously focus on it and de-centre it to investigate its constructions as an apparently distinct domain but also to explore under-researched arenas that help to construct it and were constructed by it. In contradiction to the excess of significance found in sexuality, a break away from grand meta-narratives frees up sex for analysis such that the "excess of significance" contained in and through sex cannot be taken for granted. From this point of view, the framing and analysis of sexuality is a contested terrain. The framing of sexuality is an exercise in the politics of sexuality. For example, Treichler, (1999: 35) argues that HIV/AIDS (which implicates sex, sexual behaviour, sexuality) is a story of metaphor in that it attaches itself to and invigorates discursive dichotomies of self – not self, first world – third world, civilized – not civilized. In other words, the subtext in AIDS literature plays into and reinforces pre-existing social divisions (also see Stillwagon, 2006). HIV/AIDS has resurrected colonial discourses of an "African sexuality" (Fassin, 2007; Farmer, 2001; Treichler, 1999; Wilton, 1997; Heald, 1995; Ahlberg, 1994).

Writing cannot thus be reduced to method (and content) (Clifford, 1986: 2). Texts do more than inform. Importantly, *they perform* (Treichler, 1999). Treichler, (1999) argues that like AIDS in the first world, AIDS in the third world is readily articulated to pre-existing interests and agendas. Following in this vein, Farmer, (2001) posits that the myths and mystifications surrounding discourses on HIV/AIDS often serve powerful interests in spite of the best intentions of the researcher. This is especially the case when structural violence and cultural difference are conflated to account for HIV/AIDS patterning (*ibid*). Farmer, (2001) argues that the lasting legacy of these tendencies which he calls "immodest claims to HIV/AIDS etiology" is to mask the effects of social inequalities on the distribution of HIV and AIDS and its outcomes. Herein lie the politics of framing HIV/AIDS and by extension, sexuality in a particular way. It is thus my view that questions relating to methodology (and their bearing on the overall research project), sexual risk, teenage pregnancy and others cannot be adequately addressed in isolation. Questions of differential access to power, to material resources, to *dominant discourses that justify these differences* and their historical precedents merit consideration to begin to deconstruct the politics of sexuality. These considerations are particularly salient in South Africa with its history of apartheid and its continued legacies. To argue otherwise constitutes a myth that feeds a particular fundamentalism.

Apartheid aimed to maim, dwarf, thwart, violate and desecrate the black body, spirit and soul. This objective is realized in ideology, planning and practice. Apartheid was an almost perfect project as is evidenced by the continuing discrepancies in the quality of life along racial lines. True to apartheid ideology and planning, white South Africans continue to enjoy a better quality of life and have better life chances than their black counterparts. Is it not conceivable, therefore, that the bodily *hexis* (Bourdieu, 1991) of black South Africans should, to one extent or the other, reflect this? Our sense of place and "being-in-the-world" (Csordas, 1994), in relation to our sense of place of our white counterparts, is etched in our consciousness in ways that reflect the symbolic power that we were systematically dispossessed of and thus lack (cf. Bourdieu, 1989). This is thus articulated: "The American image of the Negro lives also in the Negro's heart; and when he has surrendered to this image life has no other possible reality" (Baldwin, 1951: 38 in Marshall, 2005). This is in the same manner that Fanon, (1952) argues that the systematic brutalisation, subjugation and misappropriation of the "negro" result in "inferiority complex". Holland, Ramazanoglu *et al,* (1994) argue that there is a material reality to people's lives which can be accessed through an analysis of their lived experience in relation to other groupings. These ideas are encapsulated in the idea that history is etched and buried in individual bodies as well as in the body-politic – the embodiment of history (cf. Fassin, 2007; Csordas, 1994). Hence, not only do "bodies remember" and act out that history, *they also act from that history* (Fassin, 2007; my emphasis). Jean Comaroff, (1985) also alludes to the fact that when social and cultural continuities are fractured and individuals are wrenched from their human and spiritual contexts, possibilities exist that they can no longer recognise or realise themselves. I reiterate the identity-making potential of sexuality – herein is said to be found the ultimate meaning of humanness (Vaughan, 1991). The eventual consequence of this lack of self-recognition and self-realization is that it cements white supremacist ideas as argued by the quote below;

> And the nation echoed and enforced this criticism, saying: Be content to be servants, and nothing more; what need for higher culture for half-men? ...and behold the suicide of a race! (Du Bois, 1999: 14-15).

I, therefore, argue that the discursive frame in which sexuality is embedded is a strategic lever of symbolic power. Sexuality is fraught with symbolism that feeds to all sorts of fundamentalisms. Therefore, theories on sexuality more than inform, they *perform* a political role. The burgeoning, but not absolute trend in post-1994 South Africa to organize statistics according to all other demographics except race in the quest for so-called non-racialism masks a particular fact; that social ills apply disproportionately to black Africans. This fact can, however, be extrapolated from the recent Gini coefficient that characterizes South Africa as the most unequal society in the world. True to apartheid logic and planning, these inequalities manifest uncompromisingly along racial lines in both the level of HIV vulnerability and alienation from the whole coloniality of power, knowledge and being symbolised by Rhodes as encapsulated in the Rhodes Must Fall Movement.

Accounting for Differences

The framing of the sexuality of black people has not escaped the racist agenda espoused by apartheid, in particular, and colonialism, in general. In particular, I invoke Fabian's, (2002) argument in *Time and the other: how Anthropology makes its object* that Anthropology is trapped in portraying its object of study in the "there and then", while it portrays itself in the "here and now". The paradigm of difference that informed the colonial impulse is at the core of such a conceptualisation....By so doing, Anthropology (in this instance although this sub-text underlies all disciplines) fails to highlight that the traditional object of its study is in a mutually constitutive relationship with its traditional practitioners. In other words, by portraying the objects of its study in terms that do not recognize the relationship between the traditional subjects of anthropological study, the so-called natives and its traditional practitioners – Western (-derived) scholars – Anthropology yields a partial and thus distorted view. For instance, framing so-called natives in terms of "there and then" discounts the many historical processes that lock the natives and the rest in a closely interlinked embrace. In other words, theories that invoke "culture" as opposed to "structural inequality", for instance, to explain differential patterning of HIV/AIDS vulnerability cannot help but be caught in this "there and then" worldview of so-called natives.

Comaroff and Comaroff, (1992: 4) argue that the notions of culture and tradition, which are generally used to explain the sociological character of so-called natives, freeze "the natives in their natural state". These notions deny the interconnectedness of the world and deny the natives history. More than that, these notions mask the many differences wrought by all sorts of processes that make up "the native" as well as the many similarities that emanate from these. Even further, individual intentions and collective proclivities are summarily attributed to those attributes that are common to all natives – culture and tradition – that render them undifferentiated from each other. This is in contradiction to the recognition of complexity and ambiguity bestowed on "non-natives". Natives are understood to "have" culture which, by implication, is

82

thought to be something that adheres to them as a second skin and precludes the complexity inherent in the notion. The fact of the contamination of their cultures and traditions by foreign, parasitic forces is conveniently played down. Here, culture in the Enlightenment evolutionary sense and not in the contemporary sense as meaning-making and signifying practices (see Garuba and Raditlhalo, 2008).

From this point of view then, to respond to questions that pertain to the making and remaking of a people we either look to culture or history as if the two are mutually exclusive. On the contrary, history and culture imply one another as implied by the following quote: "culture is a historically situated, historically unfolding ensemble of signifiers in action, signifiers at once material and symbolic" (Comaroff and Comaroff, 1992: 27). To argue the point further, Fiske, (1992: 154) in a piece titled *Cultural studies and the culture of everyday life* posits that;

> Social experience and therefore culture is inescapably material; that the culture of everyday life is concrete, contextualised and lived. The embodied, concrete, context-specific culture of everyday life is the terrain in which differences between unequally positioned people are practiced, and the practice is not just a performance of difference but a producer of it.

In other words, to understand culture, we necessarily have to look to history and *vice-versa*. The point that culture is material, is further underscored by Thornton's, (1988) argument that an understanding of culture entails deconstructing how and why differences in use of materials and behaviours, for instance, come about. He further argues that cultural skills to survive in a particular context are equally available to all. The exceptions, where they exist, have nothing to do with "evolution" but rather with specific social relationships of political power, economic exchange and control of cultural resources that have led to cultural deprivation, poverty and powerlessness of some people relative to others (Thornton, 1988: 26). Therefore, culture is not given, it is *made* in a context (see Garuba and Raditlhalo's, (2008) analysis of the different uses of culture in

Anthropology). The very unfortunate and bizarre understanding of culture in terms that occlude the above complex reading emanates from the division of labour in knowledge production with anthropology given the task to study the Anthropos who is locked in tradition and is thus not part of the modern world that has to do with politics and the economy.

According to Stillwaggon, (2006); Farmer, (2001); Wilton, (1997) and Treichler, (1999) the explanation for African AIDS emerged from a characterization of Africans as the social Other, vastly different from Europeans in culture and social norms. The especially crude and reductive notions of culture that form the substance of AIDS literature in Africa find a ready articulation in the idea of culture in Western scientific racism (Gilroy, 1992). Stories about witchcraft (Ashforth, 2002), conspiracy theories (Niehaus, 2005) and sex rituals (the virgin cleansing myth) are clearly catchy and reaffirm many readers' notions of an exotic Africa. Farmer, (2001) asserts that the anthropologic literature on Haiti has tended towards the exotic. He argues that such literature follows a template that generates a discourse of the Other. I argue that the same is generally true of South African AIDS literature. This literature follows the maxim, "if it bleeds, it leads" – it has not caught up with the evolution from cultural meaning to structural violence (cf. Hunter, 2010) to account for HIV/AIDS.

Both Stillwaggon, (2006) and Farmer, (2001) argue that AIDS literature that foregrounds inequality and political economy is scarce. Most AIDS literature prioritizes overdetermined cultural narratives – culture is viewed as the primary domain of signification in the patterning of HIV vulnerability (*ibid*). Nichter and Lock (2002) caution that it is all too easy to misconstrue rates of a disease as traits of a people; and when this happens victim blaming is not far off. Bibeaut and Pederson, (in the same volume: (2002): 158) argue for an urgent reintroduction of the social, political and economic dimensions in interpreting sexuality and the AIDS epidemic in Africa. They argue that analysis has been "too heavily biased on the side of biology and culture" (*ibid*). Even scarcer has been the analysis of the spirit and letter that give rise to such understandings. We should thus be wary of analysis that gives precedence to individual intention and action without situating this in a context or one that does the opposite by collapsing individual motivations into culture. As Comaroff and Comaroff (1992: 10-11) point out that analysis should "... situate the gestures of others, their words and their winks and more besides within the systems of signs and relations of power and meaning that animate them". Implied here is the mutually constitutive relationship between the individual and society. These convictions stand in contradiction to the obsession with "culture" as a root factor in sexual expression that essentially obscures the complicity of race and class in the making of sexuality. Race and class in South Africa are closely linked.

Therefore, any sociological question in South Africa today, be it teenage pregnancy, gender relations, HIV vulnerability, financial and other exclusions cannot escape the prism of apartheid logic and consequence. I argue that to understand contemporary South Africa, one needs to understand the history of South Africa which Terreblanche (2002) characterises as – from slavery, to systematic exploitation to structural exclusion. Try as we may to divorce these social ills from these historical processes, we cannot, as evidenced by their uncompromising racial overtones. The important comprehension that sexuality, class, and politics cannot easily be disengaged from one another must serve as a basis of a materialist view of sexuality in historical perspective as well (Padgug, 2007: 16). The webs of significance should go even further to implicate colonialism that not only destroyed the fabric of African societies. The fundamentalism not to see black lives through this complexity is a tool that obfuscates and masks the complicity of a complex matrix of power that constitutes Euro-modernity. It remains important to ask how social forces come to be embodied as individual pathology. I argue that failure to properly contextualise any story render the story, just that – a story. More than that, "the story" cannot speak for itself, it is subjected to interpretation. I argue that a story is subjected to a particular canon and may thus do more than "represent", it also "evokes" (cf. Tyler, 1986). The story of AIDS in Africa and in South Africa, by implication, was subjected to a colonial canon highlighting the need to always ask: "what knowledge? Whose knowledge and to what end".

Power-Knowledge: The Making of Sexuality

Foucault, (1978) asserts that "man", over time, through various processes, became a subject of scientific enquiry. Central to Foucault's (1978) arguments is the assertion that the need to isolate man as a subject of scientific enquiry is for administrative purposes; the more is known about a people, the easier it is to control and manage them. The African is the "man" who has been subjected to the disproportionate gaze of research because of his problem status (Ndlovu-Gatsheni, 2013). While this (imperial) gaze may seem one-sided, signalling unequal power relations, it is not necessarily so. The difference between the two vantage points is that one is coming from above, is incessant and definitive while the other is coming from below, may be disrupted and is reactive (see Rosaldo, 1986 for a comparative analysis). The curious gaze that has been historically visited on black people by white scholars evokes at once the unequal power relations between black and white, the definitive power of such a gaze, and the voyeurism borne out of a Eurocentric fascination with what is perceived as an exotic sexuality (see Marshall, 2005 for instance).

A classic case in point is that of Sara Baartman, the so-called Hottentot Venus (Queresh, 2004). The very convictions that informed the Sara Baartman case still exist today; the sanctity of the Euro-scientific enterprise, its purported impartiality and its definitive nature. If nothing else, an instructive lesson from this case is that Western science should be ripped off its cloak of objectivity and impartiality. In the social sciences in particular, researchers should be transparent about their private and professional assumptions and how these may influence the research enterprise. As with the debate on "culture" that has been raging on for decades (Stillwaggon, 2006), the debate on text and context (Asad, 1986; Clifford, 1986; Pratt, 1986, Rosaldo, 1986, Tyler, 1986) has not been taken seriously in much of the AIDS literature. Ethnographers largely fail to make explicit the cultural lenses through which they interpret phenomena (Wilson, 1988; Comaroff, 1985). Through this practice, they sidestep the all-important question in the social sciences; "whose canon is it anyway"? Rabinow, (1986) reminds us of the strategic role played by such practices. He argues that denying attachment to political ends facilitates the accumulation of symbolic capital that places the text beyond reading from an ideological point of view. The text is elevated to being "scientific" and therefore not "political", again gravitating to the compartmentalization of social life.

Feminists argue that male knowledge and perspective is defined as the objective truth that represents the view of society at large (Brayton, 1993). I extend this argument to say that in South Africa (especially in the HIV/AIDS field) the dominant voice that represents black people's lives and experiences has been that of white, middle class scholars. Their view invariably becomes *the* view, with other views systematically silenced and made unintelligible (see Fassin, 2007 for a similar analysis). This view has implications in the portrayal and definition of a people vis-à-vis others; representation is never merely descriptive, it serves a regulatory and constitutive function (Marshall, 2005; Du Bois, 1999; Gilman, 1985; Foucault, 1978). Said, (1978) argues that Western scholarship has contributed to a stereotypical assessment and definition of the West's Other who is seen as different, separate, eccentric, backward, sensual and passive…one who is conquerable and inferior. This amounts to her feminization - open to rape, appropriation and misuse. As already argued, the West in this instance is not regarded as a place as such but as a project which while emanating from and representing a particular Eurocentric viewpoint claims to be neutral and universal. Du Bois, (1999) argues that black bodies suffered a double jeopardy; disadvantaged social positioning and a disempowering discursive position in academic literature as argued by the quote; "The native is the creation of the colonial state; colonized, the native is pinned down, localized, thrown out of civilization as an outcast, confined to custom and then defined as its product" (Mamdani cited in Ndlovu-Gatsheni, 2016: 1).

Ethnography is thus an imperialist enterprise (cf. Said, 1987; Asad, 1986; Clifford, 1986; Tyler, 1986). Clifford, (1986: 2) makes the point that "ethnography is always caught up in the invention, not the representation of cultures". He further elaborates on this point by saying that every version of an "other" is also a construction of a "self". In this light, how are we then to read the canonical gaze of white scholars on black bodies? Said, (1978) argues that the incessant probing into the Other by white, middle class scholars is akin to the mission of conquest and ownership – "by knowing the Orient, the West came to own it". With few exceptions, it is the poor and marginalized who are invariably the objects of anthropological research. Asad, (1986: 163) makes the point that "scientific texts" become "a privileged element on the potential store of historical memory for the non-literate society concerned who have no means to contest it." The poor and non-literate who animate the canon have little control over the use of and the connotations carried by that research. Where researchers go back to disseminate research findings, the poor and non-literate are likely to believe that research proceeds as the final word on their lives. While this may not impact their everyday lives in any substantial way, it has potential to influence their consciousness.

If we move further from the geo-politics inhabiting the Cartesian principles that animate the sciences in general and focus on the social sciences and humanities in particular, where the researcher is the primary tool of data gathering, questions relating to his/her social location and the invariable interests she/he represents are important. From the stand-point theory, the ego-politics of the researcher are key to deconstructing the lens through which data are collected, conceptualized and analysed (Collins, 1997). Hooks (1992: 343) suggests that theory is always written from some "where" and this "where" is a matter of social positioning. In the same vein, there is no thinking process outside some materiality (Grosfoguel, 2012; Alcoff, 1991). Therefore, it cannot be a matter of little importance who the researcher always is and who the researched *always* are. The implications of this speak to the entrenched power dynamics between the researcher and the researched (cf. Alcoff, 1991; Wilson, 1988). More than that, if the knower comes to know from a particular position with associated interests, the act of knowing is not innocent. It is implicated in the struggle for common sense knowledge – the dominated come to see themselves through the eyes of the dominant who have an interest to preserve and perpetuate their material and symbolic edge (cf. Marshall, 2005; Du Bois, 1999; Bourdieu, 1989). It is, thus, a matter of infinite importance who has the power to ask questions of whom, probing into personal information that is then taken away to be used as the researcher sees fit. This point is captured by a dialogue between Evans-Pritchard and a Nuer man called Cuol (Rosaldo, 1986: 91); "Why do you want to know the name of my lineage"? "What will you do with it if I tell you? Will you take it to your country?" Here, Cuol shows resistance to the occidental authority inherent in the researcher; his responses highlight understanding of the fact that Evans-Pritchard represents particular interests that may be detrimental to his own. To this end, Brayton, (1993) argues that questions about the motivations for the researcher to study people of other races, cultures, ages, abilities and classes need to be addressed as part of the research process and should not be taken for granted.

Scholarship on HIV/AIDS in Africa: Engendering African AIDS

The framing of "black sexuality" in contemporary South African scholarship is unhinged from history when "nothing much seemed unhinged from history and political economy, the connections, historically deep and geographically broad came into view with minimal effort" (Farmer, 2001: 23). He writes, "When Nancy Scheper-Hughes wrote about the "mountain of uninspiring social science literature of AIDS, a morass of repetitive, pious liturgies about stigma, blaming and difference", I knew just what she meant (Farmer, 2001: 23). Lerclerc-Madlala's notions of "infect one, infect all" (1997) that paint a picture of barbarians running amok. Nor was I inspired by the "virgin cleansing" myth as "cultural" (Leclerc-Madlala, 2002) nor Niehaus', (2005) conspiracy theories nor Ashforth's, (2002) witchcraft for AIDS theory are cases in point. Decrying these tendencies, Fassin, (2007: xix) characterizes South African scholarship on HIV/AIDS that takes this vein of analysis as "ineffective and unjust". Beside the lack of deep analysis that generally characterizes this work, it smacked of cultural racism. This corpus of work locates difference in essentialist notions of culture; painting their subjects' sexuality as essentially different from theirs. Following Gilman, (1985), these pronouncements on sexuality are essentially talking to the idea of what it means to be human. The characterizations carried by this work thus questions the humanity of those studied or questions their intelligence one way or the other – they are portrayed as puppets of "culture".

So, Foucualt's, (1978) idea of the "deployment of sexuality" and that of "a network or regime of sexuality" suggests that sexuality is being used to consolidate its power with the end result of subjugating every other individual attribute to it. It is thus that sexuality gains its regulatory, meaning and identity-making ability. Implicit in this argument is a presence that is orchestrating and influencing the interplay between sex (biology) and sexuality (socio-political identity). Foucault, (1978) refers ominously to this presence as "the invisible hand" whose purpose is to cement the *status quo*. Investing the relationship between sex and sexuality with particular meanings whose end result is the definition of what is normal and what is not is an expression of power. From this point of view, sexuality ceases to be a private matter of individual choice and becomes a public matter to be administered and regulated by "bio-powers" interested in achieving a particular end. Sex is made here to foreground and thus totalise one's identity. For Foucault, sexuality is an "especially dense transfer point for relations of power" (1978: 103), that is, power produces sexuality and gives it meaning. The notion of sex being "put into discourse" reflects the interplay between power and knowledge. Sexuality is shaped by discourse and representation. In other words, "sexuality" cannot be taken at face value, it necessarily invites a dialogue. Further, Foucault, (1978) argues that the question to ask about sex is not so much whether one says yes or no to sex, whether sex is thought of as important with far reaching consequences or not. Rather, according to Foucault (*ibid*), *the central issue is to account for the fact that sex is spoken about, to discover who does the speaking, the positions and viewpoints from which they speak*. From this point of view, Foucault elevates sex from individual politics to broader politics about socio-political power and influence.

The politics of location: Who speaks for whom and why?

Following Foucault's injunction above, this section is an attempt to account for the fact that sex is spoken about, to discover who does the speaking and the positions and viewpoints from which they speak. This is an important consideration owing to the often hidden centrality of the researcher in works done in the name of academic research particularly in South Africa. Very few researchers declare themselves as social actors in the research project. This observation is also made by Lynn Wilson, (1988) and Jean Comaroff, (1985) that the conventional acknowledgements of authors tell little about the authors themselves as well as the processes that shape the final product. For instance, the much-acclaimed partnership between Kate Wood and Rachel Jewkes is silent on the fact that both researchers hail from the United Kingdom and on how this could have influenced the lenses through which they interpreted data (collected in a language that they were not familiar with). This work is silent on how they, as researchers, were perceived and how this may have influenced the kind of data that they were able to gather (see Wilson, 1988 for example for her deconstruction of these issues). In general, the section on methodology in most South African HIV/AIDS literature largely explains methods and fails to talk to questions of "methodology" which entail the thinking process in the methods chosen and the interpretations arrived at. The methods section usually goes something like; "This research was based on ethnographic fieldwork that took place primarily between 1996 and 1998 in the greater Marianhill area of Durban. An open-ended questionnaire was used as a guide for in-depth interviews with key informants representing a wide cross-section of members from the Marianhill community" (Leclerc-Madlala, 2002: 4). With few notable exceptions, very little is said about who the researcher was and how s/he grappled with "the field" and how this influenced the resultant products. This approach then engenders arguments that are couched in neutral, objective terms, thus hiding the partiality and contingency of such arguments.

I argue that this is a political choice. It is one that seeks to hide the power dynamics embedded in the arguments made. For instance, it cannot be an inconsequential matter that in South Africa, notorious for its racist tendencies, the dominant discourses on black people's lives remain that of white scholars. More than that, many of the dominant scholars in the field of HIV/AIDS and sexuality/gender including Leclerc-Madlala, (2003, 2002, 1997); Wood and Jewkes, (2007, 2001, 1998); Posel, Kahn and Walker, (2007), for instance, lack reflexivity. They write from "a position of unrecognized specificity" (Lorenz-Meyer, 2004: 8). In other words, these practices entrench a tradition where scholars fail to do what Brayton, (1993) calls "accounting for one's investments" – declaring their private and public interests and reflecting on how these influence their worldview and thus impact their work. In my view, South African scholarship has conveniently ignored the radical democratization of knowledge that dictates that the class, race, culture and gender beliefs of the inquirer be placed on the same critical plane as the subjects of inquiry (Tedlock, 1991: 80).Therefore, in sum, South African scholarship on sexuality is characterized by three important characteristics; 1) the expert voice on black sexuality is predominantly white, 2) the scholars seldom write themselves in their findings, such that their politics are hidden from view and 3) their explanation of black sexuality seldom includes issues of colonization and the attendant political economy which necessarily implicate them as beneficiaries from the ills associated with black sexuality about which they write. In other words, I argue, that these scholars do what Roland Barthe, below, says about myth:

> Myth does not deny things, on the contrary, its function is to talk about them, simply. It purifies them, it makes them innocent, it gives them natural and eternal justification, it gives them clarity which is not that of explanation but that of a statement of fact. The myth of masculinity is to pass itself of as natural, universal, free of problems (cited in Rutherford, 1989: 23).

So, while there is a legion of scholarship on sexual behaviour, sexuality and gender relations in South Africa, especially following the HIV/AIDS epidemic, its character is the same; white scholars writing about black sexuality in terms that are not only simple, but also hide the lenses through which they come to know. In my view, South African scholarship on black sexuality gives "clarity which is not that of explanation but that of a statement of fact". For, if clarity was of explanation, then the forces that have conspired to engender what I call "black sexuality", for lack of a better term, would perforce form the basis of analysis and explanation, at the centre of which is apartheid. Instead, these scholars engage in fantastical statements of fact about the importance of "black culture" in the making and shaping of "black sexuality". Much like Farmer below asserts:

> Culture is now being taken up wholesale to explain, justify and excuse non-existent, inadequate or failed intervention campaigns and *the research base that spawns them*. Culture is becoming a favoured invocation of such projects which are usually grounded in traditional social science theory focused on individual behavioural change or in information campaigns developed in pristine ignorance of structural factors and the myriad material environments in which behaviour acquires shape, meaning and consequence(Farmer, 2001: 74, my emphasis).

More than that, "black culture" is a hold-all for social norms that condone violence, pressure to prove fertility, multiple concurrent relationships, virgin cleansing myth and sex for gifts. For instance, Leclerc-Madlala's work as is the work of other prominent writers on issues of sexuality in South Africa, emphasizes and gets stuck at what she calls "local explanatory models" (*ibid*: 28). She invests a lot of energy explicating the role of what she calls "Zulu cosmology" about body dirt, 'vaginal anomalies', cleansing cures and the like to "reveal the systematic logic upon which is based the idea of virginity cleansing as a therapeutic response to HIV/AIDS amongst people who self-identify as Zulu" (Leclerc-Madlala, 2002: 1). In other words, she finds justification for child rape in "Zulu culture". This is contrary to a measured analysis that does not take for granted that "Zulu culture" is essentially different from hers, that there could be no justification in "Zulu culture" for this crime, as she calls it. Posel, (2005) posits that the virgin cleansing myth is a sign of a moral panic than a practice embedded and justifiable by cultural belief. So, to the question why gender relationships among black teenagers are violent, Wood and Jewkes, (1998: 2) refer to "social norms" that I surmise are spawned by "black culture". Their analyses inevitably blame "black culture" that is inherently violent:

Violence in dating-relationships must be understood in the broader context of life in Ngangelizwe where beating was used in a whole variety of contexts as a strategy for punishment and a way of gaining ascendancy and control over others. Thus girls fought with other girls, neighbours with neighbours, boys with other boys, husbands beat wives, parents beat children, and teachers and circumcision school leaders beat their pupils. In this way the use of violence was 'normal'.

This analysis fails to highlight the various interconnections between apartheid and its legacies that perpetuate an untenable and perilous livelihood for black men and black women and the impact on gender relations (Moffett, 2006; Posel, 2005). The analyses lack a historical perspective. The authors revert to a fundamentalism that foregrounds the local and thus fail to situate values in their proper context. Therein emanate the racist tendencies that seek to advance as fact, based on an "immutable" premise of "black culture", the patterns apparent in "black sexuality", that differ along racial lines in South Africa.

The myth in such scholarship is to pass itself as impartial and free of politics. This cannot be the case, as the knower comes to know through explicit processes that render the knowledge situated and thus open to debate. The myth is also made by the simplistic frameworks through which black sexuality has come to gain its ontological form – what Treichler, (1999: 39) calls the "official story" of what HIV/AIDS "really" means. In other words, in this scholarship, sex is spoken about in objective terms that are apolitical, the people who speak are white scholars who fail to deconstruct their positioning and discourse. These scholars speak from a point of view of being outside the *making* of "black sexuality" (cf. Comaroff and Comaroff, 1992 for instance). These tactics essentially obscure the fact that we are situated knowers whose politics are implicated in the things we (have) come to know (Mama, 1995). The knower is inevitably involved in the struggle for legitimate naming which underscores the symbolic power that comes from this act-practice and is further underscored by it (cf. Bourdieu, 1989).

The relationship between power and knowledge is a central one in any scholarly enterprise. To sever this relationship is also a political ploy. Foucault, (1978) argues that power sustains itself by hiding how it functions. Therefore, by circumventing the imperative to "account for one's investments", scholars essentially hide the relationship between power-position and power-knowledge thereby ensuring that their work sidesteps being challenged on an ideological level. The salience of this "politricking" in sexuality studies cannot be overemphasized given the violence that has been wrought by racist discourses through which the sexuality of black people has been framed. Indeed, the scramble to study "African AIDS" is an indication of a belief that the dynamics that ferment HIV/AIDS in Africa are different from those of the rest of the world. Implied by such tendencies is the idea that HIV/AIDS prevalence in Africa is a function of particular, situated knowledge systems and concomitant behaviours and practices and not so much a question of political economy (see Patton, 2003; Singer, 1997). The slew of research in Africa in the wake of the HIV/AIDS epidemic that sought to explain the pandemic in cultural and individual behaviour terms to the neglect of the socio-economic backdrop that give them a particular shape is a case in point. The conclusion that HIV/AIDS in Africa, or anywhere else for that matter, can be explained through simplistic notions of culture and individual choice is a product of a particular worldview that in turn informs a particular way of thinking, feeding a cycle that self-perpetuates. I argue in line with Farmer, (2001), Marshall, (2005), Du Bois, (1999) and others that, generally as a perceptible trend, the incessant gaze on Africa by Western scholars is not only informed by a particular way of thinking, but is also self-interested in that it cements the prevailing power dynamics.

Foucault's, (1978) assertion that even as Western society is given to verbosity regarding sexuality, this is accompanied by an incessant *will to ignorance* about whether its political economy is instructive. The implication of this is that, in general, attention is focused on the micro-politics of sexuality – *who does what, with who, how often, how and why*, to the neglect of macro-analyses that seek to deconstruct the role and influence of bio-powers such as religion, medicine, the state and the social sciences in how and why sexuality assumes the kind of aura that it does. All these institutions are culpable in the framing of African sexuality, for instance. More than that, questions relating to how sexuality is influenced by politics and the economy remain largely hidden from analyses. Instead, discounting these factors has fed racist discourses on black sexuality and are a cause of deep-rooted and widespread prejudices and discrimination.

The views that frame black sexuality as fundamentally different from white sexuality are so entrenched not only in academic discourse (see for instance Ashforth, 2002; Leclerc-Madlala, 2003, 2002, 1997; Niehaus, 2005; Varga, 2004, 2003, 1999; Wood and Jewkes, 2001, 1998), but have the potential to be internalised in the collective memory of black people one way or another. Be it in the highly visible brutal violence perpetuated by men against women, the prevalence of sexual violence against women and children and the negative feeling against men that these cause. The pervasiveness of these social ills in black communities must surely impact self-image in a negative manner. The question to ask is in what terms do we frame the above? Certainly, scholarship that couches these social ills in individual and/or (socio-) cultural terms abounds. Upon chronicling the many ills that disproportionately bedevil black people in South Africa, my friends and I always puzzle as to who or what "bewitched" us? For "bewitched" we must be given the cycle of varying kinds of violence that we visit upon each other. Fanon, (1952) chalks such tendencies to what can be called "self-image", which for black South Africans, was deliberately and systematically brutalized. To make sense of how subjectivities are structured, I invoke Bourdieu's notion of *habitus* which he argues provides individuals with a sense of how to act and respond in the course of their daily lives (Bourdieu, 1989). This sense is not so much a state of mind as a state of the body, a state of being. It is the common sense understanding of their social position which flows from the dominant views about them in the struggle for symbolic capital (Bourdieu, 1989). The notion of *habitus* is an attempt to move beyond objectivism without relapsing into subjectivism. That is, to take account of the need to break with immediate experience while at the same time relating it to social life (*ibid*). In the same vein, Butler, (2005) posits that the subject exists in relation to the social and the "I" cannot, therefore, own itself completely.

To underscore an earlier assertion that the resources from which we borrow to fashion ourselves are not equal, I add to the idea of *habitus* as shaping our worldview and view of ourselves, discourse. Here, discourse is not only ideological but is intimately linked to the distribution of power. Thus, as argued by Bourdieu, (1989: 21) "objective relations of power tend to reproduce themselves in relations of symbolic power." I like to put this notion thus: the words I speak to you are spirit and life. Following this realization, Du Bois, (1999: 15) characterizes the effects of (white) scholarship on black souls; "while sociologists gleefully count his bastards and his prostitutes, the very soul of the toiling, sweating black man is darkened by the shadow of vast despair..." thus embodying his race. Marshall, (2005: 2517) asks; "But what does it mean to embody one's race? And what is the discursive and structural relationship between race and disease?" To which he replies by invoking Du Bois' deconstruction of what is the effect of being "social problems" on black bodies and souls. Du Bois, (1999) argues that to embody race is *to be inscribed in a particular set of discourses* which render black bodies Other, peculiar, pathological and disgraced. Therefore the results of white supremacist discourses are manifest not simply in the political, economic and socio-cultural realms, but in the bodies and souls of black folk. Du Bois therefore foregrounds the problem of the oppressed internalizing the categories of the dominant and by so doing complicates the notion of subjectivity.

Conclusion

I have argued that it is a fundamentalism – a myth borne out of an almost evangelical zest - to adhere to the "scientific method" without asking fundamental questions about its genesis; the spirit and letter that gave rise to it. I have sought to show the links between the many ills that sow disenfranchisement not only in South Africa, but in Africa as a whole, that has suffered immense violence from the colonial impulse. Using the Rhodes Must Fall Movement in South Africa, I draw parallels with how the question of HIV/AIDS was studied in South Africa. I argue that it is not a coincidence that both these seminal processes began at the university as the university is argued to be the space that perpetuates coloniality by its unproblematic embrace of the "scientific method" of Rene Descartes. Fundamentally, the "scientific method" is shown to be a potent tool in the arsenal of colonialism and as such, is an important part of the colonial matrix of power. In particular, the "scientific methods" encourage ignorance about links between the "here and now", the "here and there" and "us and them". It thrives on compartmentalising and atomising issues as it takes its cue from a systematic and deliberate shutting out of the relationships between their areas of focus. This posture and strategy has the bigger consequence of playing down the complicity of the colonizer in the lives and experiences of the colonized, allowing for a situation in which the victims of colonization are blamed for the ills they experience. As such, the apparent benevolence of research in Africa hides the sins of the colonizer on colonial soil. Research itself, beyond its role in encouraging ignorance, plays a cynical role in cementing the superiority/inferiority status to the colonizer/colonized respectively. The fundamentalism of understanding research in a-political terms is thus highlighted. As such, there is a need to move away from thinking of African peoples whose traditions and cultures have been summarily condemned by research to actually question the logics of research that conceive of African knowledge as raw and thus in need of filtering through Eurocentric prisms.

In this chapter, I have sought to draw links between the ongoing Rhodes Must Fall Movement and how the HIV/AIDS pandemic has been conceptualised in South Africa. I argue that South Africa is a microcosm of all the politics that have been argued to be the case of research in Africa. The parallels include the alienating effect of "the scientific method" valorised in the university that are essentially violent to the black body. The violence comes in the form of the silencing and flattening effect of research. This is done through imposing a Eurocentric ethos in apprehending and communicating the African experience. I argue that when students cry out that "Rhodes Must Fall!" they are questioning the wholesale narrative that seeks to paint Africans as inferior vis-à-vis their white counterparts that pervades the curriculum. The undercurrent of "curing their ills" found in HIV/AIDS does the same by adopting and perpetuating a simplistic understanding and explaining HIV/AIDS in South Africa. The role of the politics of research and that of structural factors which are global and deeply historical in nature are thus underplayed. These simplistic explanations used the detail of the local to hide the complexity of the issues by underplaying the complicity of the global. I have thus argued that the detail is the devil as it plays a cynical role that needs to be unmasked. I have also argued that it matters who speaks and what informs that speech at an individual, personal and geo-political levels. Also to be unmasked are the webs of significance that make the students who are crying for Rhodes to fall are the children of the victims of the HIV/AIDS epidemic. Who then are the perpetrator and benefactor of the misery systematically visited on the same people, in many guises, through time immemorial?

References

Ahlberg, B. M., 1994. Is there a distinct African sexuality? A critical response to Caldwell, *Africa: Journal of the International African Institute* 4, (2): 220-242.

Alcoff, A., 1991. The problem of speaking for others, *Cultural Critique*, no20: 5-32.

Asad, T., 1986. The concept of cultural translation in British Anthropology, in Clifford, J and Marcus, G. E., Eds, *Writing Culture: The Poetics and Politics of Ethnography*. University of
California Press: California.

Ashforth, A., 2002. An epidemic of witchcraft? The implications of AIDS for the post-Apartheid state, *African Studies* no 61: 121-143.

Barthe, R., 1957. Mythologies, in Chapman, R, and Rutherford, J., Eds*, Male order: Unwrapping masculinity*. Lawrence and Wishart: London.

Bibeaut, G, *et al*, 2002. Dynamic products of history: Scientific racism in medical social sciences, in Nichter, M. and Lock, M., Eds, *New Horizons in Medical Anthropology: Essays in honour of Charles Leslie*. Routledge: New York.

Bourdieu, P, 1991. Language and symbolic power, in Thompson, J.B. *Studies in the theory of ideology*. Polity Press: Cambridge.

Bourdieu, P., 1989. Social space and symbolic power, in *Sociological Theory* vol 7, no 1: 14-24.

Brayton, J., 1993. What makes feminist research feminist? The structure of feminist research within the social science, http://www.unb.ca/PAR-L/win/feminmethod.htm-downloaded 15 April, 2009.

Caldwell, *et al*, 1989. The social context of AIDS in sub-Saharan Africa, in *Population and Development Review* vol 15, no 2: 185-233.

Cesaire, A., 1952. (Translated by Joan Pinkham 1972) Monthly Review Press: New York

Charmaz, K., 1999. Stories of suffering: Subjective tales and research narratives, in *Qualitative Health Research* vol 9, no 3: 362-382.

Chigumadzi, P., 2016. Hair and land issues woven together in South Africa, African Independent: News without borders.

Chow, R., 1993. Writing diaspora: Tactics *of intervention in contemporary cultural studies*. Indiana University Press: Bloomington.

Clifford, J. 1997. Notes on (field) notes, in James, A., Hockey, J. and Dawson, A. Eds. *After writing culture: Epistemology and praxis in contemporary Anthropology*. Routledge: New York.

Clifford, J., 1986. Introduction: Partial truths, in Clifford, J and Marcus, G. E., Eds, *Writing Culture: The Poetics and Politics of Ethnography*, University of California Press: California.

Collins, P. H. 1997. Comment on Hekman's "Truth and method: Feminist Standpoint theory revisited: where is the power", in *Culture and Society* 22 (21): 385-381.

Comaroff, J, *et al*, 1992. *Ethnography and the historical imagination*, Westview Press: Boulder Colorado.

Csordas, T.J., 1994. Introduction: the body as representation and being-in-the-world, in Csordas, T. J, Ed, *Embodiment and experience: the existential ground of culture and self,* Cambridge University Press: Cambridge.

Du Bois, W. E. B., 1999. The souls of black folks, in Gates, H.L. and Oliver, T.H., Eds, Norton & Company: New York.

Dussel, E. 2014. Anti-Cartesian meditations: On the origin of the philosophical anti-discourse of modernity, in *JCRT* vol 13, no 1: 1-53.

Edwards, R., 1990. Connecting method and epistemology: A white woman interviewing Black women, in *Women's Studies International Forum* 13 (5): 477-490.

Fabian, J., 2002. *Time and the Other: How Anthropology makes its object.* Columbia University Press, New York.

Fanon, F., 1952. *Black Skin, White Mask* (translated by C L Markmann, 1967). Grove Press, New York.

Farmer, P., 2001. *Infections and inequalities: The modern plagues.* University of California Press: Berkeley.

Fassin, D., 2007. *When bodies remember: Experiences and politics of AIDS in South Africa.* University of California Press: Berkeley.

Foucault, M., 1978. *The history of sexuality vol 1: An introduction* (Translated by Hurley), Pantheon: New York.

Garuba, H, *et al.,* 2008. Culture in Sheperd, N. and Robins, S, Eds, *New South African Keywords.* Jacana: Johannesburg.

Gilman, S. L. 1985. *Difference and pathology: Stereotypes of sexuality, race and madness.* Cornell University Press: New York.

Gilroy, P., 1992. Cultural studies and ethnic absolutism, in Grossberg, L, Nelson and Treichler, P, eds, in *Cultural Studies.* New York: Routledge.

Gordon, R. G. 2014. Disciplinary decadence and the decolonisation of knowledge. *Africa Development* 39 (1): 81-92.

Gordon, R.G., 2005. Through the zone of non-being: A reading of Black Skin/White Masks in celebration of Fanon's Eightieth Birthday, in *The CLR James Journal* vol 1, no 1: 1-43.

Grosfoguel, R. 2016. What is racism? In: *Journal of World-Systems Research* 22 (1): 9-15.

Grosfoguel, R. 2008. "Decolonizing political economy and postcolonial studies", in *Eurozine Transmodernity, border thinking, and global coloniality", www.eurozine.com.*

Hall, S. 1997. *Representation: Cultural representations and signifying practices,* Sage: London.

Hanisch, C. 1961. *The personal is political: Second wave and beyond.* Memo to SCEF in Notes from the second year. http://www.carolhanisch.org/CHwritis/PIP/hntml.

Harding, S. 1998. "Is science multicultural?: Postcolonialisms. Feminisms and epistemologies, Indiana University Press: Bloomington and Indianapolis.

Heald, S. 1995. "The power of sex: Some reflections on the Caldwell's "African sexuality thesis", in *Africa* vol 65, no 4: 489-505.

Herdt, G., *et al*, 1992. Eds. *The time of AIDS: Social analysis, theory and method*, Sage Publications: Newbury Park.

Hira, S., 2012. Decolonising the Mind: The Case of the Netherlands, *Human Architecture: Journal of the Sociology of Self-Knowledge*: Vol. 10: Iss. 1, Article 7. Available at: http://scholarworks.umb.edu/humanarchitecture/vol10/iss1/7

hooks, b., 1981. *Black women and feminism.* South End: Boston.

Hunter, M., 2010, *Loving in the time of AIDS: Inequality, gender and rights in South Africa*: Indian University Press: Bloomington.

Leclec-Madlala, S., 2002. On the virgin cleansing myth: gendered bodies, AIDS and ethnomedicine, in *African Journal of AIDS Research* vol 1, No 2: 87-95.

Leclerc-Madlala, S., 1997. "Infect one, infect all": Zulu youth response to the AIDS epidemic in South Africa", in *Medical Anthropology* vol 17, no 4: 363-368.

Maldonado-Torres, N., 2012. The crisis of the university in the context of neo-apartheid: A view from Ethnic Studies, *Human Architecture: Journal of the Sociology of Self-Knowledge*, X, Issue 1: 91-100.

Maldonado-Torres, N., 2007. On the coloniality of being, in *Cultural Studies* 21: 240 -270.

Mama, A., 1995. *Beyond the mask: race, gender and subjectivity.* Psychology Press: Routledge.

Marshall, W. E., 2005. AIDS, race and the limits of poverty, in *Social Science and Medicine* vol60, no 11: 2515-2525.

Navaro-Yashin, Y., 2003. 'Life Is Dead Here' Sensing the Political in 'no Man's Land', *Anthropological Theory* vol 3, no 1: 107–125.

Ndlovu-Gatsheni, S.J., 2016, Why are South African universities sites of struggle today?, in *The Thinker*, no70: 52-61.

Nhemachena, A. 2016, 2016, Double-Trouble: Reflections on the Violence of Absence and the 'Culpability' of the Present in Africa, In: Mawere, M *et al.*, Ed, *Violence, Politics and Conflict Management in Africa: Envisioning Transformation, Peace and Unity in the Twenty-First Century.* Langaa RPCIG: Bamenda.

Nhemachena, A.; *et al.*, 2016. The Notion of the "Field" and the Practices of Researching and Writing Africa: Towards Decolonial Praxis, in *Africology: The Journal of Pan African Studies*, vol.9, no.7.

Padgug, R. A., 2003. Sexual matters: On conceptualizing sexuality in history, in Parker, R and Aggleton, P., Eds, *Culture, Society and Sexuality: A Reader.* Routledge: London and New York.

Peters, P. E.; Kabekwa, D. and Walker, P. A., Eds, "Contestations over "tradition" and "culture" in a time of AIDS", in *Medical Anthropology* 29 (3): 278-302.

Patton, C., 2003. Inventing African AIDS, in Parker, R and Aggleton, P., Eds, *Culture, Society and Sexuality: A Reader.* Routledge: London and New York.

Posel, D.; Kahn, K.; and Walker, L., 2007. Living with death in the time of AIDS: Rural South Africa case study, in *Scandinavian Journal of Public Health Supplement* no69: 138-146.

Queresh, S. 2004. Displaying Sara Baartman: Reclaiming the past, in *History of Science* vol 42, no 2: 236-238.

Rabinow, P., 1986. Representations are social facts: Modernity and post-modernity in Anthropology, in Clifford, J and Marcus, G. E., Eds, *Writing Culture: The Poetics and Politics of Ethnography.* University of California Press: California.

Rosaldo, R., 1986. From the door of his tent: the fieldworker and the inquisitor, in Clifford, J and Marcus, G. E., eds, in *Writing Culture: The Politics and Poetics of Ethnography.* Berkeley: University of California Press.

Rubin, G. S., 1984. Thinking sex: notes for a radical theory of the politics of sexuality, in Vance, C.S., ed, in *Pleasure and Danger: Exploring female sexuality.* Routledge and Kegan Paul: Boston.

Said, E., 1989. Representing the colonized: Anthropology's interlocutors, in *Critical Inquiry* vol, 15, no 2: 205-225.

Said, E., 1978. *Orientalism*. Vintage Books: New York.

Singer, M., Ed, 1997, *The political economy of AIDS: Critical approaches in the health social sciences*. Baywood Publishing Co: New York.

Singer, M., 1990. Reinventing Medical Anthropology: Toward a critical realignment, in *Social Science and Medicine* vol30, no 2: 179-187.

Stoler, A. L., 1991. Carnal knowledge and imperial power, gender, race and morality in colonial Asia, in di Leonardo, M, ed, *Gender at the crossroads and knowledge: Feminist Anthropology*. University of California Press, Berkeley.

Spivak, G., 1988. Can the subaltern speak, in Nelson, C. and Grossberg, L., Eds, *Marxism and the interpretation of culture*. Urbana: Chicago.

Stillwagon, E., 2006. *AIDS and the ecology of poverty*. Oxford University Press: Oxford.

Tedlock, B., 1991. From participant observation to the observation of participation: The emergence of narrative ethnography, *Journal of Anthropological Research* 47: 69-94.

Terreblanche, S., 2002. *A history of inequality in South Africa 1652-2002*. University of Natal Press: Pietermaritzburg.

Thornton, R., 1988. Culture: A Contemporary Definition, in Boonzaier, E. and Sharp, J., eds, *South African Keywords: The Uses and Abuses of Political Concepts*. David Philip: Cape Town.

Treichler, P., 2003. AIDS, homophobia and biomedical discourse: An epidemic of signification, in L. Parker and P. Aggleton., eds, in *Culture, Society and Sexuality: A Reader*. Routledge: London

Treichler, P. A., 1999. *How to have theory in an epidemic: Cultural chronicles of AIDS*. Drake University Press: Durham.

Tyler, S. E., 1986. Postmodern ethnography: From document of the occult to occult documentation, in Clifford, J and Marcus, G. E., Eds, *Writing Culture: The Politics and Poetics of Ethnography*. University of California Press: Berkeley.

Vaughan, M., 1991. *Curing their ills: Colonial power and African Illness*. Stanford University Press: California.

Wa Thiong'o, N., 2009. *Something torn and new: An African renaissance*, Basic Civitas Books: New York.

Weeks, J., 1995. *Sexuality* (second edition). Taylor and Francis Group: London.

Wilson, L., 1988. Epistemology and power: Rethinking ethnography at Greenham, in *Anthropology for the nineties: Introductory readings.* Cole, J.B., Ed. Free Press: New York.

Wilton, T., 1997. *Engendering AIDS: Deconstructing sex, text and epidemic.* Sage Publications: London.

Wood, K., *et al*, 2007, Showing roughness in a beautiful way: Love, coercion and rape in South African youth sexual culture, in *Medical Anthropology Quarterly* vol 21, No 3: 277-300.

Wood, K., 2001. "Dangerous" love: Reflections on violence among Xhosa township youth, in Morrell, R., ed, *Changing men in Southern Africa.* University of Natal Press: Pietermaritzburg.

Wood, K., *et al*, 1998. "He forced me to love him": Putting violence on adolescent sexual health agendas. *Social Science and Medicine, No 47,* 233-242.

Wood, K., *et al.*, 1997. Violence, rape, and sexual coercion, *Gender and Development* 5 (2): 41-46.

Chapter Four

Poverty and Fundamentalism in Africa

Oliver Mtapuri

Introduction

This chapter looks at poverty from a perspective which argues that the conscious and deliberate perpetuation of poverty is a form of fundamentalism with its associated principles and values. There are people who are parasitic and are incessantly feeding off and on the sweat of the 'povertised' of society. The chapter explores how poverty prevents the fulfilment and enjoyment of human rights and results in the deferral and postponement, abandonment and foregoing of the destination of people as happiness, freedom, self- and collective affirmation, and self-actualisation. It explains why poverty, as a form of fundamentalism, affects many Africans relative to other groups from different continents. Furthermore, it explores the ways in which what I call appropriates are complicit in the perpetuation of poverty and the fundamentalism associated with it. It also examines how the measurement of poverty speaks to the 'fundamentalisation' of poverty. This is evident in the manner in which poverty statistics are derived and interpreted to express the primacy of the exclusivity of the rich and a system of neoliberalism in which the 'trickle-down effect' – a hollow hypothesis - that should benefit the so-called poor has yet to materialise for inclusivity.

The first part of this chapter discusses the povertisation of the masses through the processes of appropriation. The term 'povertised' is deliberately used to show that the povertisation of the masses is a deliberate outcome of a process of making people poor – a form of poverty production. Poverty is neither accidental nor inevitable. Povertisation gives this notion the elements of a process as opposed to being an event; it systematises poverty, and makes it endemic and fundamentalist. Povertisation occurs when humankind's systems are ambivalent or less concerned about poverty; when poverty is taken as a normal state in the lives of those who endure and experience it by those benefiting from its perpetuation that do not seem to care about the suffering of others. Such systems include institutions such as governments, municipalities, non-governmental organisations (NGOs), private firms and individuals. Povertisation exists when spaces to productively produce food have been appropriated; when markets and trade have been appropriated; as have places which are supposed to be called home, have also been appropriated; when mineral resources, the land, the sea, earth and its diversity, knowledge production and indeed, everything of value has been appropriated. These processes of appropriation, by whatever means (negotiation, force, trickery, sorcery, deceit, bribery, 'legal', illegal) I shallrefer to as appropriatism and those who appropriate are appropriates. Those who are the victims of appropriatism are the approcriats. Appropriates benefit from the perpetuation of poverty to create their kingdoms which thrive on the povertisation of others to create a form of poverty fundamentalism with its own belief systems, norms and values. The following section examines poverty with a focus on the genesis of fundamentalism.

Poverty and Fundamentalism

By definition, fundamentalism can be seen as a political or religious movement or even an attitude which has a set of simple principles which it adheres to, steeped in its former founding principles. It is normally characterised by separation, exclusion and extremism (Pavlovic, 2009). As such there are a number of forms of fundamentalism, including religious and non-religious manifestations such as economic liberalism or free market ideologies. Fundamentalism originated as a Christian movement among the American Protestants during the late 19th and early 20th centuries who subscribed to conservative evangelicalism which urged its members to actively affirm a 'fundamental' set of Christian beliefs and values in the face of the threat of modernism. Usage of the term spread and it gained prominence in describing the same phenomena in other religions like Islam and Hinduism and even in qualifying non-religious movements in areas like economics and politics. For a movement, attitude or idea to be regarded as fundamentalist, it must strictly observe some set of basic principles with extreme positions, rigidity and inability for dialogue (Pavlovic, 2009). While fundamentalism might have originated in America and Europe, like other phenomena, it quickly spread to other parts of the world and is very common in Africa today. Indeed, scholars have linked it to some of the main challenges facing the continent today. Hence, in this instance, the link to poverty and inequality.

Using the definition above, of fundamentalism as a movement or an attitude, poverty fundamentalism is the attitude that we observe in those who believe in the perpetuation of poverty. It includes acceptance of the perpetual existence of poverty and thus regarding it as normal. The normalisation of poverty is intended to induce the thinking that it is a consequence or exigency of life and should be expected. As such poverty is considered normal and inevitable. As such, such a situation props up or supports their world and ensures its 'sustainability'.

In terms of observing the basic principles, the principles appropriates uphold include measurement, separation, exclusion, and extremism, and not accepting alternative views of the total eradication of poverty. Appropriatism adheres to the principle of 'universality' of poverty and characterises those without/the poor as lazy; but ignores the brute force of appropriation and dispossession by any means possible. Appropriates believe that poverty should be measured to show headcounts, severity and depth and so forth. They also believe that poverty should be a marker of those without; their separation arises from counting, place (spatial), and material and ideological factors and emphasising difference. Their exclusivity can be seen in the creation of private clubs, private theatres, private bars, Very Important Person (VIP) and Very Very Important Person (VVIP) status, private security and many other things which are appropriated for private use. VIP and VVIPs are accorded special and exclusive treatment – they use exclusive entrances, have special sitting areas and tend to pay more for the services they receive. It is all about their money which allows them to buy this special treatment. Appropriates advocate the supremacy of money, capitalism, individualism and neoliberalism and similarly packaged ideological-isms. Poverty fundamentalism is characterised by separation, exclusion and extremism. Extremism derives from the non-acceptance of alternatives of distribution, re-distribution, justice, equity, equality, sharing, fairness and egalitarianism. The values that underpin it include extravagance, glorification of opulence, labels, brands, wealth and money, greed, ruthlessness, conquest, a sense and feelings of entitlement, superiority, adventure, avarice, self-centredness and selfishness. As such, it involves obeying a set of basic principles without question but assuming extreme positions and strictness; these characteristics are seen in extreme positions of rejecting alternatives that de-povertise and empower the masses of the people; and the rigid notion that 'one is either in or out' without dialogue in which the status quo is a *fait accompli*. De-povertisation is deeper than poverty alleviation and poverty reduction as it aims at banishing poverty from the face of the earth for good.

Poverty in Africa

Despite the fact that, in terms of size and natural endowments, Africa is bigger than the combined area of Europe, the United States and China, many Africans struggle to make ends meet (Seidman *et al*, 2006). The average African is worse off today than he was three decades ago despite the inroads made in terms of trade and technology which have promoted growth on other continents (Schaefer, 2005). The population of Africa is about 700 million, which is more than twice that of the United States, its average real per capita growth in Gross Domestic Product (GDP) is below its 1970 levels. Statistics reveal that 200 million Africans do not have access to proper health care and hygiene and 47% does not have access to safe water while the power supply is constantly intermittent and in some place non-existent (Marke, 2007). These are the statistics that are typically conveyed through various media including print, television and radio to illustrate a state of destitution and insolvency without taking into account how much is plundered by multinational corporations through illegal extraction and exportation of the continent's mineral and other resources. The formidable forces of the appropriates are behind these reversals in growth and deepening problems including povertisation because they thrive on the existence of prolonged human made African catastrophes which they create irrespective of the consequences for the African people. Indeed, an unstable and weakened Africa becomes their playground and paradise to extract a free lunch for themselves and their descendants in perpetuity.

The Economist (in Ikejiaku, 2009) estimates that about 40% of Africa's wealth is privately held outside the continent while Hardoon (2016) notes that African money amounting to around $500 billion is deposited offshore in tax havens and this costs African countries an estimated $14bn annually in forfeited tax revenue. Reclamation of these billions should not be negotiable but imperative in the interests of social justice as most of it was ill-gotten using deceit, cheating, corruption and trickery. This money could benefit Africans, particularly children, the youth and women in terms of their education, health and overall well-being. Carey (2007) observes that, compared to other regions, African economies have suffered widespread structural imbalances over the past 50 years. The World Bank (2005) noted that sub-Saharan Africa is part of the world's poorest regions where close to half the population survives on less than US$1 per day. While these money metric measures portray the continent as poor, they do not take into account how much was looted from Africa. An image is thus created of a helpless continent when nothing is written about the wanton theft of its resources. The World Bank should also be concerned about how much is stolen each and every day, how this could be stopped and measure the extent to which this could have advanced African development. The World Bank has both the financial and expert capacity to do so. Africa is not poor based on its mineral and natural resource endowments. Africans should be proud of this reality and walk tall in the knowledge that they are rich materially, be confident in themselves and claim respect from the looters of the world. The time has come for Africa to withhold foreign debt repayments that prop up the economies of Western countries. While statistics from the Millennium Development Goals (MDGs) Assessment in 2007 (UN, 2007) showed that poverty had reduced in some of the African countries, Mazrui (in Ikejiaku, 2009: 17) noted that while the

111

continent 'is the first home of humankind, it is the last to be made truly inhabitable' on earth due to poverty and underdevelopment. As such, it is obvious that povertisation is one of the most serious challenges facing the African continent today. This is associated with the incessant rape of the continent for its resources now and 50 years ago. While this was previously achieved through conquest and subjugation, it is now perpetuated in more subtle ways, including direct resource externalisation, under-invoicing, tax evasion, capital flight, fraud, corruption, bribery and debt repayment with the complicity of current African governments.

Several factors have been linked to the occurrence of poverty in Africa; these are discussed below.

Poverty, Wars and Development in Africa

Africa has witnessed countless civil conflicts and unrest that sap its resources and cripple its economy. These localised conflicts claim millions of innocent lives – Africa's talent and human resources – sucking in neighbouring countries, and exacerbating regional instability. Examples of countries that have recently experienced civil war and political instability include Sierra Leone in 1991; DRC in 1998; Ivory Coast in 2000 (Rice et al, 2006), DRC in 2013; Sudan in 2010-2016 and Burundi in 2015.

Studies have shown that wars have devastating impacts on a nation's socio-economic development. The living conditions of affected populations are greatly compromised, not only as the conflicts unfold but for several years after the war (Collier, 2007, Collier et al, 2004, Gurr and Marshall 2005). Armed conflict worsens poverty in Africa as it continues to experience volatile political environments fomented by appropriates to create an enabling environment to loot and plunder and continue with the povertisation of Africa. This is a sine qua non upon which their own prosperity is predicated and thrives. Solomon and Wart (2005) noted that armed conflict, political violence, civil wars and government collapse and ultimately the state, represent the biggest challenges to security, peace, happiness and stability. When conflict occurs, the society's development is affected. Justino (2010) notes that the cost of

112

conflicts include the loss of human life and the obliteration of infrastructure, physical capital, health and educational facilities, human capital, and industry and the disruption of socioeconomic activities. Wars have thus been identified as a major cause of persistent poverty in many parts of the world; they destroy infrastructure, institutions, production, assets, communities and networks; kill, maim and injure people (Collier, 2007). Conflicts also lead to insecurity and destabilise peace processes; thus, no nation can progress when it is bedevilled by war, instability and povertisation through appropriation. Economic growth slows as existing investors are likely to withdraw while new ones are scared off. Few investors will risk investing their money in an environment where assets are lost or destroyed as a result of fighting, robbery, theft and looting (Bundervoet and Verwimp, 2005; Gonzalez and Lopez, 2007).

Wars also lead to the destruction of productive assets which limit people's access to key sources of livelihood and may in turn impair their productive capacity and erode their economic position. Furthermore, their ability to regain their social and economic position in a post-conflict environment remains compromised (Justino and Verwimp, 2006; Verpoorten 2009). While individuals, households and investors lose property, Ikejiaku (2009) noted that governments divert scarce resources towards the purchase of military equipment and funding war operations. Further costs are incurred in rebuilding infrastructure and rehabilitation, to the detriment of socio-economic welfare and development, thus further orchestrating the processes of povertisation and subsequent appropriation.

The effects of war on education, health and labour at the individual and household levels are felt decades after the conflict and although these effects are largely linked to macroeconomic development, they may also significantly contribute to increasing poverty [povertisation of the masses of the people] and deepening inequality, especially for the most vulnerable population groups (Alderman et al, 2006; Bundervoet et al, 2009 and Shemyakina, 2006). The development economics literature has explained the appearance of poverty traps as a result of conflict related disruption of socioeconomic activities by colonialists and post-colonialists alike. Households can be trapped in poverty if their capacity to engage in productive activities is compromised in such a way that they are unable to accumulate physical, financial and human capital beyond certain critical thresholds. They are unlikely to recover unless an intervention such as aid can place them onto a recovery path (Banerjee and Duflo, 2005; Carter and Barrett, 2006). Hence, wars and resultant povertisation are regarded as some of the main contributors to increasing poverty in Africa. The following section juxtaposes poverty, inequality and democracy in Africa.

Poverty, Inequality and Democracy in Africa

The adoption of multi-party democracy in the early 1990s generated widespread and renewed optimism and excitement about the birth of a democratic society in Africa, a process that gained support from virtually all segments of society (Somolekae, 2008). Before this, the continent had largely been ruled by single party regimes and military dictatorships who instead of serving suppressed the masses, thereby perpetuating poverty. Citizens' democratic aspirations were not confined to political democracy (the granting of civil and political rights, holding of periodic elections), but embraced calls for economic empowerment and distributed social welfare. To the disadvantaged people, democracy thus meant the betterment of their lives through delivering socio-economic goods. Political democracy therefore needed to be directly linked to socio-economic development for it to be regarded as meaningful and be accepted by the masses (Somolekae, 2008). Barkan (2006:18) noted that by the end of the year 2000, all except Comoros, Congo-Kinshasa, Equatorial Guinea, Rwanda, and Somalia of sub-Saharan Africa's 47 states had adopted multi-party politics. However, political freedom is not sufficient if it is not backed up by economic freedom. While political freedom is a necessary, it is not a sufficient condition for full emancipation. Economic freedom that is required for total liberation is the hardest to achieve. The physical removal of the coloniser did not remove his/her economic tentacles that maintained a stranglehold on Africa and its resources. The invisible hand of colonialism and neo-colonialism is as present as it was during and after colonialism – and as ferocious as it ever was. It is ferocious because it is the last reed that colonialists and post-colonial shenanigans are holding on to for survival of the post-colonial empire. What makes this so sad is that Africans are conniving in this exercise.

Modernisation theory contends that democracy is linked to the industrial phase of capitalist development (Adejumobi, 2000). Capitalist development favours features such as secularism, urbanisation, bureaucratisation and individualism. Capitalism supports the upholding of democratic values and the existence of a middle class in order to maintain a so-called liberal democratic order. As such, liberal democracy represents an outcome, and not necessarily a cause of socio-economic development. Africa needs a socio-economic and political system that is home grown and takes into account its post-colonial legacy and slavery, to remove the shackles of empire in all its forms. This requires a new breed of cadres with Africa at heart. This breed, which is fearless and down-to-earth, must have a commitment to total liberation in order for Africans to achieve a better life. This line of thinking is termed radical Africanism. Its characteristics include decolonisation, de-povertisation, refusal to pay foreign debt, de-appropriation of spaces, resources, knowledge, the attainment of total economic freedom, African sovereignty and self-determination.

The debates regarding the nexus between democracy and development are contemporary. There seems to be no consensus on whether democracy should be construed as a means to an end or an end in itself. Edigheji (2005) posed the question of whether African nations can be both democratic and developmental at the same time. Some are of the view that liberal democracy provides the basis for socio-economic development. This is supported by the argument that libertarian values such as the rule of law, respect of human rights, freedom of speech and association, separation of powers, multi-party politics and free and fair elections create an apt context for socio-economic development to thrive. Thus, it is posited that liberal democracy promotes economic empowerment, facilitates a stable investment environment and mobilises national energy and resources for economic development. Those in support of this view in Africa are quick to point to states like Botswana and Mauritius as countries with stable liberal democracies that have achieved fast economic growth over the past decades (Adejumobi, 2000). Bhorat and Van Der Westhuizen (2012) observe that between 1965 and 1990, per capita growth in Gross National Product (GNP) for Botswana and Mauritius was 8.4% and 3.2%, respectively. They also noted that South Africa recorded some of its most positive economic growth in its history during the first decade of democratic rule. From this perspective, it is not democracy but conformance to the status quo that enables plunder to continue unabated without questioning empire or simply being in complicity with it for convenience and immediate short-term gains. The lesson is that Africa has vast potential for growth. Those states which manifest characteristics of radical Africanism are punished following episodes of concerted isolation and demonization. This is done in order to discredit radical Africanism that it does not work.

Other scholars posit that creating a symmetrical link between democracy and development is to overburden democracy. As such, democracy is regarded as a worthy political project on its own and should not be forcibly linked to neither economic development nor poverty reduction. The political environment and rights provided by democracy are ends in themselves that create a society characterised by freedom of speech and association and other rights that are regarded as important to society. While they may not necessarily lead to material betterment, they would have accomplished their primary objective (Rodrik, 2006). Research has also shown that there is a weak correlation between democracy and development. For example, Tang and Yung's (2008) study on growth and democratization among high-performing Asian economies concluded that there is no long-run relationship between democratic accountability and GDP growth. Gasiorowski (2000) also argues that political democracy may have adverse impacts on macro-economic growth particularly in developing countries. He suggests that democracy gives rise to high inflation rates and retarded economic growth in these countries due to competition for resources and yawning fiscal deficits.

The type of political regime may not necessarily be a determinant of the rate of socio-economic growth and development of any country. Many authoritarian regimes have infused both fiscal and economic discipline accompanying structural reforms which resulted in impressive economic growth and development. In terms of Africa, Imam et al (2014) argue that Libya under Gaddafi's authoritarian leadership made notable economic gains. On the Asian continent, nations like China, Qatar, Hong Kong, and North Korea are among the many examples of authoritarian governments that are doing very well economically (Tang and Yung, 2008). While it has embraced democracy, Africa is witnessing the steady deterioration of social welfare and living standards (Adejumobi, 2000). This discussion highlights that the relationship between democracy and development is complex and is not easy to establish because povertisation takes place in both democratic and authoritarian states.

It is also important to note that the introduction of democracy across Africa has seen increased economic inequality as the gap between the rich and the poor continues to widen. In Africa, inequality manifests along racial lines as well as between rural and urban divides (Bhorat and Van Der Westhuizen, 2012). A number of observers (Bermeo, 2009; Kapstein & Converse, 2008; and Wells & Krieckhaus, 2006) have revealed the harmful consequences of high levels of poverty and economic inequality for the quality and sustainability of democracy. The former have been linked to reduced voter turnout, subdued political participation and high crime rates, all of which impact negatively on the quality of democracy. Citizens that believe that democracy has failed to address their challenges see no point in participating in its processes. For them, electing someone to power is like helping them up the ladder and once they are at the top, they forget about those who assisted them. Increasing income inequality has the potential to divide citizens into haves and have-nots, appropriates and approcriats, and foment social conflict in a vicious cycle. The Fees Must Fall campaign by university students from poor and disadvantaged backgrounds in South Africa is a good example; economically privileged students – some of whom are sons and daughters of appropriates – are opposed to the protests and continue paying fees. People want jobs, food, good conditions in which to raise their families, zero crime, and good health and education, and to be able to run their businesses, travel, save, have a decent pension, and enjoy happiness and freedom – with or without

117

democracy. If democracy can deliver these essentials, people will be all for it.

Religious Fundamentalism

The religious landscape of the contemporary world is filled with groups who are regarded as fundamentalist. These groups exist among all religions; from Christian Evangelicals, to Jewish Haredi, various Hindu sects, Islamists and Buddhist radicals (Gang and Epstein, 2004). The term religious fundamentalism is often used to refer to religious groups that follow a strict canon and repudiate more open religious tenets. It can be used interchangeably with the term sectarianism to refer to a hard-core group whose attributes differ substantially from those of more tolerant mainstream groups. An important characteristic of religious fundamentalism is strict allegiance to the holy text that is regarded as infallible and not subject to critical interpretation. As such fundamentalists must express their absolute faith in their holy text and must have trust in their own capacity to comprehend its contents and apply it to themselves, and to others. Their understanding and interpretation of the word is the best and must be imposed on other people. According to Suter (n.d.), religious fundamentalism defines people by what separates them. It emphasises differences in humankind, rather than what brings humanity together. It can be argued that it obtains inspiration from a form of xenophobia (hatred of non-members). For religious fundamentalism, difference matters. However Suter argues that the chain of causation is not clear; it is believed that there could be other hidden motives, which allow leaders to use the fear of globalization of the other for their own purposes.

This discussion is restricted to two major religions that command the largest following in Africa, Christianity and Islam. While Hinduism is among the world's major religions, it does not enjoy a significant following in Africa as Islam and Christianity do, and hence might not be of much importance in the context of this chapter.

Christian Fundamentalism

Viera (2007) noted that Christianity in Africa is involved in some development work in the areas of education, health, housing and farming cooperatives as well as relief services. While this aims to lure as many followers as possible, it is also linked to the emergence of 'Social Gospel' in the US and 'Christian Socialism' in the UK early during the last century. This is a breakaway movement from the traditional privatized and supernatural Christianity which believes that the gospel must not only preach about saving souls but saving the human being in totality. As such it should not be restricted to life-after-death but should seek to address the challenges that the human race faces during the earthly life. In this regard, salvation is not only equated to liberation of the human being from sin and hell but also from fear, hunger and anything that obscures God's image in human beings, distracts human potential and dehumanizes people. It further argues that God is not only found in heaven but is present wherever human needs are addressed or where human life is. Seeking God should involve entering the world and committing to the struggles against the various challenges that constrain humankind and more particularly the marginalised and the approcriats.

However, while this type of theology can be seen to promote development work and poverty alleviation, fundamentalist sectors of Christianity are utterly opposed to this kind of gospel. They regard it as a denial of true Christianity and vehemently argue against the social involvement of the church. They are of the opinion that, by preaching earthly salvation, mainline churches are denying people the true gospel and promoting humanism or full-blown communism. Such fundamentalist gospel began to flood Africa in the early 1980s as countless missionaries, new ministries and churches and perpetual crusades became the order of the day. Its effects on development are clearly evident. As opposed to the mainstream church doctrine that promotes the church's involvement in human development, the fundamentalist theology militates against it and this is quite evident in Africa today. For example, dispensationalism that predicts the imminent end of the world slows development. Supported by countless Bible verses from the books of Daniel, Revelation and

Ezekiel, fundamentalists believe in the second coming of Jesus and that the 'rapture' will follow where true Christians will be removed from the earth to heaven. These books of the Bible claim that the final throes of the world will be characterised by disasters in the form of plagues, famine and unending war. They interpret modern-day crises such as wars, earthquakes, floods and starvation as the signs foretold by the prophets (Larkin, 2009).

For fundamentalist Christians, all the hardship and deprivation that they suffer today were foretold and ordained by God, meaning that they are inevitable. They are the fulfilment of the 'word' and there is nothing that human beings can do about them. This kind of thinking engenders indifference and resignation when confronted with hunger, poverty, sickness and deprivation and can be linked to the thinking of appropriates. It encourages approcriats to accept fate; they are easily and quickly defeated as the doctrine disarms them of the urgency and energy they require to confront situations that threaten their lives. Any attempt to fight back might be interpreted as resisting God's will. Because of this, people accept their povertisation and even see earthly suffering as a sign of blessedness. The socio-political effects of such a gospel are devastating. People are starving, fighting wars, and dying of disease, among other calamities simply because God planned it. Indeed, they are expected to give thanks for this situation, as they trust in Jesus and when he returns, they will be found ready (Archer, 2004; Hart, 2010).

Besides dispensationalism, the rise of the 'Faith Gospel' in the 1970s and 1980s in America which subsequently spread to Africa, was an antithesis to development and to some extent contributed to the povertisation of the masses. The Faith Gospel movement believes that 'God has met all human needs through the suffering of Christ and all Christians should share Christ's victory over sin, sickness and poverty' (Bowler, 2010: 18). As such, believers have a right to the blessings of health and prosperity won by Jesus on the cross and they can obtain such blessings merely by embracing their faith, again discouraging people from finding alternative ways to prosper and fight poverty. Furthermore, according to this doctrine, if one gives to God, God will reimburse one more than what one offered. This has resulted in huge gains for the church as people are driven to give to meet the ministry's daily running expenses. In other words, material prosperity will accrue from a miracle working God, ignoring the political and socioeconomic factors that need to be taken into account when dealing with povertisation in Africa as a consequence of appropriation. As Brouwer et al (2013: 21) assert, "The new gospel of prosperity cranked up the equation of faith another notch, and taught that the Christian, if he [sic] truly believed, was entitled to receive the material blessings of the Lord on the basis of faith alone". Leaving everything to faith and God once again supresses the effort and energy required to confront poverty and povertisation as well as inequality.

It is important to note that other sectarian Christians such as the "*vapositori*' in Zimbabwe have a different version of theology which can also be argued to promote poverty. The 'vapositori' are followers of Johane Marange, a Christian prophet in Zimbabwe from 1912-1963 who formed the Christian Apostolic Church which is currently being led by his sons. Firstly, they are against sending their children to school as a way to protect their spiritual autonomy and as a way to resist the oppressor (Chitando *et al.*, 2014). However, the Johane Masowe Apostolic Church (formed by Johane Masowe 1915-1973), allows children to attend school and be vaccinated. The relationship between poverty and lack of education is widely documented and these children are likely to be employed in menial jobs when they grow up that will not enable them to pull themselves out of poverty and the processes of povertisation. Moreover, the Johane Marange Apostolic Church does not allow their members to seek medical care as they believe that prayer will heal all diseases. Parents or breadwinners have been lost to diseases that are easily curable, such as malaria and tuberculosis, leaving behind a host of children condemned to a life of poverty. These strong religious beliefs can be related to what Brouwer *et al* (2013; 22) argue that'...they (fundamentalists) have transformed and energised the experience of worship while also adopting strong fundamentalist loyalties to Biblical inerrancy, creationism, and millenialist dispensationalism'.

Islamic Fundamentalism

The term 'Islamic fundamentalism' is most often used in the limited sense to refer to Muslim individuals and groups that advocate Islamism, which is a political ideology supporting and promoting the substitution of secular state laws with Islamic law. Singh (2016) notes that Islamic fundamentalism resorts to the use of coercive methods to defeat moderate, secular and liberal forces in order to create a new socio-politico-economic order in accordance with strict Islamic law.

Milton-Edwards (2005) traced the history of Islam; its origins, growth and impact on global politics and concluded that Islamic fundamentalism was born out of both external and internal factors that operate in societies that were predominantly Islamic. Suter (n.d.) sees it as a defence mechanism that was adopted by Islam as it fights the threats posed by modernism to its religious group's traditional identity. Omotosho (2015) argues that there is a cognitive conflict between Western and fundamentalist worldviews and observed that Islamists' ambitions are considered to be moral imperatives and not just mere interests. Put differently, the Islamic fundamentalist aims to maximise not self-interest but rather the soul, destiny and the moral condition of his or her whole community.

The growth of Islamic fundamentalism in Africa led to the emergence of groups such as Boko Haram in Nigeria and al Shabaab in Somalia. In Nigerian, the term 'Boko Haram' is derived from the Hausa and the Arabic Languages, respectively to mean "Western or (non-Islamic) education sin (or forbidden)" (Sergie and Johnson, 2011). The sect represents casual labourers and the Almajiris in the northern parts of Nigeria where it has established a religious complex, made up of a mosque and an Islamic school. Because of its extremism, the group is labelled as a terrorist movement and its brand of fundamentalism poses a real threat to the unity, security, and stability of the country (Ohaeri, 2011). The restoration of civil rule in Nigeria in 1999 and the consequent liberalisation of the political atmosphere provided an opportunity for the reintroduction of the Sharia legal system in predominantly Muslim states in northern Nigeria. Sharia has further reinforced religion in the politics of these states and it is fully entrenched in laws and policies. It can be argued that Islamic indoctrination and the introduction of Sharia are fundamental to the insurgence of Boko Haram (Omotosho 2015).

One of Boko Haram's main objectives is to introduce Sharia law in Nigeria, whose population of 140 million is divided between Islam and Christianity. The group also rejects Western education and civilization, guided by a Quranic teaching which says anyone who is not governed by what Allah has revealed is a transgressor. As such, it is forbidden for Muslims to participate in any social or political activity linked to the Western society, including voting in elections, wearing conventional trousers and shirts or receiving secular education. Because part of its political goal is to achieve an Islamic state, its Quranic School became a fertile ground for recruiting jihadists to fight the state (Albert, 2008). Some Islamist fundamentalists believe that Boko Haram's demands symbolise people's anger and rejection of their socioeconomic conditions and are an attempt to wipe out a system that does not give them a sense of belonging (Omotosho, 2015).

Education is acknowledged as one of the fundamentals of human development, and studies have shown that poverty is more prevalent among uneducated populations. Besides discouraging education, Islamic fundamentalism is also highly patriarchal and gives men total control of their wives. Women are not usually allowed to participate in socioeconomic activities as their place is in the home where they are supposed to look after the home and children. Studies have also shown that when women are not adequately empowered, poverty is bound to be the end result. In the event that the father, who is the sole breadwinner, dies, the family is likely to be condemned to poverty.

Fighting terrorism means that governments draw on funds that could be used to promote development and poverty reduction. At local level, violence also disturbs people's socioeconomic activities, with homes, property, livelihoods and investment lost. Some people are forced to flee and end up as refugees in foreign nations where they are dependent on handouts from donors. Kenya is home to the world's biggest refugee camp which houses Somalis that fled from violence perpetrated by Al Shabaab in their home country while Cameroon hosts Nigerian refugees who escaped Boko Haram attacks in northern Nigeria. Many families lose breadwinners or are orphaned during such attacks. This suggests a traceable link between fundamentalism, povertisation and poverty in Africa.

Economic Fundamentalism

Given our earlier definition of fundamentalism as going beyond religion to include economic ideologies, this section examines fundamentalism in its economic context. Economic fundamentalism is also known as market fundamentalism. This term was introduced by Soros (1998) to replace 'laissez faire'. Soros went on to argue that the best interests in a given society are achieved by allowing its participants to pursue their own financial self-interests without any restrictions or regulations. The term is widely used to refer to an allegedly unjustified belief in the capacity of markets to solve all problems in society usually for the benefit of appropriates.

Market fundamentalism believes in the supremacy of the free market unrestrained by government interference, labour unions, or any other form of intervention that may constrain the operation of market forces, without regard to how much social disorder, suffering or exploitation results. Monopolies were simply assumed to be self-limiting (Stiglitz, 2009). Market fundamentalists also argue for cutting and/or eliminating expenditure on social services where possible. In this regard, governments should not be involved in social welfare programs. The social consequences are explained by claiming that when the poor suffer, it is a result of their own laziness. Market fundamentalists also support deregulation. They argue that government involvement in the market distorts their profits. Government regulation should thus be reduced or eliminated, even in monopolistic situations. Policy makers therefore not only become non-interventionist and active deregulators, but also profess scepticism on key economic concepts such as equilibrium exchange rate, full employment, neutral levels of the interest rate and core inflation, among many other issues (Padoa-Schioppa, 2009).

Market fundamentalism is also a strong advocate for privatisation. Because government is assumed to be inefficient, lazy, bloated and uneconomical in providing goods and services, it becomes reasonable to entrust private sector enterprises with the delivery of such services. As a result, any activity that involves the provision of goods or services to citizens should be privatized. It is claimed that this will also promote competition among service providers and thus improve the quality of products offered in the market. Privatisation entails the abandonment of the concept of 'community' or the 'common good' since, for its adherents, this translates to some form of communism that is antithetical to the neoliberal agenda. Public health and education should thus be replaced by private initiatives, as anything else is regarded as a reflection of lethargy, indolence and governmental dependence (Bidstrup, 2002).

Economic or market fundamentalism is linked to neo-liberalism/capitalism which "puts an absolute value on the operation of the market and subordinates people's lives, the function of society, the policies of government and the role of the state to this unrestricted market. Neo-liberal policies support economic growth as an end in itself and use macro-economic indicators as the primary measurement of a healthy society. It assumes almost a religious character, as greed becomes a virtue, competition a commandment and profit, a sign of salvation" (Ike, 2004:9). It also promotes global free trade in which goods from one country can move to another without any hindrance.

However Akani (2008:38) argues that the optimistic vision of economic fundamentalism is challenged by many significant facts. Firstly, the gap in per capita income between the wealthiest nations and poorest nations is ever yawning. Secondly, many developing countries are experiencing reversal in economic progress – stagnation and slower growth while income inequality is deepening at the global level between nations and within the developing countries. Odoziobodo (2014) opined that market fundamentalism requires that every nation irrespective of its level of development, nature of its economy, and place in the global economy, must follow a common set of policies. These include: (1) giving free reign to transnational corporations to operate in their countries (2) opening up economies to imports and focusing on exports in which the country has a comparative advantage; (3) curtailing government's role in the economy to merely promoting and supporting private enterprise and the market and (4) abdicating price determination to market forces - the prices of goods, labour, currencies and the allocation of resources. Akani (2004:26) believes that economic fundamentalism is a process that is driven and coordinated by forces that are recognized and distinct and justify their roles and interests in the process - appropriatism. It is driven by the United States with the express assistance of institutions that include international appropriatist organizations such as the World Bank, International Monetary Fund, London Club, World Trade Organization (WTO), the G-7 (now G-8), Organisation for Economic Cooperation and Development and others as well as large appropriatist corporations such as IBM, Berkshire Hathaway, Heinz, General Motors, JPMorgan Chase, Wells Fargo, Exxon Mobil, Shell and Chevron.

Odoziobodo (2014) argues that economic fundamentalism/capitalism has done more harm than good to African nations. He argues that African economies have been destroyed by plunging them into debt and relegating them to puppets by stripping them of their control over their economies. The state played a big role in regulating imports and exports before the advent of free economic activity which allowed local manufacturing and production of goods. Through the experiments of the IMF/World Bank of liberalisation, privatisation and deregulation of economic activities, competition has become feverish between African and advanced world economies through opening up of their small economies. Structural Adjustment Programmes that facilitate appropriatism resulted in massive deindustrialisation in most of the sub-Saharan African nations that adopted them, with Zimbabwe and Zambia, being the most notable examples in Southern Africa. The gross impact of market fundamentalism was increased poverty and povertisation of the masses in Africa, as industries failed, competition increased and unemployment ran rampant, condemning the majority of the working class and those who depended on them to poverty and further povertisation. Fundamentalism breeds fundamentalism. It is borderless and its excesses or some tenets of it endanger humanity instead of protecting it as happiness, freedom, self and collective affirmation, and self-actualisation – the destination of humankind – are foregone in the interests of the few – the appropriates and their institutions.

References

Akani, C., 2004. *Globalization and the People of Africa.* Enugu: Fourth Dimension Publishing Company.

Albert, I.O., 2008. An Alternative Explanation of Religious Fundamentalism in Northern Nigeria. *Institute of African Studies.* Ibadan: University of Ibadan.

Archer, K., 2004. *A Pentecostal Hermeneutic for the Twenty First Century: Spirit, Scripture and Community* (Vol. 28). A&C Black.

Barkan, J. D. 2006. Democracy in Africa: What Future? In Ndulo, M. (Eds.) Democratic

Reform in Africa: Its Impact on Governance and Poverty Alleviation. James Currey and

Ohio University Press, Great Britain, pp 17-26.

Bidstrup, S., 2002. Free Market Fundamentalism: Friedman, Pinochet and the "Chilean Miracle" accessed 18 Oct 2016 at on http://www.bidstrup.com/economics.htm

Bowler, K., 2013. *Blessed: A history of the American prosperity gospel.* Oxford University Press.

Brouwer, S., Gifford, P. and Rose, S.D., 2013. *Exporting the American gospel: global Christian fundamentalism.* Routledge.

Carey, S.C., 2007. European aid: Human Rights versus bureaucratic inertia?. *Journal of Peace Research, 44*(4), pp.447-464.

Chitando, E., Taringa, N.T & Mapuranga, T.P., 2014. On top of which mountain does one stand to judge religion? Debates from a Zimbabwean context. *Journal for the Study of Religion. 27(2),* pp. 115-136.

Edigheji, O., 2005. *A Democratic Developmental State in Africa?: A Concept Paper.* Centre for Policy Studies.

Gang, I.N. and Epstein, G.S., 2004. Understanding the Development of Fundamentalism. Bonn: IZA

Hardoon, D., Fuentes-Nieva, R. and Ayele, S., 2016. An Economy for the 1%: How privilege and power in the economy drive extreme inequality and how this can be stopped. Oxfam Briefing Paper.

Hart, D.G. and Miller, G.T., 2010. Piety and Profession. American Protestant Theological Education, 1870—1970.

Hill, C., 2001. International Business Competing in the Global Market Place. New York: McGraw Hill.

Ike, O.F., 2004. The impact of globalization on Africa: A call to solidarity and concern. *Globalisation and African Self-determination*, p.19.

Ikejiaku, B-V., 2009. The Relationship between Poverty, Conflict and Development. Journal of Sustainable Development, l(2), pp. 15-28.

Imam, M., Abba, S., and Wader, M. M., 2014. Libya in the Post Gaddafi Era. *The Journal of Social Sciences and Humanities Intervention,* 2(2), pp. 1150-1166

Karam, Z. and Janseen, B., 2015. Inside ISIS Strategy to Indoctrinate Children, *The Epoch Times, 24* -30 July 2015 accessed 27 October 2016 at

http://printarchive.epochtimes.com/a1/en/us/orc/2015/07/24/OCEET20150724A13.pdf.

Larkin, C., 2009. *Dispensational truth, or God's plan and purpose in the ages.* Cosimo, Inc.

Milton-Edwards, B., 2005. Political Goals of the Holy War Islamic Fundamentalism Since 1945, London: Routledge, accessed Online at

http://www.tribuneindia.com/2005/20050703/spectrum/book1.htm on 24 Oct 2016

Odoziobodo, S.I., 2014. Africa In An Age Of Globalization: What Is Her Future? *International Journal, 4*(4), pp.2307-227X.

Omotosho, M., 2015. Dynamics of Religious Fundamentalism: A Survey of Boko Haram Insurgency in Northern Nigeria. *Dynamics, 4.*

Padoa-Schioppa, T., 2009. Market Fundamentalism and the Abdication of Politics. *The Federalist Debate*, (1), p.4. Available on http://www.federalist-debate.org/index.php/current/item/167-market-fundamentalism-and-the-abdication-of-politics accessed 21 Oct. 2016.

Pavlovic, P., 2009. Fundamentalism or Tolerance: What Is the Public Role of Religion in Modern Society? In Hadsell, H. and Stückelberger, C., Overcoming fundamentalism. *Ethical Responses from Five Continents*. Nairobi: Globethics.net

Rodrik, D., 2006. An Interview with Dani Rodrik: Home-Grown Growth: Problems and Solutions to Economic Growth. *Harvard International Review*, pp.74-77, on http://www.grips.ac.jp/teacher/oono/hp/course/lec04_leadership/leadership.htm accessed 27 Oct. 2016

Scott, B.R., 2006. *The political economy of capitalism*. Division of Research, Harvard Business School.

Sergie, M.A. and Johnson, T., 2014. Boko Haram. *Council on Foreign Relations*, 7(10), p.2014.

Singh, A., 2016. Islamic Fundamentalism and International Terrorism. *Global Journal For Research Analysis*, 4(5).

Stiglitz, J.E., 2009. The current economic crisis and lessons for economic theory. *Eastern Economic Journal*, 35(3), pp.281-296.

Soros, G., 1998. Capitalism's last Chance? *Foreign Policy*, pp.55-66.

Suter, K (n.d) Religious Fundamentalism, available on www.global-directions.com/articles/religion/religiousfundamentalism.pdf accessed 20 Oct. 2016

Tang, S.H.K. and Yung, L.C.W., 2008. Does rapid economic growth enhance democratization? Time-series evidence from high performing Asian economies. *Journal of Asian Economics*, 19(3), pp.244-253.

Viera, P.A., 2007. Christian missions in Africa and their role in the transformation of African societies. *Asian and African studies*, 16(2), pp.249-260.

Chapter Five

Questioning the Cult of the State: Evangelicals on the Zimbabwean National Pledge 2014-2016

Munetsi Ruzivo

Introduction

Like a thunder bolt the Minister of Education, Dr Lazarus Dokora, announced to the Zimbabwean nation that all pupils in both primary and secondary schools will in the future be required to recite the National Pledge. The announcement was met with mixed reactions among the citizens, for instance, the Evangelical Fellowship of Zimbabwe lashed out at the Minister for making the National Pledge mandatory in schools. Some citizens saw nothing wrong in the National Pledge and these formed a bulwark that supported government position on the issue. Paradoxically, while the Evangelical Fellowship of Zimbabwe was critical of government, beliefs underpin both the vocation of the Evangelical Fellowship of Zimbabwe and government's requirement that school pupils recite the National Pledge. In both cases, there is imposition of beliefs on school pupils by the government as well as by Evangelical Fellowship of Zimbabwe. This makes one question why the Evangelical Fellowship of Zimbabwe wants to maintain religious organisation monopoly to impose religious beliefs on pupils. This chapter will, firstly, investigate circumstances surrounding the introduction of the National Pledge by government in all secondary and primary schools in Zimbabwe. Secondly, the chapter explores arguments proffered by government officials and its supporters on the need for the National Pledge. Thirdly, the chapter argues that in secular state no form of religion should influence government policies. The chapter interrogates the position of both government and Evangelicals on the teaching of religious propaganda of either civil or religious nature. Although civil religion tends to thrive in secular state and may appear to be not exclusive and intolerant to other varieties or forms of

131

religions in Zimbabwe it may be as intolerant and fundamentalist as evangelical groupings.

The Historical Background

The annunciation by the Minister of Education Dr Lazarus Dokora that all pupils will be required to take a National Pledge must be understood against the background of the long held desire by the Zimbabwean Government to reform its education system and align it with international standards. In 1998, a Presidential Commission of Inquiry into Education and Training (popularly known as the Nziramasanga Commission because it was led by Dr C Nziramasanga) was set up and charged to inquire into the following: the relevancy, quality, orientation in a rapidly changing socio-economic environment, the basic principles and philosophy of Zimbabwe's educational and training needs and aspirations on the eve of the twenty-first century, fundamental changes to curriculum at all levels, the establishment of an appropriate framework for organisation and management of education and training systems, the issues of gender and gender equity as regards access to education (Zimbabwe Report, 1999: xxi).

The findings of the Commission were published and made public but were never implemented for a variety of reasons that bordered on economic challenges amongst a host of others problems bedevilling Zimbabwe. The Deputy Minister of Education Dr Paul Mavhima pointed out that the Commission had not been implemented because of lack of funding. He pointed out that some neighbouring countries had gone ahead in implementing the findings (www.sundaymail.co.zw//2-education-news-7-september-2014/).

Minister Dokora was aware that the *Zimbabwe Report of the Presidential Commission of Inquiry into Education and Training* popularly known as the Nziramasanga Commission had not been implemented since its submission to government in 1998. The third task of the Commission was to inquire into the basic principles and philosophy of Zimbabwe's educational and training needs. It is the third principle that the Minister of Education identified as lacking in the Zimbabwean education system. Since the Nziramasanga

Commission had found out that the Zimbabwean education system lacked an undergirding philosophy Minister Dokora with the assistance of stake holders in the education system decided to formulate and implement the philosophy. No one had queried the Commission's findings for the past 16 years. And yet no one had paid attention to the recommendation that there was the need to have basic principles and a philosophy of Zimbabwe education system inculcated into the curriculum. Most people did not anticipate the implications of the findings at the implementing stage of the Commission's findings. In its *Education Medium Term Plan 2011-2015*, the Ministry of Education made it clear that it wanted to carry out a curriculum review for both secondary and primary education (Georgescu, 2013:2). In 2014 the Patriot newspaper, an official Mouthpiece of the Zimbabwe African National Union Patriotic Front (ZANU PF) party carried out an article Pledge of allegiance a must for Zimbabwe, written by Davet Muzvidziwa. The writer of the article argues:

> Allegiance refers to a devotion or loyalty of a person to a group or your country. It is a solemn oath with both physically and emotionally that one will always be there for his or her country first. Because of allegiance many people have fought bitter wars in defence of the territorial integrity of their countries (Patriot, 2014: 5).

The writer maintains that the idea of pledging allegiance to their offices as in the case of soldiers and policemen as well as heads of state and other state functionaries is not new in Zimbabwe. The question for him is whether the pledge of allegiance can be extended to all the citizens. Muzvidziwa mentions that Germany and the United States of America place uncompromising importance to the citizen pledge of loyalty. A brief history of the pledge of allegiance in the USA is given.

The United States of America National Pledge was published and given national publicity through the official programme of the national public school celebration of the Columbus Day in October 1892. It had been published in the Youth's Companion a Boston based Youth's Magazine. Mr Francis Bellamy a former Baptist

Minister dismissed from his ministerial post for preaching against the evils of capitalism wrote the National Pledge (Bishop, 2007:26).The Pledge was intended to reflect the commitment of public schools to assimilating the growing number of migrants in the USA. Bellamy was a socialist who preached against the evils of capitalism. In a nation dominated by robber barons and big businesses the Pledge was seen as a call for change. At stake was the issue of promoting fairness, equality, egalitarianism and opportunity (Bishop, 2007:26). Jeffrey Owen Jones and Peter Meyer observe that Reverend Bellamy lived during the period of great changes in American history, the age of quarrels and contradictions, of religious awakening and heady materialism as well as mighty migrations and merging of ideas. People confessing various faiths and from various nations were making their way to the USA (Owens & Meyer, 2010:49, 74). He viewed the pledge as an inoculation against subversion. There was fear of communism, migrants, materialism, freedoms and radicals. It seems Bellamy wrote the pledge for patriotic reasons. He wanted to turn the arriving migrants to sing the American patriotic tune. Bellamy's pledge of 1892 thus ran:

> "I pledge allegiance to my flag. And to the republic to which it stands: One nation Indivisible, with liberty and justice for all."

The Minister's Position on the National Pledge

The Pledge of allegiance was to become part of the cult of the state, that is, the civil of religion of the American people. The Pledge was ratified and approved and officialised by the USA government in 1942. The wording of the National Pledge was modified several times to accommodate a few additional words such as 'one nation under God' and 'My'. There are similarities between the USA and the Zimbabwean National Pledge of Allegiance as both aim at cultivating and fostering a patriotic spirit among the citizens. The National Pledge should be understood against a background of growing social discontent among civil society organisations such as Tajamuka, National Vendors Union of Zimbabwe, This Flag, National Electoral Reform Agenda (NERA) and numerous church related non-governmental organisations. After failing to get audience from government officials on issues bearing on the state of the economy and massive corruption in government, members of civic organizations organized demonstrations and strikes code named 'stay away' (www.newsday.co.zw/2016/07/04/breaking-riots-rock-harare/).

The climax of the demonstrations and strikes was the birth of This Fag movement led by Pastor Jealous Mawarire The civic society made use of the media to appeal to the Zimbabwean people to take courage and declare to government that they had had enough. Pastor Mawarire made his appeal via social media. He made use of Twitter to disseminate information and to make an outreach to reach the public. The internet in Zimbabwe is no longer a preserve of the elite but has been embraced religiously with the same faith that religion has been embraced. In much the same way that people do not critique their religious ministers, pastor Mawarire's message via social media went viral. Whilst churches for a long period of time has been the source of truth and alternative trusted voice, the internet has emerged as a serious contender to the space that was a preserve of the churches. In a way the internet has become a new religion in the sense that they provide the alternative source about their government activities and it brings to the surface that which the governments seek to conceal. The core of Mawarire's message was:

This is the time…
that a change must happen.
Quit standing on the sidelines
and watching this flag fly
and wishing for a future that you are not wanting
at all to get involved in.
In this flag...
every day that it flies it is begging for you
to get involved.
It's begging for you to say something.
It is *begging* for you to *cry out*
and to say "Why must we be in the situation that we are in?

Pastor Mawarire rejected the notion that Zimbabwe belonged to a group of the political oligarchy. In his view there is no Zimbabwean who is more patriotic than the other. For Mawarire living one group of people to define the national agenda was the very cause of why Zimbabweans were suffering. This way Mawarire refused to be silenced or pushed aside by the cult of the state. There is a connecting thread between Dokora's call for adoption of the Pledge of Allegiance and Evan Mawarire's call for Zimbabwean citizens to stand up and define chat their destiny. Mawarire, on one hand rejects the idea that the political oligarchy defines the socio-political and economic agenda of the country without the involvement of the citizens. Dokora on the other hand stands for the political elite of the country. The people that opposed Dokora's Pledge of Allegiance also opposed the country's political oligarchy and demanded greater involvement in socio-political and economic issues. This is tantamount to an outright rejection of exaltation of the cult of the state and the manifestation of its power trappings and paraphernalia. It looks like a confrontation of tow cults; the global cult of the internet versus the cult of the state. The global cult of the internet does not respect sovereignty and territorial integrity claims of modern states. It speaks directly to its audience via instruments of social media such as cell phones, Twitter, Facebook, Instagram and WhatsApp just to mention a few. The Global cult of the internet uses its power of global connectivity to direct the thinking of its adherents in a certain direction. It provides its adherents with references tools and readymade answers from a variety of search engines such as Yahoo, Google, YouTube, Microsoft Network and many others. The cult of the state relies on the state's powers of coercion to force citizens to accept its programmes such as the National Pledge.

On the part of the cult of the state the Pledge of Allegiance was part of the broader national curriculum review. Appearing before the Parliamentary Portfolio Committee on Education (PPCE), Dokora informed members of the (PPCE) that the proposed curriculum was intended to compel all students in both primary and secondary schools in Zimbabwe to salute the flag and recite a Pledge of patriotism if approved by Government (www.newsday.co.zw/2016/04/18/dokora-defends-national-pledge). In Parliamentary debate of 7 April 2016 the Honourable senator Chimhini asked the Deputy Minister of Education Professor Mavhima where the Pledge was coming from and whether sufficient consultation had been done? To this question Professor Mavhima answered:

> Each of the Zimbabwean primary and secondary education level would be required to recite the pledge. Infant Primary schools ECD (A), ECD (B), Grade 1 and 2 would recite a very simple pledge which talks about almighty God in whose hands our future lies. I salute the national flag. Those are the three lines that the pledge says. I commit to the dignity of hard and honest work. If you go to our constitution you will find those words actually being plucked from our constitution (http://www.parlzim.gov.zw/senate-hansard/senate-hansard-07-april-2016-vol-25-no-40).

The Deputy Minister further clarified the issue that was raised by Professor Mavhima. He said that secondary schools would have a longer one. The Pledge according to the Minister emphasized matters of diversity, freedom, acknowledgement of heroes of the liberation struggle, commitment to honesty and dignity of hard work. The Minister also revealed to Parliament the words of the Pledge said by pupils from grade 3 up to form 6. According to the Minister the Pledge starts with the same words:

> 'Almighty God in whose hands our future lies'. Then it says one aspect, respecting the mothers and fathers who laid in the national liberation struggle, basically Chimurenga, *imvukela*. It then goes to say 'acknowledging the richness of our natural resources. It also says, 'also acknowledging the richness of our cultures and traditions. It goes on to say, 'I salute the National Flag and I commit to the dignity of honesty and hard work. (http://www.parlzim.gov.zw/senate-hansard/senate-hansard-07-april-2016-vol-25-no-40).

The curriculum was expected to motivate pupils to cherish their Zimbabwean identity, values, history cultural traditions preparing and orienting them for participation in voluntary service and leadership in the country.

Responses to the National Pledge

Responses to the proposal were prompt. The Movement for Democratic Change-T proportional representational MP Nicola Watson pointed out that some religious sections of society were likely to resist the Pledge on religious grounds. Another MP from the MDC-T formation pointed out that the newly constituted Zimbabwean state in early 1980 forced school children to salute the flag. This was however dropped as people because of dire poverty sold the flag in the street whilst others made it part of their household interior decorations. The point raised here by the two MPs was that Dokora should have desisted from thinking that he was reinventing a wheel. What he was trying to do had been tried before and had not worked and there was no logic of repeating it. Dokora insisted that he did not see anything wrong in Zimbabwe having its own version of the pledge since the Americans had their own (www.newsday.co.zw/2015/06/12/dokora-curriculum-to-force-pupils-salute-flag/).

Online responses to the *Daily Newspaper* were brutal and punishing. One respondent by the pseudonym Tendai Chaminuka asked Dokora the basis for comparing Zimbabwe and America as regards the Pledge of Allegiance. He further asked the Minister whose children were to salute the Zimbabwean flag every day? He reminded the Minister that nearly all ministers Children were studying abroad saluting the American flag or flag of other nations. The point that was being raised here was that ministers and their families should lead by example. The National Pledge should not be for the poor citizens who are unable to send their children abroad. If the National Pledge is to be meaningful to Zimbabwe, then children of the ministers should be educated in Zimbabwe where they would recite the National Pledge with their compatriots. Another respondent to Dokora's Pledge pointed out the lack of principles on the part of the minister and his party. On one hand Dokora's Zanu PF party preached that Zimbabwe will never be a colony again and on the other Dokora suggested that he and his party modelled their Pledge on that of the USA the very country his party demonises (https://www.newsday.co.zw/2016/04/18/dokora-defends-national-pledge/).

One major weakness observed by a respondent to the online *Herald* article on the Minister's announcement of the National Pledge was that the Pledge did not allow for the differences of religion and did not observe the constitutional right of the children to address the God of their parents. This argument is premised on the fact that Zimbabwe is a multi-faith country with Moslems, Jews, Hindus, Buddhists and African traditionalist. Given this diversity, which God is addressed by the National Pledge? The Minister needed to clarify this issue to avoid being accused of being biased against non-Christian religions.

Other online respondents to the *Herald* article accused government of unleashing a brutal method of brainwashing unsuspecting kids in an attempt to instil in them party values at a tender age so that the party is guaranteed of future supports from the young generation. Other respondents pointed out that a few years ago the national youth service had been introduced for this purpose but was itself a disaster. One respondent made it clear that only when government leaders stopped corruption and began leading by example only then would his or her kid make the Pledge of Allegiance.

What triggered this brutal response to the Minister? Was it simply the issue of the National Pledge or there were other considerations? Some of the people opposed to the National Pledge were angered by the Ministers ban of Scripture Union. In reality Dokora had not banned Scripture Union. According to the Sunday Mail of 24, April 2016 the Ministry of Education Sorts and Culture instructed a religious organisation called Scripture Union to suspend its activities in Zimbabwean schools until a new curriculum was in place. According to Daniel Chinengundu after forcing schools to adopt the National Pledge in the second term of 2016, Dokora restricted scripture union from visiting schools and conducting its meetings, banned the Lord's prayer and stopped the distribution of Bible is in schools by the Gideon's Foundation (http://www.sundaymail.co.zw/govt-halts-scripture-union-in-schools/).

The move did not go down well with Evangelical Christians who accused Dokora of being a front for Islamic interests. An organisation called Prayer Network of Zimbabwe organised a demonstration against the Minister and even wrote a petition to the Minister pleading that he retracted his list of bans. A body member Rody Takaruza was cited in the *Daily News* warning government not to adulterate but respect Christian values that were being taught to their children. A lady named Jenni Williams accused Government of interfering in religious affairs (www.dailynews.co.zw/articles/2016/05/19/churches-demostrate-against-dokora-s-national-pledge).

The Pledge according to the Evangelicals and their partners was not Christian. Divine Destiny leader Ancelimo Magaya described the Pledge as devilish and unconstitutional. The Sunday Mail reported that Christian organisations were suspicious that the move was aimed at banning the Lord's Prayer. Goodwill Shana former President of the EFZ expressed his concerns:

> The national pledge (in the US) did away with prayer in schools. The general concern is the process will have Christian values done away with. The process itself was not open, it will be wonderful to have consultation. I think EFZ (Evangelical Fellowship of Zimbabwe) is concerned with inroads the multi-faith agenda is making in trying to be as inclusive we slowly find ourselves doing away with Christian values. While we think, a pledge doesn't appear outwardly negative but in the process where is it going. From the Constitution, I have a right of association and (that applies) for children as well. The pledge isn't on the curriculum and it's an imposition and it might play the role of violating my Constitutional right. When you read newspaper articles (on the pledge) you see that the language used is arrogant, that it's not optional, what kind of language is that? ... Our country doesn't need division, imposing is not the way. I have made (known) my concerns to EFZ – that the church should register concerns strongly. We

shouldn't just be against it but let's have dialogue with the series of stakeholders involved. Politicians say we (church) are important but exclude us in these important decision processes (http://www.sundaymail.co.zw/churches-reject-national-pledge-at-schools/).

The Secretary General of the EFZ Mr Blessing Makwaringa told Fatima Bula that their members were not comfortable with the Pledge. In his view some people with conservative views on issues of faith were deadly against the Pledge. He further questioned the logic of forcing the kids to recite the Pledge without parental consent. In Makwaringa's opinion the whole charade or absurdity was tantamount to idol worship. Another former Secretary General of the EFZ was of the view that the general trend in the world was the movement towards interreligious dialogue and understanding. But he was quick to point out that with Zimbabwe it would not work. He accused the Minister of attempting to teach their children values that were unchristian and of making a unilateral decision with catastrophic consequences on the lives of the children. In the interview with Fatima Bulla Rev. Tavaziva pointed out that Lord's Prayer was not forced on anyone. Those not interested in it could keep quite but kids were not free to do so with the National Pledge (http://www.sundaymail.co.zw/churches-reject-national-pledge-at-schools/).

Sharp reactions from Matabeleland region followed. A number of churches made their position clear that their schools were not going to recite the National Pledge. The Brethren in Christ Church made a statement that the Pledge violates Chapter 4 Section 60 (2) which stipulates that no individual may be forced to make an oath that goes against their rights or beliefs. They also cited Chapter 2 Section 19 (b) which states that the state is empowered to protect children from anything that places their moral or spiritual development in danger. The Brethren in Christ Church issued a statement:

As BCC Zimbabwe Conference together with the likeminded organisations with likeminded organisations, we are unequivocally

141

against the pledge and its implementation. We therefore appeal to the Ministry of primary and secondary education and government to rescind the decision. Our position as BICC Zimbabwe Conference is that we will neither participate nor encourage our institutions, members and our children to participate on matters contrary to our beliefs and conscience (http://www.chronicle.co.zw/churches-defiant-on-national-pledge/).

The Government owned paper, the *Chronicle* of 2 May, 2016, reported that the Christian Alliance of Zimbabwe spokesperson Reverend Useni Sibanda made it clear that children of Christians will not recite the Pledge. In a more combative mood Revered Sibanda said that their children would not recite the Pledge because it violated their constitutional provisions. He was saddened by the fact that government had not consulted parents before the promulgation of the Pledge. In his organisation's view the Pledge was now a ritual that militated against the Christian values (http://www.chronicle.co.zw/churches-defiant-on-national-pledge).

In spite of the EFZ and its affiliates and allies position on the Pledge, the Ministry dug in and argued that the words of the Pledge were culled from the Constitution of the country and therefore anyone who rejected the Pledge was automatically rejecting the Constitution of the country. In the *Chronicle* of 2, May, 2016 the Permanent Secretary in the Ministry of Education said that parents had been consulted during the curriculum review process (http://www.chronicle.co.zw/churches-defiant-on-national-pledge).

When the Minister was summoned to appear before the Parliamentary Portfolio Committee on education the Minister informed the committee that he issued the ban because schools had become the target of many church organisations that were going there without any formal arrangement with government. The temporal suspension of activities by church related organisations in schools, according to the Minister, was meant to monitor what they were doing (https://openparly.co.zw/2016/06/15/i-didnt-ban-scripture-unions-dokora/). The Minister's position on the issue was that since he was in the process of coming up with a new curriculum the temporal moratorium was meant to rationalise some religious teachings in schools so that they could align with the new curriculum. According to Minister Dokora all organisations were supposed to examine the new curriculum framework and see how best they could contribute to it (The Sunday Mail, 2016: 2).

The National Pledge issue became so divisive among school teachers with some supporting the introduction of the Pledge and others opposed to it. Some school teachers were of the view that the National Pledge instilled discipline in the kids. They saw it as an anticorruption fighting tool that mould kids into patriotic citizens. Those opposed to it argued that the Pledge infringed their right to religious freedom (Herald, 6 May 2016). The Deputy Minister of Home Affairs insinuated that government should consider forcing civil servants to recite the National Pledge specifically designed for them. The level of resistance was great.

An academic wedded in and joined the fray. This was Peter Kwaira a lecturer at the University of Zimbabwe. He saw nothing wrong with the National Pledge since it was derived from the Constitution of Zimbabwe. According to Kwaira consultation was done during the constitutional making process of 2013and also during the curriculum review of 2014-2016(Sunday Mail, 2016:5). Kwaira corroborated the Minister's position on the Pledge. The Minister had earlier on warned Christian and teacher organizations that were rejecting the National Pledge and seeking to sue government that they were free to proceed as Zimbabwe was a democratic state (zbc.co.zw/index.php/68131-you-are-free-to-challenge-national-pledge-in-court-dokora).

The point missed by Kwaira is that Minister Dokora culled the Pledge from the Constitution and made it something to be recited in the form of a civil prayer. When people complained of lack of consultation they were simply stating that Dokora did not inform them that he intended to cull words from the Constitution and make it mandatory for their kids to recite them. Moreover, the general disgruntlement in the country over the state of the economy was translated into a force opposed to any endeavour of any Government official no matter how good the endeavour might be. One respondent to the online herald pointed out that forcing children to recite the Pledge would not change their perception of a government that is perceived as violent and corrupt. The respondent went on to point out that respect was not won by coercion but doing good. Government was getting resistance on the National Pledge and even on the bond notes because it was imposing. (http://www.herald.co.zw/civil-servants-need-national-pledge 6 May 2016/).

What irked Evangelical Christians and their affiliates was that the Minister behaved as if the National Pledge had become law before the President had approved it. *The Daily News* captured it well when it observed that schools had started implementing the government controversial National Pledge. Mr Matthew Sologani filed an application with the Constitutional Court ordering the barring of the implementation of the National Pledge by Minister Dokora, the Attorney General, Prince Machaya, Mashambanhaka School Secondary and Chizungu Primary School. His argument was the Pledge infringed on his religious beliefs (www.dailynews.co.zw/articles/2016/04/18/schools-national-pledge-roars-to-life).

Fierce resistance was mounted by Christians in Bulawayo who attempted to gather more than 20000 signatures to force the Minister to backtrack on the Pledge. Interdenominational meetings were held in Bulawayo and these were followed by several meetings of the allies of the EFZ. Women of Zimbabwe arise wrote to the Minister Dokora and informed him that the Pledge violated children's rights enshrined in the Constitution. The WOZA document states:

> Chapter 2 section 19 subsection 3 (b) which states that the state must take appropriate legislative and other measures to ensure that children are not required or permitted to perform work or provide services that are inappropriate for children's age; or place at risk the children's wellbeing, education, physical or mental health or spiritual, moral or social development (www.wozazimbabwe.org/wp-content/uploads/2016/05/Open-leter-to-Minister-Dokora-6 may2016.pdf).

WOZA women further stated that the manner in which the Pledge was introduced violated the people's freedom of conscience.

Chapter 4 Section 60 states that no person shall be compelled to take an oath that is contrary to their religion or belief. Basically Woza raised five objections and I will here summarise them. The first one is that the Pledge bonds our children to work in Zimbabwe where there are no jobs, the second one is that the Pledge contains military language, third it is a lie that children will be inheritors of our economy given rampant corruption in the country, fourth the Pledge is a diversionary tactic to political and economic problems bedevilling the country, fifth the Pledge says nothing about those who perished during the Gukurahundi (Matabele disturbances in the early 1980s)issue and finally the pledge is equated to the Lord's prayer (www.wozazimbabwe.org/wp-content/uploads/2016/05/Open-leter-to-Minister-Dokora-6may2016.pdf).

On the celebration of the 36th independence children's party that was graced by President Mugabe at the National Sports Stadium, the kids recited the Pledge after the national anthem even after the matter had been taken to the Constitutional Court by Evangelical Christians and their allies. What surprised many was the sense of urgency with which the Minister approached National Pledge issue. *The Standard* newspaper of 8 May 2016 commented that Minister Dokora had become unpopular for making rush decisions relating to the education sector and in this case relating to the National Pledge issue (www.thestandard.co.zw/2016/05/08/dokoras-war-gods-people/). Evangelicals where aware that the National Pledge issue emanated from the Nzira Masanga Commission whose findings we have already discussed above had not seen the light of the day. The Minister was so quick to dust the report and extract some lines from it which he then stitched together to come up with the National Pledge. Legality of what the minister did will be a matter that will be decided by the Constitutional Court of Zimbabwe since Evangelical Christians and their affiliates have already taken the first step of approaching the courts for justice.

Religious versus State Fundamentalism

Evangelicalism refers to a subset of Protestant Christianity that is distinguished by both doctrinal and practical characteristics but not by denominational affiliation or even necessarily by self-labelling. Generally, there are five fundamentals that characterise Evangelicals and these are conversion namely that life has to be changed; activism expressing the gospel in effort; Biblicism which is a particular regard for the Bible; the virgin birth and crucicentrism which stresses on the sacrifice of Christ on the cross. From the definitions of evangelicalism, we can see that it embodies religious fundamentalism which in America referred to those who wished to defend the fundamentals of faith. It denotes those who by the intensity of their conviction cling to the traditional Biblical view of inspiration (Bebbington, 1989:181). Evangelicals were generally opposed to modernism. Does Evangelicalism embody religious fundamentalism? Paul Freston (2008), observes that the two have a complex relationship. In his view there is an overlap in the sense that some Evangelicals can be fundamentalists whilst others many not. Fundamentalism emerged as a movement that reacted against globalisation whilst Evangelicalism may have contributed to it (Freston, 2008:6). Fundamentalism reacts generally against processes of secularisation and modernisation. Although Evangelicals in both the United States and Zimbabwe come from a background of conservative Protestantism, their faith has nevertheless globalised. They have emerged as the greatest exporter of American culture, political agendas as well as religious ideas (Yates 2002:70). On a more general note the Zimbabwean evangelicals share the same fundamentals of faith and exhibit the same complex relationship with globalists.

The Evangelicals in Zimbabwe are more on the conservative side as regards a number of issues. In 2013 they expressed their concern over the constitution by making an appeal to Constitutional Parliamentary Committee to amend the constitution by removing ungodly elements from it. The ungodly elements referred to where immorality, homosexuality, same sex unions and marriages, abortion on demand and the possible silencing of churches from preaching against the ungodly acts, shutting out of churches from preaching in schools, work places and public places (http://www.3-mob.com/?p=10882#.WFFxRoVOLIU). Evangelicals approached the National Pledge issue from a conservative background that regarded aspects of the Zimbabwean Constitution as ungodly. Evangelicals are seen by government as importers of foreign values, ideas and political agendas. In their complaint to COPAC the Evangelicals predicted that the Constitution if left as it was it would lead to the silencing of churches and preaching in schools. The National Pledge could be seen in the same light. In the view of the Evangelicals the National Pledge was ungodly and this is the reason why the Evangelicals reacted as we have observed against the Minister's declaration. They reacted in their usual conservative nature of preserving the fundamentals of their religion.

Government's stand reveals its interest in promoting civil religion in the form of a cult of the state. Civil religion here is defined as, 'a collection of beliefs, symbols and rituals with respect to sacred things and institutionalised in collectivity' (Bellah, 1970:175). This religion tends to share certain traits with both African traditional religion and Christianity. In its manifestation it is not objectionable to Islam and other religions. This civil religion is well articulated in the National Pledge. This civil religion believes in the existence of transcendental being called God who is described as almighty (line 1 of the National Pledge). There is belief that this Almighty deity guides the nation and that the fate of the nation lies with this deity. The God acknowledged in the Constitution is for the purposes of maintaining the cult of the state. The values of freedom, justice, honesty and hard work expressed in the Pledge are at the core of the Zimbabwean Government civil religion. The symbols of civil religion enshrined in the National Pledge are: the fallen national heroes, traditions and culture. The recitation of the Pledge every morning on school assembly and the gesture of saluting all become rituals of the state cult of civil religion with a specific purpose of instilling patriotism to the national interest (www.herald.co.zw/national-pledge-officially-launched). The National Pledge is part of the state cult of civil religion. It is modelled along religious lines such that it becomes less objectionable to religious people and yet it does not appeal personal inner feelings because it is simply at the service of the higher ideals of the state. Africans are aware of the machinations of African rulers that they want the state to be worshipped, they do not worship it although they comply with its dictates. They participate in the rituals of the state cult without subscribing to its ideology. Many do so to preserve their status and gain. What they fear is the backlash from the state should they challenge it in the way evangelicals do.

In spite of the protests by evangelicals whose long term goal is to see the creation of a confessional state, government stance shows that its form of religion is civil and opposed to the Evangelical vision of a Christian state. Government through the Ministry of Education wanted to strengthen issues to do with the value system, heritage and self-understanding of the nation (www.herald.co.zw/national-pledge-officially -launched). The state though clearly defined as a secular state maintains what it deems fundamentals and these are at the core of its civil religion as we have already observed. Whilst in the churches there are those who have been chosen to be presiders of church services, civil religion has at the local level the headmaster presiding as high priest at the local school whilst at the national level it is the President who becomes the high priest of the nation. On behalf of his Government the Minister exhibited an uncompromising attitude for the purposes of maintaining the fundamentals of a civil religion which is meant to redirect and reorient the nation towards creating a strong sense of national identity for political reasons. For the Government of Zimbabwe, the best laboratory for this experiment were primary and secondary schools. The *modus operandi* of this religion is the appropriation of the idea of sacrifice and commitment inherent in major religions of the world for purposes of coming up with values and beliefs that are beyond questioning. The values and beliefs enshrined in this religion will be a standard for measuring one's loyalty to the nation (Ruzivo, 2013:1-2).

Conclusion

In the above deliberations we have observed the introducing of the National Pledge was met with mixed reactions. More outstanding were Zimbabwean Evangelicals who argued that the Minister Education, Sports and Culture had not consulted enough. Evangelicals saw the Pledge as tantamount to idolatry. They cited some clauses in the Constitution that forbid the use of children to perform work or provide services that are inappropriate for their age.

Others argued that the Pledge did not only militate against their belief systems but infringed upon the religious rights of their children. Government viewed Evangelicals as importers of foreign values and political agendas. It was precisely for this purpose that Government mooted the idea of the National Pledge in order to mould children into responsible citizens who cherish their own culture, history and identity. Government on the other hand argued that it was effecting the 1998 Presidential Commission recommendation that the school curriculum be undergirded by basic principles and a philosophy of the Zimbabwean education system. Government supporters argued that the Pledge would instil discipline and a philosophy of *Ubuntu* to pupils. What we see at the end of the day are two competing forms of religious fundamentalism one fronted by the state in the name of civil religion and the other promoted by Evangelicals and backed by globalists.

References

www.zbc.co.zw/index.php/68131-you-are-free-to-challenge-national-pledge-in-court-dokora-). Accessed 11/12/2016.

Bebbington, W, D., 2005. *Evangelicalism in Britain: A History from the 1730s to the 1980s.* London & New York: Taylor& Francis.

Bellah, R, N., 1970. *Beyond Belief Essays on Religion in a Post-Traditional World,* Los Angeles: University of California Press.

Bishop, R., 2007. *The Pledge of Allegiance: The News Media and Michael Newdow's Constitutional Challenge,* New York: State University of New York.

Freston, P., 2008. Introduction: The Many Faces of Evangelical of Evangelical Politics in Latin, in Freston, P., Ed., *America Evangelical Christianity and Democracy in Latin America.* Oxford: Oxford University Press.

Georgescu, D., 2013. Zimbabwe Curriculum Review: A Concept Paper hosted on https://www.academia.edu/3008036/Zimbabwe_Curriculum_Review_-_Concept_Paper.

http://www.3-mob.com/?p=10882#.WFFxRoVOLIU   accessed
    15/12/2016.

http://www.chronicle.co.zw/churches-defiant-on-national-pledge/
    accessed 12/12/2016.

http://www.herald.co.zw/civil-servants-need-national-pledge/
    accessed 09/12/2016.

http://www.parlzim.gov.zw/senate-hansard/senate-hansard-07-
    april-2016-vol-25-no-40accessed 15/12/2016.

http://www.sundaymail.co.zw/churches-reject-national-pledge-at-
    schools/ accessed 14/12/2016.

http://www.sundaymail.co.zw/govt-halts-scripture-union-in-
    schools/accessed 30/11/2016.

https://openparly.co.zw/2016/06/15/i-didnt-ban-scripture-
    unions-dokora/ accessed 10/12/2016.

https://www.newsday.co.zw/2015/06/12/dokora-curriculum-to-
    force-pupils-salute-flag/ accessed 15/12/2016.

https://www.thestandard.co.zw/2016/05/08/dokoras-war-gods-
    people/ accessed 15/12/ 2016.

Jeffrey, O, J., *et al.*, 2010. *A Pledge: A History of the Pledge of Allegiance.*
New York St. Martin's Press.

Nziramasanga, C, T., *et al.,* 1999. *Zimbabwe: Report of the Presidential
Commission of Inquiry into Education and Training* Harare:
Government Printers.

Ruzivo, M., 2013, Civil Religion in Zimbabwe: Unpacking the
Concept. In Chitando, E., ed., *Prayers and Players: Religion and
Politics in Zimbabwe.* Harare: SAPES.

The Patriot October 17-23, 2014.

The Sunday Mail 8, May, 2016.

Yates, J., 2002, American Evangelicals: The Overlooked Globalizers
and Their Unintended Gospel of Modernity. *The Hedgehog Review*,
vol. 40 (2) 66-90.

www.dailynews.co.zw/articles/2016/05/19/churches-demostrate-
    against-dokora-s-national-pledge accessed 28/11/2016.

www.herald.co.zw/national-pledge-officially-launched
    accessed 30/11/2016.

www.sundaymail.co.zw//2-education-news-7-september-2014/
    accessed 20/11/2016.

Chapter Six

Foot Soldiers of the New Empire or Horizontal Saviours? Interrogating Civil Society Organisations and Fundamentalisms in Twenty-First Century Africa

Artwell Nhemachena & Bankie F. Bankie

"While NGOs can have a positive influence on society at large, one must be aware of their backgrounds, who is in charge of them, and from whom they are getting funding because the nature of the NGO is changing; it is being more and more integrated into the imperial apparatus of domination and exploitation. NGOs are fast becoming missionaries of empire" (Global Research, 3 March 2012).

"Likewise, if each man makes himself judge of the principles of government, you will at once see the birth of civil anarchy or the annihilation of political sovereignty. Government is a true religion: it has its dogmas, its mysteries, and its ministers. To annihilate it or submit it to the discussion of each individual is the same thing; it lives only through national reason, that is to say through political faith, which is a creed" (de Maistre *et al*, 1996: 87).

Introduction

This chapter is informed by reports such as those by The Guardian, (26 August 2015) that: "ninety-six countries have taken steps to inhibit NGOs from operating at full capacity, in what the Carnegie Endowment, calls a viral-like spread of new laws under which international aid groups and their local partners are vilified, harassed, closed down and sometimes expelled" (see also Daily Nation, 8 November 2015; The Herald, 3 June 2016; Chronicle, 23 October 2013; The Herald, 4 July 2009; Perkins, 2007). In all these cases, the connecting thread appears in the form of allegations that some civil society organisations have assumed the roles of missionaries of the [new] empire or the old empire that has [with African independence] simply morphed into an invisible absent present [theological] leviathan (see Nhemachena, 2016). The critical question herein is: civil society organisations are missionaries of which empire when empire has long been pronounced dead and has already received countless scholarly obituaries with the declarations of independence of African states? However, in tandem with Kwame Nkrumah's (1965) warning that after colonialism there will be neo-colonialism [which is a stage of imperialism], other writers like Hazelwood, (2014: 98); Maxwell, (2000: 5) and Cherep-Spiridovich, (2000: 20) have similarly warned of the existence of an *invisible* [global][1] government that is directed by a kind of [*invisible*] secret masonic society that deploys financial muscles to direct world affairs, including [surreptitious] wars. Hazelwood (2014: 98) points out thus:" They are an unseen government behind the scenes who dictate and control our governments today. The men stay behind the scenes and they use financial influence in political life…The reason for their secrecy becomes clear when you consider their major goals, which is to establish a one world government, consisting of a world economy, and a world religion. You can see the beast and the religious whole rising up to rule this world system today".

Underscoring ways in which a very few people in the West[2] control the world and in the process play God, Maxwell, (2000: 5) observes: "The real menace of our Republic is this invisible government which like a giant Octopus, sprawls its slimy length over city, state and nation. Like the octopus of real life, it operates under cover of a self-created screen…At the head of this octopus are the Rockefeller Standard Oil interests and a small group of powerful banking houses generally referred to as international bankers".

Similarly, writing from an international law perspective, Reinold, (2012: 1076, 1077) also underscores the existence of a project for a one world government that is underpinned by Western proponents of the 'rule of law', which is an integral aspect of the emerging global constitutionalism. Reinold, (2012: 1076, 1077) writes thus: "…in a pluralist *post-national* [our emphasis] setting, the project of *global constitutionalism* [our emphasis] is continuously challenged by states

---

[1]We use the term "global" not necessarily in the purported "inclusive" sense but in the sense of the dominant western or Euro-American one "world" government
[2]We use this term to refer not only to Europe but to Euro-America

from the periphery…The ICC [international Criminal Court] was thus established as an institution dedicated to promoting the rule of law, which is an integral component of the project of *global constitutionalism* [our emphasis]".It can be argued in this chapter that while the 'rule of law' as it is conventionally purveyed appears to be universal and innocently all-inclusive, it is premised on hegemonic Western jurisprudence that is set to be the jurisprudence of the envisaged 'one world government' dominated by the West. In this sense, civil society organisations that are uncritically informed by Western discourses of "inclusion" into a one world government dominated by the West and its logics are arguably complicity in the constitution and sustenance of empire even as they paradoxically claim to be agents of emancipation.

Discourses about empire and ways in which it sustains itself [including as a quasi-theological entity] are replete in contemporary scholarship (see for instance, Ndlovu-Gatsheni, 2012; 2013). Calling for de-imperialisation that he defines as abandoning Eurocentrism and the spirit of imperial domination, Ndlovu-Gatsheni, (2013: 349) insists on the need to abandon Western arrogance which, he argues, breeds and perpetuates the idea that Europe and North-America have everything to teach non-Europeans and nothing to learn from other people and their civilisations. Thus for Ndlovu-Gatsheni (2012: 48),Africa is entrapped by global imperial designs and technologies of subjectivation that masquerade as emancipatory while in reality serving the perpetuation of coloniality which he defines as: "…an invisible power structure that sustains colonial relations of exploitation and domination long after the end of direct colonialism".

While civil society has been defined as the terrain on which closed states and political societies are forced to be open to democratising initiatives within the context of global shift in forces (Conkle, 1999: 339), it is necessary for scholars to unpack what the discourses and practices of civil society, openness, democratisation, globalisation entail in the context of key ideas such as *invisible* global government, *secret societies* and fundamentalism that informs this chapter. In the discourses that presume the existence of peripheral closed states and political societies that are further presumed to need global civil society assistance in order to open up, there are erroneous

153

presuppositions that the global is necessarily open and democratic enough to export their surplus openness and surplus democracy to states and polities that happen to be still closed and undemocratic. In discussing fundamentalism, this chapter challenges this presupposition that the global is open and democratic since the global is by virtue of its definition prematurely circumscribing and encompassing. The chapter contends that the global is a form of fundamentalism in so far as it defines, confines and presumes that there are no alternative worlds to the global that the West has constituted and imposed on other people as a *fait accompli*. In other words, the notion of the 'global' that has been constituted to define and confine others has neither been subjected to democratisation processes nor to competing metaphysical lenses arising from the rich variety of epistemic and ontological heritages of the world(s). Because the global is understood herein as circumscribing and encompassing including without open and sincere discussion, the chapter challenges notions that assume that there is openness in the global. The argument, therefore, is that just like the nation-state which it has increasingly become opposed to, the global is a creed for the West; it is a religion with its evangelists and missionaries that proselytise it while also assuming that there are no alternative or challenging perspectives to that global entity that humanity has increasingly been tricked and cheated into worshipping.

For the above reason, the chapter proceeds to argue in support of the vignette by de Maistre *et al,* (1996: 87) who state that:" Government is a true religion: it has its dogmas, its mysteries, and its ministers"; however it is not necessarily national governments that are religions but also the emergent "one world government" and its global constitution. These are increasingly constituting a religion seeking to proselytise by suppressing peripheral states, peoples and religions including Christianity that are deemed to be as atavistic as to retain what some scholars (Poxon, 2001; Latour, 2005) call the "old" [Supreme] God that they hold as legitimising religious fundamentalism. In other words, the West conceives itself as the alpha and omega resolving problems arising from the presence or absence of God as well as resolving problems arising from the humanely realm across the planet. This, it is argued in this chapter is a manifestation of the tip of an emergent Western religion [read atheism] in which the global [read West] seeks to displace and replace God and, thus, becoming the new Supreme being in the Nietzschean sense of Supermen, that tower over the entire world.

While religious fundamentalists have been criticised for dogmatic beliefs in the sacred Godly texts, secular fundamentalists [including worshipers of the deity called global] also rely on methods of secular interpretation that mirror the methods by which religious fundamentalists interpret the Bible (Conkle, (1999: 339; 340). Interpretations of constitutions, human rights and democratic provisions are often insular, dogmatic and absolute such that they are deemed to be immune to alternative questions, evidence, arguments, and adaptation to local indigenous and contemporary circumstances. Just like fundamentalists or absolutists believers who understand themselves as appointed carriers of sacred gospels and have no compunction about killing heretics or doing anything else to advance their cause (Conkle, 1999: 340-1), human rights, democracy and rule of law activists consider themselves as receivers of [secular] absolute [universal] truths over which wars with [secular] heretics can justifiably be fought. Thus, from the United States of America to the most peripheral state in the world, there has been the emergence of constitutional worship [which is a form of secular fundamentalism wherein the constitutional text is deemed to be the source of absolute, plain, unchanging truth which cannot be challenged on the basis of societal, philosophical or other values that lie outside the text (Conkle, 1999: 343-4).

The dogmatism and insularity of liberal democracy is evident in assumptions that there is no [viable] alternative to liberal democracy. Similarly, fundamentalism and its insularity and dogmatism are witnessed when Bretton Wood Institutions claimed that there was 'no alternative' to free market policies, which African states were forced to implement. When Western states summarily describe states in the global south as axis of evil, as pariah, as failed, as patrimonial, the underlying dogmatic assumption is that the West defined ways have 'no alternatives'. Equally, when Africans are made to believe that there are 'no alternatives' to Western economic, health, political, social, educational, legal, cultural and religious models there is also need to interrogate these claims using the lenses of fundamentalism. Western models of development and civilisation that presume that there are 'no alternatives' to Western development as well as alternative civilisations, including alternative modernities all speak to Western fundamentalisms that are imposed on Africa and other communities of the south. Impositions of these Western economic, educational, developmental, cultural, legal, social, political and religious models amount to dogmatically proselytising these insularities and they have the effect of turning the West into a heaven of gods and goddesses from whose shrines the entire planet is, by fiat, expected to prostrate. The effect is that while Western secularism dismisses the *Heavenly* God, the West itself [in spite of its claims to atheism] surreptitiously and *immanently* assumes the seat of God who is dismissed by their [secular] epistemologies and practices.

The upshot of the above is that Western liberalism is an intolerant and dogmatic liberalism, which does not even tolerate the presence of God. It is a liberalism that has deployed its [old and new] missionaries to evangelise "multiplicity" and "inclusion" as if the God that they dismiss has never been inclusive and reckoning of multiplicities. The point here is that claims that beliefs in Heavenly God spurs fundamentalisms is more about human beings seeking to depose God and becoming new Supreme beings in His place. If civil society organisations proselytise the gospels of empire, they can well be understood as new missionaries of empire evangelising the goodness of empire and enforcing [at a planetary level] the commandments from the shrines of empire. Similarly, if global civil society is funded by secret society organisations and by individuals bent on creating a 'one world government' and a global constitution, the question is whether such civil society organisations live up to exigencies of transparency and openness which they proselytise in the peripheries. Much like colonial missionaries who preached honesty, fidelity and commitment to God while they paradoxically cheated Africans into signing away their land and resources, such civil society organisations are runners with the hares and hunters with the hounds.

The proliferation of civil society organisations with independence of African countries begs questions about the underlying resilience of the colonial *mission civilisatrice*. It begs questions about why civil society organisations proliferated in and focused on "civilising" Africa [rather than focus on civilising the (neo-)colonially brutal Western societies] that was the victim of multiple forms of brutalisation. To focus on civilising the victims of enslavement and of (neo-)colonisation rather than focusing on Western perpetrators of (neo-)colonial brutalities presupposes resilience of colonial assumptions that colonists' offences against Africans did not constitute incivilities. The fact that Western organisations, foundations and individuals [some of whom are tainted by crimes of colonialism and enslavement] are returning to the continent to "civilise" postcolonial Africans underscores the paradoxical assumption that in spite of their brutalities and barbarities Westerners still possess surplus civilities to export to those that they have brutalised and are still brutalising in many ways. Apart from arrogantly presupposing that Western enslavement and colonial brutalities are civilising for Africans, this logic repeats the old missionary logics. Thus, replacing old missionaries, who erroneously presumed that Africans needed Godly salvation more than the incoming Western colonial plunderers with whom missionaries were complicity, civil society organisations arguably misplace their projects of *mission civilisatrice*. The focus on the mission of "civilising" victims of brutalities rather that (neo-)colonial brutalisers presupposes Godly immunity to colonisers. It presupposes fundamentalism in which colonisers continue to enjoy immunity while the missionaries that they sponsor evangelise their "goodness" and the indispensability of their [secular] shrines. A closer look at (neo-)missionaries and the questions of deliverance is necessary in order to understand the resilient coloniality of empire.

Deliverance to Godly Freedom or Deliverance to the Imperial Leviathan? Coloniality and the New Empire

When colonial missionaries preached about deliverance and freedom, it did not occur to some Africans that it was more about deliverance of Africans from their own autonomous and sovereign institutions to the servitude and bondage in the meshwork and network of empire. It was far less about deliverance from sins as in fact the missionaries themselves were sinning against God as they colluded in the barbaric colonial and enslavement projects. If it was about deliverance to God, missionaries would not have been the ideal midwives since they, along with some of their churches, participated in enslavement of Africans as well as in the colonial plunder and expropriation of African land, labour and livestock (see for instance Nhemachena, 2016; Schmidt, 1992). Thus, little did it occur to Africans being converted by missionaries that when the missionaries preached deliverance, they meant delivery not necessarily to God as precolonial Africans knew Him but to the imperial leviathan that was masquerading as an immanent God. In this sense, [some] Africans who already knew God [who had various vernacular names] were justifiably surprised when missionaries claimed to monopolise knowledge and access to God: thus, the only God that Africans did not know about, and that missionaries were bringing to Africans for the first time was the imperial leviathan posing as God.

It was not deliverance from sin that missionaries of the colonial era brought because sin was integral to the colonial projects in which many missionaries participated directly or indirectly. It was not deliverance from sin because Africans already knew and distinguished what was sinful and what was righteous: they knew that witchcraft and sorcery were sinful and were thus against these practices; they knew that it was sinful to engage in sodomy, homosexuality, bestiality and that those that engaged in these activities did not merely need tolerance but were sick and needed treatment via rituals, spiritual and herbal treatments. Therefore, unlike colonists and contemporary worshippers at the global shrines who insist merely on tolerance, even if without treatment, for the sick and demonically devious, Africans knew pretty well that tolerance was not enough and so they had to go further than that. In a world where tolerance has become a dogma from global fellowship, there sadly is increasingly tolerance for anything including tolerance of sin, tolerance of hunger, tolerance of illnesses, tolerance of murder, tolerance of plunder and looting which are resilient and increasing since the colonial era. In other words, to tolerate something or someone does not necessarily imply that the tolerated *ipso facto* gets freedom or deliverance. Tolerance is in fact an apology for the status quo which if interpreted broadly and in terms of (neo-)colonial plunder and looting translates to toleration of looters and plunderers. In this sense, tolerance delivers Africans to the exigencies of the imperial leviathan that seeks to continue to plunder and loot and to in fact play God.

Just like the colonial missionaries who assumed that Africans were living in states of nature without Godly orderly hierarchies, civil society organisations that present Africa as inherently disorderly continue to work on dogmatic imperial presuppositions that Africa is inherently and demonically disorderly. Civil society organisations continue to write and present frightening statistics [often without historically situating these in the history of enslavement and colonial barbarism] about African disorderliness that can only be saved by the Western saviours' exorcism of the demons in the continent. If civility is about caring for others, Africans' hospitality has been unparalleled in history as even early colonial travellers and missionaries benefitted from this hospitality (Nhemachena, 2015); if civility is about playing intermediary roles, Africa had systems that mediated not only between the state and individual citizens, as is presumed in Western theories, but there were also systems that mediated between good and evil spirits- that is between what in vernacular Shona in Zimbabwe are called *mweyayetsvina* (evil spirit) and *mweyamitsvene* (holy spirit) and between God [*Mwari*] and Evil [*mweyayetsvina*]. What these practices underscore is that Africans had wider spectrum of systems of civility including intermediaries: they did not only need intermediaries between the individual and the state [as presupposed in the West] or between the individual and the market but they also had systems of civility that mediated between the local and the foreign; and these were evident in some of the rituals (see Bhila, 1982) that were performed in precolonial trading stations/forts where Africans interacted with foreigners including Western traders.

Thus, while civil society organisations that are informed by Western epistemologies and ontologies privilege acting as buffers between the individuals and their states, African modes of civility also underline the exigencies of mediating between the local and the foreign, the visible and invisible [as indeed the beasts or leviathans

159

from which Africans needed buffers could be foreign, local, visible or invisible]. Because these realms are little if at all understood by civil society organisations that are premised on Western epistemologies, such organisations summarily dismiss African alternative spaces of civility. To the extent that African spaces of civility encompassed buffers between the local and the foreign, such African epistemologies threaten to deconstruct Western civil society organisations themselves which can be understood as manifestations of foreign leviathans. The dogmatic and stereotypical approach to civility by civil society organisations [that proliferated at independence in Africa] informed by Western epistemologies and ontologies point to a form of fundamentalism that target Africans and their states as barbaric, uncivilised and demonic paradoxically without noticing the incivility of Western plunder and looting, against which Africans also need buffers. This form of fundamentalism ignores the fact that the West often creates problems in Africa so that it can subsequently pose and posture as saviour of the continent, in ways that render for it economic and political capital.

Although there are times when some civil society organisations protest on a global scale against Western institutions including against social political experiments with the New World Order (Lenco, 2012: 8), civil society organisations generally have their epistemic and ontological foundations in the same Western systems, that dismiss African systems of thought and civility. In other words, Western civil society organisations fight [when they do] the Western systems from inside the belly of the Western beast and so much as old missionaries failed to effectively fight from within the Western systems, contemporary civil society organisations are arguably bound to have minimal or negligible scores against the imperial leviathan. They are mainly critical not only of African popular epistemologies and ontologies but also of African nation-states and territoriality. For this reason, Passavant *et al*, (2004: 149) note scholarly arguments to the effect that power is deemed to have shifted from the state to the supranational level; states are argued to have been eclipsed in world politics by transnational corporations and by nongovernmental organisations. Passavant *et al*, (2004: 149) note thus: "For Hardt and Negri, many of these NGOs...are best understood as moral instruments by which the empire's powers of interventions are advanced by circumventing the power of the state..." Also, in African family matters, Benson *et al,* (2008) argue that family focused NGOs champion particular cultural arguments honed in American style culture wars.

These activities of some civil society organisations are linked to the constitution and sustenance of empire. No wonder, Edwards *et al,* (2006) argue that humanitarian NGOs are powerful pacific weapons of the 'new world order'. For Edwards *et al* (ibid: 138); "The key institutions and actors that comprise...the biopolitics of empire are the United Nations, the NGO community and global civil society". While the development of global civil society is lauded by some as the only effective means of resistance to U.S and Multinational Corporation hegemony (Fischer-Tine, 2007: 29), the challenge here is that civil society organisations unlike the states, including world powers like the United States of America which they challenge, do not have military resources and this means that they can make lots of noise which amount to sonorous nothing.

In this vein, Wallis (2008: 26, 29) notes that America has a vision of an "American peace" based on unquestioned U.S military preeminence but also that American leaders like George Bush have, in their efforts for religious preeminence, believed that they have divine plans that supersede all human plans. Thus, consonant with religious discourses, [former] President George Bush is noted as having used religious language more than any other president in history. Wallis (2008: 29-31) observes that: "The hymn [in 2003 State of the Union that President Bush evoked] says there is "power, power, wonder-working power in the blood of the lamb"...The hymn is about the power of Christ in salvation, not the power of the "American people", or any people, or any country...Bush seems to make this mistake over and over again-confusing nation, church, and God. The resulting theology is more American civil religion than Christian faith...To confuse the role of God with that of the American nation, as George Bush seems to do, is a serious theological error that some might say borders on idolatry or blasphemy... America's foreign policy is more than preemptive, it is theologically presumptuous; not only unilaterally but dangerously messianic; not just arrogant but bordering on the idolatrous and blasphemous".

If civil society organisations are understood through the prism of old colonial missionaries who took to wittingly and unwittingly spreading the gospel of empire even as they professed to be against imperial barbarity and plunder; scholars need to question why Africans must have hope in the ability of contemporary civil society organisations effectively holding imperialism at bay as well as delivering Africans from the rapacious grip of empire. Like the old missionaries, contemporary civil society organisations not only suck from global capital that sponsors them but they also do not have the repressive apparatuses to hold back the most heavily militarised, including the nuclear armed imperial states in the world. A focus on pressuring smaller states to demilitarise and disarm repeats the old missionaries' practices that viewed African militarisation and armaments as demonic, savage and barbaric even as the same missionaries were complicity in militarisation and armaments by the colonial establishments. The difference is that now this process is occurring at a global level in ways that speak to the constitution and sustenance of global apartheid embedded in resilient global matrices of power.

Therefore, the question is whether contemporary civil society organisations are not repeating the errors of the old missionaries who conceived African state apparatuses as barbaric, savage and in need of excision even as the same missionaries were paradoxically complicit with colonial state apparatuses (now read global apparatuses)? If precolonial African states were disarmed and demilitarised in the interest of opening up space for the colonial establishment, might it be possible to argue that contemporary pressures directed at African states to demilitarise are meant to open up spaces for the global Western hegemonics so that they freely hang over the world as the sole or master leviathan to which everyone else must prostrate as to God? If civil society organisations [like missionaries of the old] genuinely seek to ensure accountability, transparency and the rule of law, why would they focus on pressurising the "weaker" states, and leaders some of whom are shipped off to imperial centres to be tried and punished

(Nhemachena and Bankie, 2016c)? If civil society organisations pressurise Africans to attend Western education, the question is whether they are not repeating the old missionary logics of delivering Africans to the imperial leviathan and away from their own epistemologies? if civil society organisations are pressurising for Africans to have access to Western-based health systems, the question is: are they not delivering Africans to the coloniality of the imperial leviathan that like the old colonial systems used health services as apparatuses for colonisation? If civil society organisations are pressuring for Africans to be included in Western human rights projects that neglect correlative human duties [as evinced in African jurisprudence] are they not delivering Africans to imperial leviathan? Are the human rights, presented or rendered without correlative duties, not another way by which empire continues to depict Africans as trapped in childhood, in which consciousness of duties to their communities is yet to emerge? In other words, Africans need to be wary of civil society organisations that dangle before them rights without correlative duties to their communities and families; they need to be wary when civil society organisations dangle before them phantoms of freedom without correlative constraints because these have increasingly become baits by which Africans, and the global south more broadly, are delivered away from their communities, states, God and ancestors but to the imperial leviathan that threatens to completely displace and replace God.

If deliverance to Godly Heavenly freedom requires consciousness of duties not only to one's community but to the Heavenly realm, the question is about where Africans are being delivered to when they are made to believe that they only have rights? If communion even with African ancestors requires observance of duties to the communities as well as to the ancestors, the question is about where Africans are being delivered to when they are rendered human rights education that instils no correlative senses of duty? If communion with God, ancestors and other Africans has entailed recognition of orderly hierarchies in the communities and states, the question is where Africans are being delivered to when they are made to believe that they can ignore hierarchies and live in increasing nihilism and anarchy?

The point here is that while humanity is made to believe that deconstruction and [secular] liberalism frees them from the Godly hierarchies portrayed as oppressive, empire itself has transformed itself into "God" positioning itself [and intolerant to its own deconstruction] at the apex of a Godless [as He is known] world. While humanity has been made to believe that freedom comes with deconstruction of own cultures, societies, religions, polities and [peripheral] states (Nhemachena, 2016), empire has paradoxically positioned itself to be its own religion, with its own old and new missionaries hiding behind secularism.

Instead of looking up to God, some Africans have been converted such that, since the colonial era, they have looked up to the empire as to God. To this new "God" that has replaced God, Africans continue to be delivered; and to deliver one another as well through uncritical embrace of imperial education, religion, culture, materialities, politics, spiritualities and epistemologies. A closer look at ways in which Africans are delivered daily to empire reveals the resilience of missionary callings as foundational to operations of some civil society.

Possessing the Genes of Missionaries of the Old? The Fundamentalism of Resilient Missionary Callings

When writing about hunting parties in precolonial and early colonial Africa, Schmidt (1992) provides us with the underlying complex logics of deliverance. Showing that deliverance is not always to where one desires, I therefore use Schmidt's (1992: 50) description of a hunting party in Africa thus: "With the nets the hunters caught antelopes such as reedbucks, waterbucks, and kudus, as well as wild pigs...In September 1870, Baines witnessed "an exciting chase", which he subsequently recorded in a drawing. In the vicinity of the Inzinghazi River, he and his companions heard "a confused clamour of many voices, the [Shona] hunting game". A large group of people, "boys, girls, and men, women, and gods were driving a duiker bok towards a long line of stake nets", he noted. Once the antelope was entangled in the meshes, it was speared by the men. During the drive Mauch recalled: the children shout and cry", directing the frightened animal into the net. Mauch remarked that such hunting parties often included the people of several villages, and frequently lasted for many days. Thus, the women, girls and young boys arrived at the hunting grounds laden with "baskets, pots, ground mealies, water, calabashes…that is with food to last for the duration of the hunt".

The logics of these kinds of hunting parties are reminiscent of the noise that old missionaries made about African sinfulness as a way to frighten and deliver Africans into the nets of colonial empire. They are reminiscent of the noise that sons and daughters of empire made to frighten and deliver Africans into the imperial pitfalls. The noise was made to frighten Africans about the alleged "evils" and "devilish" ways of their "heathen" ancestors set to "hell" so that Africans could be delivered into the imperial nets. Similarly, a lot of noise was made in order to frighten Africans away from their relatives or fellow African neighbours who were presented as evil and about to attack some of their own. Equally, a lot of noise has been made about African families and marriages in order to frighten Africans from their families and marriages and into the imperial nets of pornography, bestiality, prostitution, homosexuality, sodomy and now into the imperial industry that manufactures sex robots, dildos and virtual sexuality (see Nhemachena, 2016b). A lot of noise was similarly made by colonists about the evils of African herbal and traditional medicine so that they could deliver Africans into the net of imperial medicine, which paradoxically relied on African herbs from which Africans were forced to flee (Nhemachena, 2015). Thus, it is true that missionaries have missions to deliver Africans but not necessarily to God [whom Africans already knew prior to colonisation] but to the nets of empire. For this reason, missionaries were in fact hunters, who staged hunting parties on Africans including by setting outposts in remote areas from which they made frightening noise that set Africans running into imperial nets.

Contemporary complains by some African leaders that the International Criminal Court, based in The Hague, is hunting them and that the hunting is racistic and neocolonial (Al Jazeera, 15 November 2013; Reinold, 2012), underscore that imperial hunting parties did not end with the old missionaries. Global networks of civil society organisations share the logics of hunting parties, particularly those that are given to producing frightening statistics designed to generate moral panics about African morality, poverty, legality, including rule of law, "sloppiness", "barbarity", "savagery", "backwardness" and so on that are meant to frighten Africans [from time to time] out of their institutional hiding and into the imperial nets. The logics are even clearer when one reads the above together with Clarke, (2009: 70-3) who states that: "Through such complex and intensive efforts to convert critics into advocates, NGOs are playing a central role in mobilising governments to ratify the Rome Statute…With the goal of ensuring the universality of the Rome Statute, the primary objective of many of the activists engaged in CICC organising is to ensure implementation of the Rome Statute in as many countries as possible…Through the networking strategies of the CICC, several regional coalitions of rule of law NGOs…have been created since 2002 to work with African states towards implementation. The NCICC, for example, continues to be a central actor in pressuring West African governments to ratify international treaties and implement codes of the statute… "Today, the financial resources being brokered with international lending institutions are increasingly linked to state compliance with international rule of law and human rights standards".

The argument that the ICC and the networks of civil society organisations were minded on hunting and delivering Africans into the imperial net is particularly stark when one factors in the point that major Western powers [including those that perpetrate planetary violence] refused to sign and submit themselves to the ICC even as they arrogate the prerogative to refer African states for trial by the court which they themselves have refused to submit to. Thus, while NGOs, which have had unprecedented growth [in Africa] since the 1980s (Abdelrahman, 2004: 40), are perceived by some to be increasingly important in humanitarian tasks including issues of poverty, the environment and civil liberties (Global Research, 3 March 2012), there appear to be a dark side to these offsprings of Euro-enlightenment. For this reason, other scholars argue that NGOs are used as tools for foreign policy implementation by some powerful Euro-American states. The Global Research, (3 March 2012) notes for instance that: "Instead of purely military force, the

U.S.A. has now moved to using NGOs as tools in its foreign policy implementation, specifically the National Endowment for Democracy, Freedom House, and Amnesty International…"

Thus, while some conceive civil society organisations as torchbearers and stakeholders in the "new world order" (Drainville, 2012: 104), other scholars like Brewda, (1996) note that the British Empire has deployed NGOs against some nation states in recent years and these NGOs operate under cover of defending "human rights", "democracy", "environment" or "humanitarian relief" when they are also used to target states for discrediting, coups and revolutions. Brewda, (1996); New Atlas,(8 September 2016) and Engdakl, (2011) also note that civil society organisations like Oxford famine (Oxfam) and Amnesty International are led and controlled by some members of the British House of Lords including members of families of the nobility. It is also noted that some civil society organisations working on democracy are sponsored by, among others, petrochemical giant Chevron, Wall Street's Goldman Sachs, States Departments, agricultural and pharmaceutical giants. So, Engdahl, (2011) notes that military industry and oil industries use methods of propaganda as well as NGOs for regime change, colour revolutions and they operate a global network of bases for full spectrum dominance.

Whereas during the inception of the colonial era missionaries, who were entangled in complex webs of colonial connections (Moyo, 2015: 27), acted as pressure groups to cox African leaders to sign away their land and other resources including sovereignty, in the contemporary era civil society organisations act as pressure groups and also as missionaries. So, while missionaries of the old coxed the Ndebele King, Lobengula to sign the Moffat Treaty as well as the Rudd Concession (Moyo, 2015), contemporary African leaders are coxed and pressured by civil society organisations to sign the Rome Statute for instance that takes away their sovereignty, autonomy and subjects them to the imperial court, in the form of the International Criminal Court. Just like the old missionaries who worked extremely hard running missions, risking their lives and good health in the process (BBC World Service n. d), contemporary civil society penetrate remote areas, risking lives and good health of members and

167

officials. Of course, as the BBC World Service (n. d) notes: not all missionaries were villainous though there were some such as Moffat, the Reverend Helm of the Christian Missionary Society (CNS) who deliberately mistranslated a document which resulted in Lobengula giving away his land to the British South African Company of Cecil Rhodes. Other villainous missionaries noted include the Catholic Priest, Friar Anthonio Barroso, who persuaded Dom Pedro V, King of the Congo to sign a note in 1884. Dom Pedro V believed it was a thank you letter for a gold-backed chair when in fact it was an oath of loyalty and submission to the King of Portugal. It may be necessary to also note other missionaries who for instance persuaded the Balozi in what is now Zambia, to request "protection" of Queen Victoria and to sign a treaty (Webourn, 1968).

Therefore, like the hunters described by Schmidt above, missionaries [some of whom pretended to be real friends to Africans] frightened Africans into signing treacherous protection treaties with colonists (Webourn, 1968; Morel, 1920: 34). Consequently, vague promises enshrined in protection treaties and alliances were in fact apparatuses to divest Africans of their property (Jan-Bart, 2004: 44). Jan-Bart, (2004: 64) cites one precolonial Namibian African leader, Hendrik Witbooi stating thus: "What are we being protected against. From what danger or difficulty, or suffering can one chief be protected by another? I see no truth or sense...in the suggestion that a chief who has surrendered may keep his autonomy and do as he likes...This part of Africa is the realm of us Red Chiefs...if danger threatens one of us which he feels he cannot meet on his own, then he can call on a brother among the Red chiefs...for we are one in colour and customs, and this Africa is ours".

Hendrik Witbooi's responses to European protection treaties are at the heart of contemporary African antipathy to missionary-style interventions from the West. In such missionary style interventions, Africans are expected to always religiously prostrate and lose their sovereignty, autonomy and dignity. At the heart of contemporary scholarship that portray Africa as horizontal, as without any history and need for autonomy, as without hierarchy and without history and need for sovereignty, is the resilience of the logics of the old missionary-prostrate-style. Africa is being conditioned via ideologies, imperially inspired and led wars as well as via aid, to prostration at all intersections with the West. In a world where empire is increasingly becoming a religion, deposing and replacing God, Africa is expected to lie horizontally in the old missionary style that is sadly finding favour among some contemporary theorists on flatness, horizontality and rhizome (Deleuze and Guattari, 1987; Latour 2005). Whereas Hendrik Witbooi's remarks speak to the Zimbabwean Shona vernacular saying that "*nzou hairemerwi nenyanga dzayo*" (an elephant does not feel the weight of its tusks), this timeless African axiom has lost relevance for contemporary Africans who, after being robbed of their properties, are now being conditioned, much like animals to receiving and surviving on charity that comes with conditions of paying homage and reverence to empire. The fundamentalism of empire lies not in assuming the presence of God, but in dismissing Him as well as in its fundaments of the liberal free market that is sadly not equipped to restitute those that suffered brutalities and expropriations of colonisation and enslavement. Its fundaments lie not only in dogmas that sustains it but also in its art of dissolving others including God while entrenching its own planetary hegemony. A close look at the case studies of Mozambique and Kenya bears testimony to some arguments made so far in this chapter.

Mozambique

Worldwide aid is a US$50 billion per year industry, putting aid on a par with some industrial sectors of the global economy with similar turnover, such as the machine tool industry (UNIDO 1989). Most of the funding comes from the industrialised countries aid budgets, which are approved by their national Parliaments. These countries support aid for a number of reasons, in conformity with their national self-interests. Major factors at play are geo-political and strategic interests. For instance, a country hosting a Western military installation is susceptible to Western pressure and would have strategic value to the West.

The case study, Mozambique, attained self-government in 1975 after a long-drawn-out barbaric colonial experience under Portuguese rule, which was followed by a protracted armed struggle led by the liberation movement FRELIMO, which opted for Socialism. After 1975 war, which was led by RENAMO, continued in the country and this war was aided and abetted by certain Western countries. This was during the Cold War period that pitched the East against the West, with their proxies being the scene of armed confrontation. Mozambique did not accept funding from the Bretton Woods Institutions, the World Bank and the International Monetary Fund (IMF) or other major funders yet, emerging from a liberation struggle which was destructive, aid was its major funding source.

Traditionally 'care packages' were supplied by Western donors by way of disaster relief through groups such as Oxfam, which collected second hand clothing for sale in its shops to poor people and the money raised was spent to assist poor people in the third world. The European Union, the United States and other rich countries spent millions on farm subsidies to make their farms economically sustainable, far in excess of what they gave to the poor countries.

The export to Africa of food surpluses was a delicate issue which if not handled carefully could destroy the survival systems in subsistence economies and endanger local food production, creating consumptive habits which are unsustainable. Aid to Africa could destroy sensitive economies based on long-standing farming practices. Aid is a two edged sword, which can cut both ways, either to assist or to terminate the recipient. An aid agency can encourage a particular investor creating a win/win situation. The Mozambican situation provided few such examples.

Recent discovery of off-shore oil and gas in Mozambique may lead to development, but reports which appeared in 2016 of missing millions of funds via government contractors would indicate that the country now has endemic issues of public probity, which were not apparent in the earlier years of self-government. Meanwhile, Mozambique is aid-dependent for the foreseeable future. Instead of entering civilian politics peacefully, RENAMO never did lose its military capability and was never fully integrated into the new democratic state. It remained belligerent, threatening violence and at the time of writing is in a state of armed conflict with FRELIMO because its demands remain unheeded, such as a greater share in the oil and gas revenues.

Hanlon (1991) gives information on the early years of self-government in Mozambique and the dealings of the country with NGOs. FRELIMO emerged from a long liberation struggle. On obtaining power, it maintained a centralised approach to government. Foreign assistance was sought via channels which had proven supportive during the liberation struggle. This came as a result of agreements and accords with countries, UN agencies and some individuals. There were no freelance aid workers and all projects were under the direct control of Mozambican Ministries. The FRELIMO government had power over donors due to its ability to say "No!" It did turn away NGOs. Because of its practice of 'democratic centralism' the FRELIMO government refused to supply details of its national accounts and information on its foreign debts. It's non-membership of the IMF meant it would not be pressured to reveal its internal financial system. However, when it fell behind in its foreign debt repayments in 1983 its situation began to change. Famine reversed its financial system of the past. The country was obliged to open-up, but this opening did not improve the country's situation.

Once the gates opened, the donors poured in. Despite the aid invasion of 1983-85 the financial situation of the country did not improve and the financial crises remained or even deepened. In the period 1982-86, less money came into the country per year than in the peak year of 1981. Export earnings decreased due to war and drought. The low levels of aid reflect FRELIMO's pursuit of non-alignment and its refusal to join the Western group.

In late 1986, Samora Machel was killed when his plane was brought down. Destabilisation in Zambezia and Nampula provinces increased at this time. Oxfam and Save the Children launched an emergency appeal for Mozambique. Famine was being talked about and certain NGOs gave the impression that there might be a repetition in the Kalahari, of events previously seen in the Sahel and Ethiopia. There was malnutrition in 1987 but not death. Starvation was replaced by chronic malnourishment creating what some called a 'permanent structural emergency'.

The Bretton Woods institutions' influence in the country had increased and financial capital was mixed with the state farms and old colonial plantations. World Bank investment had been in quick return areas, such as real estate, tourism and mining and to a lesser extent in agriculture. These policies were reminiscent of the shopkeeper colonialism of the 1960s. This was not neo-colonialism but re-colonisation.

The IMF and the World Bank had sought to dominate by their conditionality thus imposing what was called 'structural adjustment'. They sought leverage and influence over Mozambique's financial health via 'co-financing', whereby existing donors were requested to jointly fund World Bank Projects. This form of leverage was called 'co-ordination'. There were more than 200 donor agencies in Mozambique. The idea was that NGOs group together for co-ordination purposes. Several agencies, bilateral and multi-lateral and NGOs have assisted government with consultants, as a form of technical assistance. The funds would have been better used if given direct to the Mozambican government. One of the consequences of these types of arrangements was the tendency for the donors to encourage government officials to compete amongst each other.

To an extent, Mozambique received aid as a form of international solidarity because Mozambique had adopted a people's approach, rather than an elite approach to development. The imposition of the Unilateral Declaration of Independence (UDI) in Rhodesia had negative consequences for Mozambique, which it hoped would be able to offset, since UDI was not of Mozambique's making. Samora Machel was of the view that the country was sufficiently well endowed so that foreign countries and trans-national corporations could benefit by way of investments and need not seek exploitive relations with Mozambique, allowing Mozambique to also benefit.

FRELIMO implemented a policy of non-alignment and respect for sovereignty, with control of the development processes. Hanlon (1991) states that some Western countries and donors refused to accept such an approach to development and this opposition led them to seek to destabilise Mozambique.

Multilateral agencies and NGOs receive most of their funding from donor governments and so act as channels for aid. Of the NGOs there are private, non-governmental organisations such as

Oxfam and Care International formed to provide aid, as well as from churches and solidarity organisations.

As a matter of policy, Mozambique excluded the international NGOs such as Oxfam. The country preferred the use of 'co-operators' – people who had been part of the solidarity movement and had a specific skill. Many were from the Left, with specific skills, working on contracts for two years working in a Ministry or on a farm, paid the same salary as a Mozambican. There was no Peace Corp or VSO program. Assistance came from developing countries such as Tanzania. There were refugees from Chile, Brazil, East Timor and South Africa. Many were technicians who were hired as co-operators and paid with Nordic funds.

Further explicating the role of civil society organisation in Mozambique, Hanlon (1991: 181) proceeds to note thus:

> In the area of health – health services had never been free, but charges were low. Over time charges were increased for purposes of cost recovery. But the funds raised failed to cover costs – so that Mozambique became increasingly dependent on donors to fund health services. Bi-lateral funds were increasingly channelled through UNICEF and NGOs to reduce Mozambican control over its health system. Hanlon informs us that some NGOs went as far as to create a parallel mission hospital system. The donors claimed aid of more than US$ 27 million for Mozambican health, including drugs in 1988. The main donors were Italy (US$16 million, US$10million), WHO (US$3million), the USSR, Norway and Netherlands(each US$2million). Others estimated the real total to be around US$20million, with at least forty donors and agencies involved in the health sector. By 1987 the Ministry of Health (MOH) was complaining about donor agencies acting without informing provincial authorities. The Red Cross and Medecin Sans Frontiers were particularly problematic, having their own planes and flying without Mozambique accompaniment. It took some two years for Mozambique to re-assert its authority. Another problem that emerged from NGOs was that of stealing MOH staffers by offering them higher salaries.

Mozambicans have been slowly setting up NGOs, but foreign NGOs were moving much faster, using their wealth and power to the displeasure of the Mozambican authorities. Some foreign NGOs tried to work with local NGOs- an arrangement called 'localisation', in order to establish Mozambican NGOs. The NGOs set up in such circumstances were subsidiaries of the foreign NGOs, being dependent on their original sources of funding. The observation about Mozambique was that foreign NGOs working in Mozambique were not usually "grassroots" organisations but rather autonomous groups created by a few prominent persons, which are close enough to obtain their government's support. Mozambicans have started creating NGOs on similar basis promoted by well-connected locals, having some autonomy, but close allegiance to FRELIMO. The Christian Council, grouping some Protestant churches sympathetic to FRELIMO was a typical example of such a formation.

Leading figures such as Janet Mondlane, Marceline Chissano and Gracia Machel set up their own NGOs in the 1980s-90s. Many foreign NGOs were pleased to see their Mozambican counterparts implementing and developing their own structures so that they would take on the responsibility of Government: however, in Hanlon's view most local NGOs lacked competency.

Another observation of Hanlon (1991) was how the donors supplied food and transport to NGOs and not to the government. This was the situation in early 1989. This was being done by the US government to the displeasure of the Mozambique government and the United Nations. This was an attempt to marginalise the Mozambique agencies created to handle food distribution.

For instance, in 1990 one NGO brought in 420 tons of maize and gave it out free to all in the district, most of whom were producing their own food. This was a disincentive to agricultural production, destroying the agricultural marketing campaign in the district. The disregard for suffering and the wish to defeat the intentions of the FRELIMO government in the area of food production were time and again evident in the behaviour of NGOs. For instance – church groups giving assistance only to their members. With this type of NGO behaviour some hungry people went without food while others received too much.

Green (1990) of the Institute of Development Studies and Advisor to the Mozambique Government noted that northern NGOs were more prone to bypass the Mozambique government than Mozambican NGOs. He was of the view that northern NGOs needed to understand that in general they were part of the problem, not part of the solution: more often they were arrogant, corrupt and incompetent. Most NGO projects in Mozambique were adjudged useless. Hanlon concluded the NGOs were increasingly being used by donors. NGOs became contractors, no different than private companies. Hanlon concluded that in general NGOs act for arrogant and racist donors who do not trust Mozambicans to carry out projects. NGO characteristics are part of the anti-government privatisation ethic of large donors. They are used to weaken and bypass the Mozambican government.

Hanlon (1991) describes the NGOs in Mozambique as 'new missionaries'. Some of the biggest NGOs are religious groups, thus in fact they are 'old missionaries'. In both Mozambique and Zimbabwe, missionaries supported the liberation struggle. In Latin America missionaries assisted in the development of liberation theology. Hanlon states that NGO new missionaries can play a role in Mozambique, but that they need to understand that 'they are, indeed, missionaries who have been sent to Mozambique as part of the recolonizing mission'. In Hanlon's view the most useful role that progressive NGOs could play would be 'as missionaries from Mozambique, rather than to Mozambique'. In that form, their role would be to bring to Europe and North America the message that destabilization continues and that structural adjustment is wreaking havoc. Instead of reinforcing a false picture of 'civil war', 'black-on-black violence' and white people helping benighted natives, the new missionaries would present a more accurate picture of Africans suffering at the hands of white re-colonizers. Some of these new missionaries have been very successful in fund raising in the west and carry influence there.

As regards NGOs FRELIMO adopted a strategy to always strengthen national structures. The policy was that donors should work through local government in an attempt to strengthen it, rather than operating in parallel, even if this might slow down aid work.

These were the views being articulated in1988.NGOs were to strengthen Mozambican institutions through training and material support. This call by FRELIMO largely went unheeded. The implications of this would be that western donors did not want to support FRELIMO. Hanlon observed that at all levels in food distribution, Mozambique being prone to flooding and other disasters – the donors deliberately setup parallel structures to government, often in competition to government structures.

Concerning where donor funding goes, Hanlon noted that the World Bank was diverting donor funds into channels it controls through co-financing and control over emerging funding, whereas Mozambican Ministers requested donors not to co-finance but instead to use funds as part of the normal bi-lateral aid frame. Donors rather gave funds to NGOs and UN agencies, particularly UNICEF. There was little evidence that such agencies used funds better than government. Much of the funding was used up by paying commissions to support their own overheads.

Hanlon (1991) provides some detail on what he calls 'recolonisation' under the aegis of the Bretton Woods Institutions, such as the IMF. This was their agenda in the 1980s, a period in which the north became richer and the south poorer. This period is often described as the 'missing decade'.

Kenya

In the Kenyan case study we turn to the book entitled: 'The NGO Factor in Africa – the case of arrested development in Kenya' by Maurice Nyamanga Amutabi (2006), in which the author uses case studies, particularly that of the Rockefeller Foundation (RF) in the area of medical research and health in Kenya, from the yellow fever campaigns of the inter-war years to health care projects post-war and post self-government, as an illustration of the behaviour of NGOs in Africa.

Amutabi expresses the view that NGOs represent the re-awakening of the democratic spirit in Africa after the phase of the one-party state and military dictatorship. They are felt to be more accountable and participatory actors than government functionaries.

The author states that in general NGOs in Africa tend to be small in size, with limited budgets, concentrated in urban areas, handling a limited range of issues, weak on research and analysis and with limited national and international networking relationships. They are dependent on Euro-American resources and support. Amutabi does not mince his words in explaining the paternal and dependent relationship between the north and African NGOs.

Paul Tiyambe Zeleza in his foreword to Amutabi's book, states that NGOs are neither neutral nor innocent bystanders in the development struggle underway in Africa. Zeleza refers to Amutabi's analysis that NGOs are in large measure representative of the neo-colonial and neo-liberal project in Africa. The Rockefeller Foundation has been in Kenya since 1924. Amutabi compares the work of RF and the Christian missionaries in their complicity and civilisational mission. The book exposes the cooperative experiences of NGOs and multinational corporations and concludes that NGOs are to be situated in the trajectory of colonialism, decolonialism and globalisation, making NGOs agents of market forces, acting in concert with the political elites and the comprador bourgeoisie.

In historical context Amutabi (2006) dates the active promotion of NGOs by organisations such as the IMF and World Bank to the 1980s. Prior to that, states had been the main dispensers of Western largesse to the south. This IMF and World Bank support to NGOs placed NGOs in a strong position in their dealings with states. Projects were designed in the north for implementation in the south. NGOs by and large come with Western social priorities such as western liberalism and gender bias, as well as a pre-disposition to marketing strategies. Those dealing with NGOs on the ground have little understanding of the power relations within which NGOs operate and what and whose interests they serve. This is not to say that RF's projects in Kenya lacked humanity. However, the overall thrust of RF's activities in Kenya places it firmly in the framework of the advancement of Western interests in Africa. The antidote, as seen in Mozambique, would be for RF to schedule the handover of its Kenyan operations to Kenyans.

Conclusions

177

This chapter has argued that there are parallels between civil society organisations and the logic of missionaries of the old in that both of them facilitate the preeminence and supremacy of empire that is understood to be positioning itself to replace God as the Supreme Being. Contemporary scholarship that is evangelising the immanence of God rather than His Heavenly transcendence are argued to be, wittingly or unwittingly, preparing the ground for empire to claim the position of an immanent God in the world. The networks of civil society organisations, transnational corporations and so on, also position empire to claim, omnipresence and omniscience in the world where such organisations operate as surveillance agents and foot soldiers of the empire. Besides, it has been argued that the imperial possession of weapons of mass destruction, including biological and chemical weapons, position it to arrogate to itself Godly omnipotence in the world. In such a scenario, scholarly discourses over the secular and the religious need to be teased out more, so that the position of empire which constitutes an invisible presence in the world can be better understood. It can be understood in terms of imperial sponsorship of emergent new religions that dismiss the conventional God as old paradoxically even as empire itself relies on old imperial logics.

In order to adequately understand the hypocrisy of empire that postures as opposed to fundamentalism while it constitutes and buttresses imperial fundamentalisms, it is necessary to interrogate how empire has been resilient. Constituting and maintaining its fundamentalisms via liberalisms that present sham alternatives to multitudes that remain trapped in imperial dogmatism, empire has been resilient for centuries. Intolerant to dissent over its liberalisms, versions of rule of law and democracy, empire has been able to stand on its insularity as it smoothers dissent to imperial patrimonialism and authoritarianism masquerading as [sterile] liberal freedom or emancipation. In all these efforts and rubrics, there are civil society organisations some of which evangelise the imperial gospels on the continent while simultaneously engaging in surveillance as the multiple eyes of empire that thrives on semblances of omniscience and omnipresence in the world. If empires [whether directly or indirectly constituted] were never about fundamentalism, the fundamental question is about how such empires manage to be resilient and to reproduce themselves. In other words, the point in this chapter is that an empire that postures as antithetical to *fundamentalisms* should not prevent scholars from asking *fundamental* questions about that empire. To be against fundamentalisms and *a fortiori* to be averse to asking and answering fundamental questions would be to soporify scholarship, and destroy the critical intellectualism, that is already suffering, particularly in the African academies.

References

Al Jazeera., 15 November 2013, Africans Push UN to Call off "Racist"Court.www.aljazeera.com/indepth/features/2013/11/africans-push-un-call-off-racist-court-2013111451110131757.html.

Albdelrahman, M. M., 2004, *Civil Society Exposed: The Politics of NGOs in Egypt.* Palgrave Macmillan: London and New York.

Amutabi, M. N., 2006, *The NGO Factor in Africa.* Routledge, Taylor and Francis Group.

BBC World Service., n.d, African History from the Dawn of Time. www.bbc.co.uk/worldserice/africa/features/storyofafrica/8chapters.4.shtml.

Beasley-Murray, J., 1999, Learning from Sendoro-Civil Society Theory and Fundamentalism, *Journal of Latin American Cultural Studies*, 8, 1: 75-88.

Benson, B. E. *et al.*, 2008, *Evangelicals and Empire: Christian Alternatives to the Political Status Quo.* Brazos Press: Michigan.

Bhila. H. K., 1984, *Trade and Politics in a Shona Kingdom: the manyika and their Portuguese and African neighbours, 1575-1902.* Longman: Essex

Brewda, J., 1996, The Invisible Empire of NGOs, Daniel Solis Report. Danielsolis.cz/the-invisible-empire-of-ngos/source EIR News Service-Special Report.

Cherep-Spiridovich C., 2000, *The Secret World Government of "The Hidden Hand": The Unrevealed in History.* The Book Tree.

Chronicle, 23 October 2013, Foreign Aid Hinders Development in Africa.www.chronicle.co.zw/foreign-aid-hinders-development-in-africa/.

Clarke, K. M., 2009, *Fictions of Justice: The International Criminal Court and the Challenge of Legal Pluralism in Sub-Saharan Africa*. Cambridge University Press: Cambridge.

Conkle, D O., 1996, Secular Fundamentalism, Religious Fundamentalism and the Search for Truth in Contemporary America. Digital Repository, Maurer School of Law: Indiana University http://www.repository.law.indiana.edu/facpub.

Daily Nation, 8 November 2015, NGOs accused of Pushing Ruto Case. www.nation.co.ke/news/politics/NGOs-accused-of-pushing-Ruto-case/1064-2948638-iiep8ki/index.html.

deMaistre, J. M. *et al.*, 1996, *Against Rousseau: On the State of Nature and on the Sovereignty of the People*. McGill-Queen's University Press: London.

Deleuze G and Guattari F., 1987, *A Thousand Plateaus: Capitalism and Schizophrenia*. University of Minnesota Press

Drainville, A. C., 2012, *A History of World Order and Resistance: The Making and Unmaking of Global Subjects*. Routledge: London and New York.

Edwards, A. *et al.*, 2006, *Sport Empire*: Meyer and Meyer Sport (UK) Ltd: Oxford.

Ekins, R., 2005, Secular Fundamentalism and Democracy, *Journal of Markets and Morality*, 8, 1: 81-93.

Engdahl, W. F., 2011, *Full Spectrum Dominance: Totalitarian Democracy in the New World Order*. Progressive Press.

Fischer-Tine, H., 2007, Global Civil Society and the Forces of Empire: The Salvation Army, British Imperialism, and "Prehistory" of NGOs (ca. 1880-1920), in same, ed, *Competing Visions of World Order: Global Moments and Movements, 1880-1930*. Palgrave Macmillan.

French, H. W., 2014, *China's Second Continent: How a Million Migrants are Building a New Empire in Africa*. Foreign Affairs.

Global Research, 3 March 2012, NGOs: The Missionaries of Empire. www.globalresearch.ca/ngos-the-missionaries-of-empire/29595.

Green, R., 1990, Poverty, Rehabilitation and Economic Transformation: The Case of Mozambique. Presented at the Institute of Social Studies in The Hague, Netherlands, I November 1990

Hanlon, J., 1991, *Who Calls the Shots?* James Currey and Indiana University Press.

Hazelwood, M., 2014, *The World System Equals the Beast of Revelation.* Archway Publishing: Bloomington.

Jan-Bart, G., 2004, Imperial Germany and the Herero of Southern Africa: Genocide and the Quest for Recompense, in Jones A, ed, *Genocide, War and the West: History and Complicity.* Zed Books: New York.

Latour, B., 2005, *Reassembling the Social: An Introduction to Actor-Network-Theory.* Oxford University Press: New York

Lenco, P., 2012, *Deleuze and World Politics: Alter-Globalisation and Nomad Science.* Routledge: London and New York.

Maxwell, J., 2000, *Matrix of Power: How the World Has Been Controlled by Powerful People Without our Knowledge.* The Book Tree: Escondido.

McAnulla, S., 2014, Secular Fundamentalists? Characterising the New Atheist Approach to Secularism, Religion and Politics, in *British Politics*, 9, 2: 124-145.

Morel, E. D., 1920, *The Black Man's Burden: The White Man in Africa from the Fifteenth Century.* Library of Congress Catalogue.

Moyo, F., 2015, *The Bible, the Bullet, and the Ballot: Zimbabwe: The Impact of Christian Protests in Sociopolitical Transformation ca. 1900-ca. 2000.* Pickwick Publications: Oregon.

Ndlovu-Gatsheni, S. J., 2012, Coloniality of Power in Development Studies and the Impact of Global Imperial Designs on Africa, *ARAS,* 33, 2: 48-73.

Ndlovu-Gatsheni, S. J., 2013, The Entrapment of Africa within the Global Colonial Matrices of Power: Eurocentrism, Coloniality and Deimperialisation in the Twenty-First Century, *Journal of Developing Societies* 29, 4: 331-353.

New Atlas, 8 September 2016, Exposing US-Funded "NGOs"https://off-guardian.org/2016/09/08/exposing-us-funded-ngos/.

Nhemachena A., 2015b, Sensing Presences: Health, Illness and resilience in Contemporary Rural Zimbabwe, in *Africology: The Journal of Pan African Studies*, vol 8, No 8

Nhemachena A., 2016a, Double-Trouble: Reflections on the Violence of Absence and the Culpability of the Present in Africa, in Mawere M et al., eds, *Violence, Politics and Conflict Management in Africa: Envisioning Transformation, Peace and Unity in the Twenty-First Century*. Langaa RPCIG: Bamenda

Nhemachena A., 2016b, Animism, Coloniality and Humanism: Reversing the Empire's Framing of Africa, in Mawere M and Nhemachena A., eds, *Theory, Knowledge, Development and Politics: What Role for the Academy in the Sustainability of Africa?* Langaa RPCIG: Bamenda.

Nhemachena A and Bankie F B., 2016, The ICC and the Global South: On International Law and the Question of an African Jurisprudence. Presented at the *Conference on the International Criminal Court and Africa*. Hosted by the Faculty of Law and the UNAM Law Review, University of Namibia; 14-15 June 2016, Windhoek Country Club, Windhoek, Namibia.

Nhemachena, A., 2015a, Envisioning African Democracy in the Twenty-First Century: MwanaWasheMurandaKumwe and the Coloniality of Contrived Democracy, in Mawere M and Mwanaka T R, eds, *Democracy, Good Governance and Development in Africa*. Langaa RPCIG: Bamenda p 1-43.

Nkrumah, K., 1965, *Neo-Colonialism, The Last Stage of Imperialism*. Thomas Nelson and Sons, Ltd: London.

Passavant, P. and Dean, J., 2004, *Empire's New Clothes: Reading Hardt and Negri*. Routledge: New York and London.

Paul, J. A., 2000, NGOs and Global Policy-Making, in Global Policy Forum https://www.globalpolicy.org/empire/31611-ngos-and-global-policy-making.html.

Perkins, J., 2007, *The Secret History of the American Empire: Economic Hit Men, Jackals, and the Truth about Global Corruption*. Penguin Group Inc: New York.

Poxon, J., 2001. Embodied Anti-Theology: the Body without Organs and the Judgement of God, in Bryden, M., ed, *Deleuze and Religion*. Routledge: London: 42-50.

Reinold, T., 2012, Constitutionalisation? Whose Constitutionalisation? Africa's Ambivalent Engagement with the International Criminal Court, *International Journal of Constitutional Law*, 10, 4: 1076-1105.

Schmidt, E., 1992, *Peasants, Traders and Wives: Shona Women in the History of Zimbabwe, 1870-1939*. Heinemann Educational Books, Inc: Portsmouth.

The Guardian, 26 August 2015, Human Rights Groups Face Global Crackdown 'Not Seen in a Generation'. https://www.theguardian.com/law/2015/aug/26/ngos-face-restriction-laws-human-rights-generation.

The Herald, 3 June 2016, NGOs, Whose NGOs? www.herald.co.zw/ngo-whose-ngos/.

The Herald, 4 July 2009, Zimbabwe NGOs-Auxiliaries of Neocolonial Agenda allafrica.com/stories/200907060019.html.

The Telegraph, 26 December 2015, Rule, Britannia! Our New Empire of Culture is Taking the World by Storm. www.telegraph.co.uk/culture/12070156/Rule-Britannia-our-new-empire-of-culture-is-taking-the-world-by-storm.html.

Wallis, J., 2008, Dangerous Religion: George W Bush's Theology of Empire in Benson B E *et al.*, eds, *Evangelicals and Empire: Christian Alternatives to the Political Status Quo*. Brazos Press: Michigan.

Welbourn, F. B., 1968, *Atoms and Ancestors*. The University of California.

Chapter Seven

Dismantling Fundamentalisms in Science: Trailing Feyerab End's Epistemological Anarchism and the Place of African Science

Tobias Dindi Ong'aria

Introduction

Philosophy of science is an enterprise that concentrates more on method to understand how science proceeds, how we get scientific knowledge, and what science is capable of doing. Hence, to talk of science bereft of method is not possible. Discourse in the philosophy of science is almost entirely about what is the most appropriate method of doing science. For African science, the concern of method equally creeps in just like in Western science. However, it is even more complicated when the 'African' notion is introduced because of definitional difficulties. First, what exactly do we call 'African science' and how different is it from 'Western Science'? Are they demarcated by geographical terms or philosophical terms, or even racial terms? This is difficult to define just like it is in religion and philosophy. This is an attempt at possibilities of redeeming African science into the discourse in philosophy of science, from a perspective of Paul Feyerabend's everything goes, into a possible existence in a cosmopolitan milieu. Can Feyerabend's epistemological anarchism offer a prospect window for African Science? If yes, how far can it be taken? And if African Science is to be relooked, are there any 'dogmas', as Feyerabend criticises in Western Science, that ought to be tolerated? I will start by exploring Feyerabend's criticism of method in Western Science as contained in *Against Method, (1975)* I will then explore African Science, or what could rightly be termed so, and how Feyerabend's contribution could offer prospects to it. Lastly I will look at what needs to be upheld in method, despite Feyerabend's criticism, if African Science is to flourish again. Specifically, I will look at how a bare minimum of logical rigour cannot be compromised if we have to talk of a science as 'African.' Basically, although 'anything goes' could be a promising idea, an extreme adherence to it has negative implications for African Science.

What is African Science?

Science receives a lot of recognition as compared to other academic fields today. It is common knowledge in our own time that several African education systems esteem science related fields of study as compared to the humanities, because it appears to be more related to the day to day needs of ordinary folk, and it seems to give responses to societal needs, perhaps in a more technical manner as compared to the reflective approaches towards our world. What then is science? And what is that which we talk of as African Science? Science in this section is talked of as a systematic study that is rigorous and logical, employing experimentation and observation, aimed at explaining the world so as to arrive at true, certain knowledge. From this understanding of science, it is apparent that science is an empirical activity, and is generally held as derived from facts of experience (Chalmers, 1999).

Due to the problems in defining African Science raised above, I will borrow Akpan's definition (2010:13) of African Traditional Science, which he terms as "activities of understanding, explaining, and exploring nature for man's use, which proceeded from African beginnings on African soil by African people". Even with this definition, we ought to exercise caution especially with the category 'African', as it does not escape complexity as a category of identity. This is because present Africa definitely is a product of hybridity in several aspects, including social, intellectual, and religious among other characteristics, we would therefore have to keep several presumptions in mind as we proceed with the category 'African.' This challenge however does not have to hinder critical reflection on African Science by whatever means, because Africa has a contribution to make to the global world in many spheres, one of them, and relevant for this discussion, being science.

Paul Feyerabend and epistemological anarchism

Feyerabend is known for criticising Western Science for its emphasis on a universal method, that is, a claim that science has to proceed in a specific way, with specific rules, whose violation renders a practice not scientific. This is clearly put forth in *Against Method* (1975) in which he insists that science ought not to stress a universal rule. He argues that it is necessary in some cirumstances to break methodological rules in scientific practice if progress is to be achieved. His claim is that for each rule, there is always a situation that necessitates an ignoring of the rules of method, and in some cases even to adopt the opposite of these rules. For Feyerabend, all methodologies do have their own weaknesses and a strict following of any of them deemed the best, would be erroneous. The only 'rule' according to him is 'anything goes' (1975). It is, he claims, "unrealistic and pernicious" to let science proceed with fixed universal rules. It is unrealistic because it does not take into consideration the talents of man and the circumstances under which they grow and develop. Similarly, it is pernicious because insistence on rules and fixed ways of doing things could only increase man's ability to grow professionally, yet ignoring man's humanity.

It is possible to create a tradition that is held together by strict rules, and that is also successful to some extent. But is it desirable to support such a tradition to the exclusion of everything else? Should we transfer to it the rights for dealing in knowledge, so that any result that has been obtained by other methods is at once ruled out of court? (Feyerabend 1975).

This way of proceeding for science, if Feyerabend is to be read between the lines, is tyrannical. He attacks it as dogmatic and even goes ahead to argue that it took over its opponents by force. For Feyerabend (1975), science took over the place of its opponents by power and not by argument, which is an assertion that paints Western science (deemed as rational) in an ironical way. In European colonies -like Africa- science and the religion of brotherly love (Christianity) were imposed on natives without any argumentation, or even convincing. These are all instances that Feyerabend advances to taint the authenticity of Western Science's insistence on a universal method of doing science.

In Africa for example, it is very difficult to draw a line that demarcates where science ends and myths begin. Many explanations of nature are mythical, passed down from generation to generation hence preserved in folklore, and believed and widely applied in trying to seek an understanding of the universe. Western science readily dismissed all these for not being logical and hence irrational. Feyerabend (1975) disagrees with such notions, insisting that science and myth are closely related. Myth is closed, and taking recourse to myths reveals a lot of issues surrounding taboo, as compared to science which is sort of open, yet both protect basic beliefs.

Feyerabend thinks 'primitive' thinkers applied more insight in their search for knowledge as compared to 'enlightened philosophical rivals'. This he suggests for he thinks Western science banked more on dogmatism than insight and that way it was able to flourish. Without this dogmatism, he argues, it would not have ruled the world as it did. He calls for an urgent re-examination of the "attitudes towards myth, religion, magic, witchcraft and all those ideas which rationalists would like to see forever removed from the surface of the earth," something he terms "a typical taboo reaction" (1975).

Such an attitude of supremacy from Western Science consumes other forms of thought and this is clearly seen in the relationship between Western science and indigenous tribes especially in Africa and Latin America. Feyerabend (1975) says:

> The rise of modern science coincides with the suppression of non-western tribes by Western invaders. The tribes are not only physically suppressed; they also lose their intellectual independence and are forced to adopt [...] Christianity. The most intelligent members [...] are introduced into the mysteries of Western Rationalism and its peak-Western Science. Occasionally this leads to an almost unbearable tension with tradition.

Criticising Western science will be met by questions seeking to justify why Western science is superior in the way it proceeds, as compared to primitive science. The advances that have been achieved by Western science are cited as a reason for this superiority, yet western science ignores the fact that there are instances where it has grown, not out of rigour but out of pure chance. Feyerabend (1975) argues that "everywhere science is enriched by unscientific methods and unscientific results, while procedures which have often been regarded as essential parts of science are quietly suspended or circumvented". Hence he argues against separation of science and non-science. This according to him does not offer any opening for the growth of knowledge. "The assertion that [...] *extra scientiam nulla salus* is nothing but another and most convenient fairy tale" he says.

All these arguments put forward by Feyerabend are geared toward doing away with a 'rule' of method and opening space for liberalism in the way in which science is practiced. These build towards his bold assertion that 'everything goes'

Reading Feyerabend in the Practice of African Science

To better see how Feyerabend's method could be of possible help to African science, I now turn to African Science to see what it really is, or could be said to be. Just like many human enterprises which arise as a response to need, science in Africa is a response to a given need that the African person is out to solve. According to Akpan (2010:15); "traditional African science could hardly be separated from technological knowledge which is generally regarded as applied science". Today, with the technological growth and a takeover of most of our societies with the Western way of doing science, it is difficult to show, especially in city settings, the practice of African traditional science. It is, in most cases, traces of African systems of doing science that can be seen. This, however, is not to say that African traditional science is not being practiced elsewhere on the continent. Despite not being as successful as western science,[3]

---

[3] This 'success' too ought to be read carefully for It might be inspired by romanticism. To see great technological developments may not necessarily measure as success if they do not respond to other humanistic needs like good ecological balance, identities of human communities, and other existential and non-material needs of the human person, like the development of a more authentic being.

there still remain aspects of traditional African science. African traditional science is to be understood better if given a historical examination to see the period when it flourished.

According to Ivan Van Sertima (1983:9), it was "mystifying" to early travellers to the African lands to come and find sophisticated ways of communication from one place to another, despite their lack of the technological infrastructures that the Western world boasted of. Sertima's characterization of African science is thus because according to him, science is part of a civilization and destruction of a civilization comes with effects such as the destruction of their systems of thought too. He suggests that Africa suffered because of the mass uprooting of populations during the slave trade, which stole Africa's intellectual heritage leaving behind only the "stunned survivor" (1983:10). By this he means the brains of Africa were all ripped off to other lands and whatever was left could not sufficiently sustain the kind of intellectual activity that was there before.

Sertima's project in *The Lost Sciences of Africa* is to expose Africa's "genius" buried for centuries, which he believes cannot remain buried forever. He therefore ventures into exposing scientific activity present in Africa in the ancient times. The scientific activity exposed by Sertima varies from sophisticated steel production by the use of technologically effective furnaces which Europe did not have at the time, to sophisticated astronomical skills. Surprisingly, despite a lack of written records of African scientific activity, the generations of the Haya people inhabiting the western shores of Lake Victoria, according to Sertima (1983:8) would describe the processes their ancestors employed down to fine details. Other sophisticated scientific systems that are to be traced to Africa in Sertima's account are the archaeological records of the Namoratunga or the stone people closely related to the Turkana of Kenya, and the famous star watching Dogon people of Mali, both of them depicting very sophisticated astronomical capabilities. Others include developed systems of mathematics, navigation, systems of writing, agricultural development, and closer home, the stunning architecture of The Great Zimbabwe (Sertima, 1983:10-16).[4]

---

[4] The Great Zimbabwe, which means 'house of stone', is an old ruined city of the Shona civilization of the 11th to 15th Century. It is located a short distance from the

All these expose an undeniably successful system of doing science that produced results, helped man understand or get closer to understanding his surrounding, manipulate nature and respond to the needs of his time. However, today many of these remain just that which Sertima terms them; "lost sciences." What happened to African Traditional Science? The most plausible explanations as earlier mentioned are to be traced to the interaction between Western science during the slave trade and colonization, a suggestion shared by both Sertima and Feyerabend.

Despite these developments, a lot more of African science still survives and though it is not as espoused as is Western science, the capability of African science is not to be underestimated today. However, of interest to this discussion, is why African science, even if it exists in traces, does not grow as steadily as does Western science. It is to be readily agreed upon that two major factors could contribute to the growth of a scientific enterprise; the first is the result of the enterprise and how it is perceived to be closer to truth, and the second, its method and how efficient the method is judged to be, irrespective of the order the two factors follow. The results of African traditional science cannot be questioned. The African people, through traditional medicine are able to successfully treat several ailments; through traditional methods like salting and smoking, they are able to preserve food for days, even months, without the luxury of freezers. The African people are also able to observe the skies and make close to accurate weather predictions just by observing winds and bird movements among others, sometimes to a degree of accuracy that beats sophisticated meteorological setups. We can rightly infer that although technological methods could offer faster, measurable results, the African systems of traditional science equally have the capacity to produce results. Could the problem therefore be in method?

Many scholars, according to Akpan (2010:18) have condemned the method of African science claiming it is "mystically and religiously inclined, superstitious, [and] more practical than

---

city of Masvingo in Zimbabwe and is evidence of very sophisticated architecture and political system of the time. The name Zimbabwe and the bird that is the national emblem of Zimbabwe derive from this civilisation.

theoretical, isolatory than community driven, esoteric and so on." Akpan suggests that these descriptions of African science are to some extent true and have therefore led to African science being described as a pseudo-science. For Akpan, the problem with African science is its tendency not to accept dead ends. He suggests that a scientific enterprise ought to acknowledge when something cannot be explained, this is supposed to aid the process of searching to restart all over again, or even to aid the scientist to re-examine how he has proceeded. Many African traditional scientists however take recourse to supernatural explanations[5] which many times cannot be justified. This trend, he suggests, stagnates African science.

Feyerabend's ideas would readily appear to be a soft landing for African Science. This would be a cushioning for a system of thought that is generally not considered as vigorous as science ought to be. Would Feyerabend then be advocating for anything, even what we would ordinarily term irrational, to be allowed to flourish?

Whereas Feyerabend would suggest that science and myth are closely related and myth should therefore not be looked at harshly, moderation in tolerating aspects outside of what is conventionally understood as science is important. Although everything could go as Feyerabend suggests, if science is aimed at understanding the universe, there must be some basic foundational minimum that scientists share. This is not a total refusal of 'everything goes,' rather it is a suggestion that a boundary that separates science from 'pseudoscience' ought to be moderately emphasized to allow for scientific growth and at the same time keep a check for non-science not to creep in. This is equal to pushing Feyerabend just a little further: Let every lily bloom, but first check to ensure it is a lily.

Radner and Radner in *Science and Unreason* (1982) suggest a number of factors that should designate a practice as either scientific or pseudoscientific. "The work of a crank," they say, "is fundamentally different from that of a legitimate scientist. There may be some features common to both, but there are others that are

---

[5] Super natural explanations are rational, in a different way, they cannot fit into formal logic's way of attempts at explaining reality; however, they hinder objectivity. The fact that African science tries to claim recognition out of its own milieu means it has to open to that outside context.

found only in crackpot work and never in genuine scientific work." If all they conceive as pseudoscience was to be followed strictly as that, a lot in African Science would have to be thrown out of the body of knowledge termed scientific. They outline a number of what they call "marks for pseudoscience" (1982) and these include anachronistic thinking, looking for mysteries, appeal to myth, and explanation by scenario, research and exegesis among others. Whereas ordinarily a reliance on these as parts of scientific practice ought to be considered irrational, the case is totally different in African science. A look at how African traditional medicine proceeds for instance cannot ignore the place of mystery and myth in explaining phenomena, some of which is corroborated. Feyerabend in such a scenario would rightly say that myth and science are not very separated. There could be a possibility that myths were developed over long periods of observation of natural phenomena, and an explanation by a myth corroborated only serves to confirm. An acceptance of myth as scientific has to consider both these two positions, that it could tell us something about the world on one hand, but on the other hand, it might be a hiding place for that which we have failed to explain.

I suggest that a 'total' following of Feyerabend's 'everything goes,' whereas it could open a window for African Science, it could as well be counter-productive for African science. I premise this assertion on the fact that African Traditional science cannot be conceived of as totally irrational, hence, such a 'liberalist' view compromises the rigour that ought to be characteristic of scientific practice. Although Western Scientists attributed the star watching successes of the Dogon to the presence of European space-men, Jesuits and other travellers among them, (Adams, 1983:27), it is clearly evident that the Dogon were successful in their scientific enterprise whether they learnt it from the westerners or not. What European astronomy had not managed to perceive as the Sirius star by an untrained eye, the Dogon had seen, even plotting its orbit, with a very high degree of success. Why then place the benchmark as low as 'everything goes' instead of striving to restore such rigour?

Could African Conceptual Frames be Fundamentalist?

On another note, African science, just like science elsewhere is aimed at the bare minimum to help man understand the universe. If it is the same universe that science in whichever culture is trying to discover, then there may be some bare minimum of standards too. Logic does not change from one culture to another, except in the form in which it is expressed. An addition of one to one will yield two in Africa just like in Europe, Latin America, or Asia; a separation of standards does not aid African science. If African science is to gain a renaissance, it must brace up to the challenge and engage at the level of the scientific community. Akpan (2010:19) has suggested that a lot of scientific activities in Africa, apart from having 'mystico-religious influences' in them, also proceed with a high degree of secrecy, perhaps with a fear of information being hijacked by other scientists. To this he asks, "If such wonderful and credible findings are not given elaborate and coherent theoretical explanation, how can others in the field acknowledge the efficacy of such discoveries?" This non exposure of scientific activity harms growth of the entire body of African science and the only way it can be redeemed is to be opened to the examination of the scientific community. For such examination to proceed there must be a bare minimum of standards. This bare minimum can be a product of dialogue, as I intend to show in an example of African Traditional Medicine.

Traditional Medicine as an example of modern-day practice of African Science

In most African societies, various plant species were employed to heal various health problems. It can be inferred that the discovery of these plants and the role they played might have followed chance, but repeated experimentation may have centred to a specific issues that they could heal, and therefore having whole communities adopting the use of specific plants for given health problems.

If society is approached as an organic whole, it will be accepted that societies devised ways of addressing the various needs they were faced with, and traditional plant medicine was a way of addressing health needs, among other possible remedies. Hence, in traditional societies plant medicine played a major role, it still does today. Apart from providing food and shelter, 80% of the world's population depends on them for medication (Ekeanyanwu, 2011:90-94). African Traditional Medicine could increase its fortunes today, and even be more fruitful beyond Africa, if it embraced an outward looking character, and an openness to scientific advances from other scientific traditions.

In the Nigerian town of Benin City, a monastery of the Benedictine monks runs a successful traditional medical clinic that is well acclaimed in its method. By marrying indigenous herbal medical knowledge and rigorous laboratory research, the monks have managed to modernise traditional medicine that responds to a wide range of the health needs of the community with reduced side effects due to the originality of their medicine (Paxherbals, 2014). Paxherbals, as the institution is called, blends modern medical laboratory methods with the traditional products, and this kind of dialogue, everyone would agree, is more beneficial than initiatives that struggle to fight for radical African identities. This is advantageous in that it encourages a dialogue of cultures and that is a fundamental step to a cosmopolitan sharing of knowledge, definitely a clear way in which Africa can contribute to scientific discourse today.

This tends to question the appropriateness of Feyerabend's epistemological anarchism especially to a morphing enterprise like African science. Consequently, although Feyerabend's epistemological anarchism could redeem some dignity for the African scientist, it has the potential of destroying the enterprise of African science too, especially where the core of advances in Africa are directed towards fierce defence of the African identity. Whereas this is important, Africa has come a long way and it is past that stage of rhetoric. The phase it must enter now is to find ways in which that identity can dialogue with the world to respond to, and shape the factual being of the African people. It is here that the African traditional scientist ought to be careful not to respond to a western fundamentalist approach by a fundamentalist response, because he stands to lose, especially because the western scientist has a wider nod globally even though it might be out of narcissism.

Conclusion

Hence an appreciation of Feyerabend's epistemological anarchism, African science, and the prospects that the former could open to the latter are a considerably important area for reflection in considering how Africa's intellectual settings could be redeemed to give a contribution to the world. I have shown following Sertima, that African science was once a vibrant and sophisticated system, but as things are, the view is bleak for African science. Looking at the place of logical rigour in science, I have argued that although Feyerabend's anarchism could help African science crawl back into scientific discourse, a radical following of it could be counterproductive as it would discourage the rigour and encourage a mythico-religious component that is characteristic of African science. Logic, being an important part of any scientific endeavour cannot be compromised.

References

Adams, H. 1983. African Observers of the Universe. *Blacks in Science: Ancient and Modern,* Transaction Books: New Brunswick, London: 27.

Akpan, C. 2010. The Method of African Science: A Philosophical evaluation, *American Journal of Social and Management Sciences*: 11-20.

Chalmers, A. 1999. *What is This Thing Called Science*, Open University Press: New York.

Ekeanyanwu, R. 2011. Traditional Medicine in Nigeria: Current status and the Future, *Research Journal of Pharmacology* 5 (2): 90-94.

Feyerabend, P. 1975. *Against Method*. Verso Editions: London

Paxherbals, 2015. *African Herbal Remedies*, www.paxherbals.net.

Radner, D. and Radner, M., 1982, *Science and Unreason*, Wadsworth Publishing Company: Belmont California.

Sertima, I. 1983. The Lost Sciences of Africa: An Overview. *Blacks in Science: Ancient and Modern, Incorporating Journal of African Civilizations*: 9-26.

Chapter Eight

Fetishisation of Knowledge:
A Case of Patriotic History in Zimbabwe

Tafirenyika Madziyauswa

Introduction

The situation that is generically known as 'the Zimbabwe crisis' extensively ramified the geopolitical landscape of Zimbabwe. The crisis culminated in emergence of new forms of discourses meant to sustain the so-called 'Third Chimurenga' as I explain later. One notable effect of this crisis is the emergence of a new form of religion fronted by prominent academics manifest in the fetishisation of knowledge. The ruling party, ZANU-PF engaged academics to disseminate a set of ideas that sought to make the ruling elites the chief narrators or gatekeepers of Zimbabwe's past. This chapter, therefore, discusses how the discourse that emerged with the advent of "Third Chimurenga" is inclusionary and exclusionary as well as monolithic and bigoted or dogmatic. This is manifest in the new form of history which Ranger calls 'patriotic history.' I elaborate on patriotic history in the sections that follow.

I argue in this chapter that patriotic history is used to legitimise intolerance to any version of the past not officialised by the dominant class. This resonates with the concept of religious fundamentalism which in its narrow and constrained sense entails dogmatism and bigotry as evident in its application in the realms of Christianity and Islam. In this chapter, I demonstrate that the concept of fundamentalism can no longer be constrained within the realm of religion, but can as well be regarded as manifesting in manifold domains.

The concept of fundamentalism(s)

For long the notion of fundamentalism has been narrowly constituted to encompass religious dogmatism and or bigotry within the realms like Christianity and Islam. Characteristically, fundamentalisms are steeped in binarism which foreclose anything deemed divergent and contrary to mainstream ideas. The gospel according to fundamentalism preaches a form of cardinal truth that is exclusionary to other versions of the truth and inclusionary to the versions that are considered politically, economically, ideologically, culturally and socially correct. However, the concept can no longer be warped in the stasis rendered by people in reference to religion, but it is a broad concept that transcends the borderlines that hem religion.

One way of liberally defining fundamentalism is manifest in the way knowledge is disseminated and repackaged as 'Third Chimurenga' in the post-2000 Zimbabwe. The fetishisation of knowledge in form of the Third Chimurenga is navigated in instances where prominent scholars are engaged to evangelise particular sets of ideas which treats anything contrary as subversive and anti-establishment. In the section that follows, I discuss how the new historiography in form of patriotic history can be viewed as typifying fundamentalisms. Thus, the discourses of patriotic history are couched in such a way as to discursively exclude the possibility of other versions of the past being versions of the past.

Land reform, Patriotic history and Third Chimurenga

In this section I seek to briefly discuss, land reform, patriotic history and Third Chimurenga in order to comprehend how these issues can be read as forms of fundamentalisms and fetishisation of knowledge (since the focus of this chapter is not on the historicisation of the land question). The land question was central to both the First and Second Chimurengas and the Third Chimurenga is seen by ZANU-PF as the final instalment in resolving the question of land (Tendi, 2010). I, therefore, delve into the land question by drawing on three major events (though they can be more than that),

that had an impact on land reform, that is, the Lancaster House Conference resolution of 'willing buyer, willing seller' principle, Ms Clare Short letter to Zimbabwean government and the 1997 donor conference convened by the Zimbabwean government. The Zimbabwean government was obligated by the 1979 Lancaster House agreement to use the 'willing-buyer, willing-seller' principle as the basis of acquiring land for redistribution of land (with 1990 as the expiration date) (Moyo, 1995; Moyo and Yeros, 2004: 9). The principle of 'willing-buyer, willing-seller' was restrictive as the government could not buy large tracts of land to resettle a landless people and the prices of land rose astronomically making hard for the government to acquire land (Tshuma, 1997).

Faced with the foregoing constraints, the ZANU-PF government was faced with another obstacle after the expiry of the Lancaster House 'willing-buyer, willing-seller' principle. The British Conservative party-led government had agreed to continue funding the land reform in Zimbabwe in 1996, but the coming into power of the Labour government of Britain in 1997 saw the new government reneging on the country's colonial financial obligations to Zimbabwe. This was spelt out clearly by Ms Claire Short, the then Labour government Secretary of State for International Development when she wrote a letter to the then Zimbabwean Minister of Agriculture, the late Mr Kumbirai Kangai stating that: "I should make it clear that we do not accept that Britain has a special responsibility to meet the costs of Land purchase in Zimbabwe. We are a new Government from diverse backgrounds without links to former colonial interests. My own origins are Irish and as you know we were colonised not colonisers."[6]

Due to a spate of land occupations by the villagers in Svosve (June 1998), Nyamandlovu (Matabeleland), Nyamajura and Nemamwa (Masvingo), the government of Zimbabwe hosted the Land Donors' Conference between9 and 11 September 1998 to raise funding for land reform attracting close 48 countries including Britain.[7] ZANU-PF in conjunction with war veterans and land-hungry peasants was later to adopt the Fast Track Land Reform

---

[6] See Zimbabwe Embassy Stockholm Documents.
[7] ibid

Programme (FTLRP) which "radically transformed the politics and economic landscape of the country" (Raftopoulos, 2009:211). According to Ndlovu-Gatsheni (2013: 152) the chaotic and violent way in which ZANU-PF-led government implemented the FTLRP after the attempts to amend the constitution failed "became the first development that provoked regional and international concerns about the Zimbabwe issues." The 2001 Southern African Development Community (SADC) Summit of Heads of State and Government met to discuss the chaotic and violent land reform that was being implemented by the ZANU- PF-led government. The FTLRP continued unabated due to the failure of initiatives of regional and continental bodies (SADC and African Union) to raise funds for Zimbabwean land reform as well as the reluctance by South Africa to oppose the land reform because Mugabe had initially agreed to delay land repossessions during the transition to democracy in South Africa so as to avert a 'racial flare-up' in South Africa (Ndlovu-Gatsheni, 2013:152).

It in view of the foregoing that Mugabe asserts that the Third Chimurenga was a war to resolve lasting colonial land inequalities between the black majority and white minority commercial farmers who were backed by the Rhodesian colonial government and Western imperialism. Mugabe contends that Britain and the rest of the Western world were vehemently opposed to land redistribution so as to safeguard their vested interests, that is, their white kith and kin in Zimbabwe, and by financing the opposition MDC, the aim was to derail equitable land reform.[8]

It should be noted that "land is a grievance going back to the First *Chimurenga* (emphasis in original)of 1896 when British South Africa Company rule was first established [and] [l]and was a central grievance in the Second *Chimurenga*" (Tendi, 2010:1). It can be argued that as Zimbabwe entered the new millennium, the land question had not be adequately addressed if the land occupations that started in Svosve are factored in since the "minority white population still controlled the majority of the most productive land" (ibid: 1). As such, land was (is) the centrepiece of the Third Chimurenga, as its

---

[8] See Robert Mugabe, *Inside The Third Chimurenga*. Harare: Department of Information and Publicity, 2001.

(Third Chimurenga's) ideology. ZANU PF regarded Third Chimurenga as the final episode of the liberation struggle of its predecessors; the First and Second Chimurengas which were against colonial rule. Thus, patriotic history seeks to preach the importance of land ownership as an extension of the ownership of history. However, as will, be discussed later on, by omitting other versions of 'truths,' patriotic history can be viewed as entrenching fundamentalisms in Zimbabwe.

Subsequently, patriotic history is a new brand of historiography that arrived in the academic scene of Zimbabwe in the late twentieth and beginning of twenty-first century. It has new cadres, new discourses which sound like a rehashing of the old nationalist discourses of the pre-independence era and the target is a small community of white farmers, their workers of alien origins and foreign sympathisers as well as supposedly local black lackeys (opposition parties).The grand scheme of patriotic history, according to Ranger includes youth militia recruited as warriors of Third Chimurenga, war veterans, authors of patriotic history like Robert Mugabe and Tafataona Mahoso and (former) ministerial historians like Aeneas Chigwedere and the late Stan Mudenge (Ranger, 2005:221).

Fetishising Knowledge

In this section, I seek like Engmann (2007) to excavate a more comprehensive and nuanced understanding of the concepts of "fetish" and "fetishism." As such the nuanced comprehension of the concepts of fetish and fetishism is done through a dissection of the discourses of patriotic history. It is in context that Deslandes (2009:2) cites a political theorist Tom Nairn who argues that "every idea, in time, acquires a fetish-like rigidity." In this light the term 'fetish' can refer to a Christian imperialist name for non-European subjectivity, a psychoanalytic stand-in for repressed dissidence, a commoditisation of the sign of otherness, a postcolonial appropriation of the third world by the first, aqueer-ing of the self towards other subjectivities, and a radical anthropological force for reappropriation (Deslandes, 2009: 2).

203

This is not further from being an apt description of the situation that characterises the post-2000 Zimbabwe where the discourses packaged as 'Third Chimurenga' have acquired a fetish-like inflexibility. As such, it is vital to consider how the ruling party, ZANU-PF, fetishises rather than how we fetishise about the ruling party. I return to this idea of fetishisation later on. In order to foreground the concept of fundamentalism, I turn to the Third Chimurenga which Ranger (2004) describes as 'patriotic history.' It is the use of the two words 'Third' and 'Chimurenga' that sounds a note of fundamentalisms into the post-2000 Zimbabwe state of affairs.

'Chimurenga' is a Shona word that refers to a struggle, a war or a fight for emancipation. The term was used to describe the uprisings that took place in Mashonaland in 1896-97. The First Chimurenga is the initial struggle of the black people of Zimbabwe against the white occupation of their land. The thrust of First Chimurenga was to purge the land of the invaders, the white colonisers, the land-grabbers and the illegal occupants of the land and return it to its rightful owners. The bid to oust the white invaders was unsuccessful and this allowed the white settlers to entrench their hold on the land and to later acquire legal status over the pieces of land. The First Chimurenga, though it was ruthlessly and crudely crushed, provided the nationalist discourse which served as a source of inspiration for the Second Chimurenga cadres. Part of such inspiration came from the famous words of [Mbuya] Nehanda, a First Chimurenga heroine who uttered the famous words "My bones shall rise again" (Lan, 1985:6).

The Second Chimurenga which was "the guerrilla war of the 1970s" (Ranger, 2005:221), on the other hand, was bloody and brutal and as well as violent. The war "went on for fifteen years, killed 40,000 people, and turned social structures and everyday relationships upside down" (Kaarsholm, 2005:4). The war wreaked havoc in the lives of many people as families were torn away from each other and some straddled antagonistic sides. The ideals of the First Chimurenga were broadened and encapsulated in the Second Chimurenga and the target of both struggles was the white coloniser and that justifies the chronology denoted by 'first' and 'second.' This is not to suggest that the two chimurengas followed each other immediately, but they were consecutive insofar as the ideals that motivated them were concerned.

However, after the Second Chimurenga there was a long lapse before the Third Chimurenga was sanctioned. Like the two 'chimurengas' before it, the Third Chimurenga ushered in its own narrative. The narrative of the Third Chimurenga "the third and last instalment of the liberation struggle first mounted in the 1890s--- entails a re-inscription of both the nation's past and the officially sanctioned national identities," (Muponde and Primorac, 2005: xiii).The (re)construction of the historical memory, identity and nation in form of patriotic history have demonstrated a tendency by the ruling party, ZANU-PF, to be inclusionary and exclusionary depending on the political divide. However, in terms of land expropriation, the Third Chimurenga was not entirely or mainly about claiming identities and memories, but it was also about land and materialities. Patriotism was, therefore, fetishised as a means to the end of reappropriation of land from white farmers. It is in this context that the act of writing an autobiography is to be regarded as a deconstructive act that undermines received historiography by portraying and presenting an alternative version of the past.

There is need to problematise the use of the term 'third' to describe the post-2000 land redistribution programmes hijacked by the ruling party, ZANU-PF. It was the war veterans and the landless peasants in Svosve communal lands that played vanguard (Sadomba, 2013: 83) since initially the ZANU-PF government was opposed to the processes The use of 'third' in the post-2000 Zimbabwe suggests a continuation of the same struggle that started in 1896. Whilst the two 'chimurengas' had a popular base in being collective struggles by people motivated to take up arms against a common enemy identified through skin pigmentation, the Third Chimurenga presents a different picture. It is not incidental that Ranger (2004) describes this new brand of history whose initiation date is the year 2000 as 'patriotic history.'

Patriotic history is buttressed by narratives that link the ruling party, ZANU-PF to the ideals of free and fair as well as timeous elections, good governance, rule of law and a respect for human rights. After all Zimbabwe is not part of England and "will never be a colony again," (The Herald, February 3 2002). If anything, ZANU-PF encapsulates traits that can only describe it as a dictatorial de facto one party state where oppositional parties are only there to make up the numbers. Raftopoulos puts it succinctly thus: "For most of the independence years, Zanu (PF) was prepared to tolerate a minimum of electoral competition, and the existence of civic bodies that complemented the delivery of the state, so long as its single party dominance was not threatened" (Raftopoulos, 2003:234). Most opposition parties fared badly in the elections and it was the new party MDC that performed beyond expectations in the March 2000 parliamentary elections when it garnered57 seats compared to ZANU-PF's 62 seats out of the 120 contested seats (Makumbe 2009: 9). Twice, within a short period (2008 and 2013), ZANU-PF regained power, amidst allegations of mass electoral rigging and intimidation as alleged by the opposition and some observers (Hove, 2016). In 2008 ZANU-PF clearly lost and used the SADC-negotiated Global Political Agreement (GPA) to stay in power.

Army commanders in Zimbabwe vowed that, they would never salute a leader who has never been to the war front, which by implication, meant they would not recognise a version of leadership proffered by oppositional leaders like MDC-T's Morgan Tsvangirai or Simba Makoni. For instance, General Constantine Chiwenga, the Commander of the ZDF was quoted three weeks into the presidential run-off election of 2008 saying: "Elections are coming and the army will not support or salute sell-outs and agents of the West before, during, and after the presidential elections. We will not support anyone other than President Mugabe who has sacrificed a lot for this country (Masunungure 2009: 70). It is this stance by the armed forces that clearly spells how the historical past has been monopolised to reflect a penchant for monolithic and homogenous tendencies. The above examples show how the war of liberation has become a fetish that has to be worshipped by being regarded as the ideal for measuring present and future political leaders of Zimbabwe.

It would be myopic to think that ZANU-PF's patriotic history like its land re(-dis)tribution was (is) driven by political violence and disempowerment of the three thousand or so white farmers. Instead the entire programme was (is) motivated and supported by specific ideological discourses—knowledge and its representation of truth. This is evident in the way the part played by ZANU-PF in liberating the country and in returning the land to its rightful owners, the blacks, is worshipped at the expense of the realities of chaotic way the land issue was tackled, formulated and implemented as well as the part played by other parties. It is vital to note that knowledge is too fluid to be contained within such theoretical boundaries as those framed by fundamentalisms, hence to constrain knowledge within such boundaries is to fetish knowledge. Patriotic history is in the same position with anthropology today, in that "is little different from an evangelical and ideological commitment to saving souls, saving situations, winning converts and 'giving back'" (Nyamnjoh, 2014:48).

Ranger posits that this new historiography ('new' as coming after independence with new political players) which he terms 'patriotic history' is either dichotomous or leaner than the nationalist historiography since patriotic history repudiates the 'disloyal questions' posed by those historians who authored and championed the narratives of nationalism (Ranger, 2004). This is characteristic of dogmatism of fundamentalisms which are insensitive and intolerant to standpoints which are diametrically opposed to dominant viewpoints. It is in line with the foregoing thinking that as "the gatekeepers of knowledge" (Nyamnjoh, 2004:5), prominent scholars like Professor Claude Mararike, Professor Isheunesu Mpepereki, Dr Tafataona Mahoso and the late Dr Vimbai Chivaura, Ibbo Mandaza and Godrefy Chikowore among others, were engaged to disseminate or evangelise/ preach the patriotic history discourse. It does not need a concerted effort to figure out that the preceding scholars were carefully selected because of their well- known views on the post-2000 Zimbabwean situation, that is, their views cannot be said to be disinterested, objective and non-partisan. Thus, patriotic history fetishes knowledge to the extent it criminalises different versions of the past. Any view that did not conform to the ones expressed by the said scholars in programmes like 'Talking Farming' and 'Madzinza Edu' (Our roots) were either deemed 'disloyal' or they were unilaterally silenced from mainstream government-owned media especially radio and television. Thus, patriotic history fetishes knowledge to the extent it criminalises different versions of the past.

Subsequently, the cultural spectrum was invaded overnight and ramified in order to be compliant to the new political goals. It was the government-owned media, both print and electronic media, which spearheaded the purge of those who could not tow the new line of 'fast track land redistribution.' Jingles like 'Machembere' (loosely means old women) or 'Rambai Makashinga' (loosely translated to remain perseverant) invaded the airspace at an interval of thirty minutes. Other jingles included *Sisonke*, Our Future, *Siyalima*, *Mombe Mbiri Nemadhongi Mashanu*, *Uya Uone Kutapira Kunoita Kurima*, *Sendekera Mwana Wevhu* and *Zesa Yauya neMagetsi* all which were meant to promote farming and land redistribution.[9]Such propaganda fetishes knowledge by promoting one version of truth Sibanda writes: The ZANU-PF government's involvement in commissioning of propaganda music [jingles] has introduced a new form of censorship in Zimbabwe [and] managed to elbow what it calls "politically incorrect music compositions from the airwaves"[10]. In order to whip the psyche of the masses, there was the unearthing of dust-covered video clips depicting the Rhodesian atrocities committed in Mozambique during the liberation war and all attempts were made to graphically display the brutality of the whites so as to justify the farm invasions and the unilateral compulsory confiscation of the land from the white farmers. It looked like a phase of retribution which the national reconciliation had averted in 1980, was being unplugged. In other words, the history of the liberation was rewritten with serious omissions regarding what transpired during the war in a manner characteristic of fundamentalisms. In order to understand how ZANU-PF evangelised knowledge, it is important to Tendi at length herein:

> There was a blitzkrieg of Patriotic History in the state-controlled media from 2000. The state-run Zimbabwe Broadcasting Corporation (ZBC) broadcast repetitive liberation war documentaries that presented

---

[9] See Maxwell Sibanda, 'Complete control: Music and propaganda in Zimbabwe' on Freemuse.org>archives.
[10] Ibid.

ZANU PF as the sole deliverer of independence, justified the land seizures as a means to redressing a colonial inheritance of racially biased land distribution, highlighted colonial atrocities, and wrote out personalities and historical events inimical to ZANU PF's quest to maintain political power. Catchy music jingles and albums, the majority of which were composed by Information Minister Moyo, reworking liberation war songs, and celebrating ZANU PF's role in liberation history, were aired on state-run national radio stations hourly.10 ZANU PF presented itself as the ordained guardian of Zimbabwe's political past, present and future. There was an obsessive concentration on history (Tendi, 2010:4-5).

Thus, publications like *Inside Third Chimurenga* (a collection of speeches and writings by President Robert Mugabe) were part of the tools used to evangelise the Third Chimurenga in a way that is akin to fetishising knowledge. Utterances by President Mugabe that 'Zimbabwe will never be a colony again' and the one directed to the then British Prime Minister Tony Blair, 'Keep your England and let me keep my Zimbabwe' (The Guardian, September 2 2002) entrenched the meta-narratives meant to uphold, support and concretise fast track land redistribution. Anything that did not advance the new positioning of the establishment was not only disqualified as anti-establishment, but was coloured in binary terms as 'white' versus 'black.' The whites as represented by Britain and her allies included those blacks in oppositional politics, hence the Movement for Democratic Change (MDC) and anyone who are assumed to support it (white farmers), have been labelled by Zanu(PF) as 'sell outs' to the 'white enemy' at home and to Zimbabwe's former colonial masters abroad (Britain) or the West in general[...], and accused of sabotaging the final phase of the nationalist, anti-colonial; revolution, the so-called *Third Chimurenga* (emphasis in original) (Hammar and Raftopoulos, 2003:11). From inception, MDC was shrouded by this allegation that it was a front for the displaced white farmers described as Britain's 'kith and kins' and their black cousins. The logic of patriotic history like colonial and colonising epistemologies sought to repudiate "is simple and problematic: it sacrifices pluriversity for university and imposes a one

209

best way of attaining singular and universal truth" (Nyamnjoh, 2012:131). It is this whitening and blackening of the Third Chimurenga that fetishises knowledge along binary lines: the 'them' and 'us.' This is worshipped at the expense of reality. Anything to the contrary is regarded as an act of dissidence from accepted norms (Deslandes, 2009).

Patriotic history is fetishistic. Patriotic history can become a fetish if it is read through the figure of difference. The new historiography is, to borrow from Derrida (1985), constructed in *differance* (in difference) to the nationalist historiography. Such an approach naturally fetishises knowledge by assuming that it contains a meaning in and out of itself (Deslandes, 2009). According to Ranger this new historiography (patriotic history) is either dichotomous or leaner than the nationalist historiography (Ranger, 2004). The evangelisation mission of patriotic history is disseminated through the carefully chosen group of scholars and a set of repackaged war songs, video clips and new songs that were used as subtle weapons to win new converts. As such any narrative that delves into alternate forms of the past is deemed subversive and counter establishment, that is, it is seen as complicit to regime-change agendas sponsored by Britain and her cronies.

It is vital to establish the links that exists between colonial epistemologies (like that of colonial Rhodesia) and post-colonial (post as in after) post-2000 Zimbabwe epistemologies in terms of their overall goal. I find this interface in Nyamnjoh's contention that "its (colonial epistemology) evangelical zeal to convert creative differences has not excluded resorting to violence, for the epistemology knows neither compromise nor negotiation, nor conviviality" (Nyamnjoh, 2012:131). This resonates with patriotic history which has been unleashed using both implicit (songs, video clips, jingles, etc.) and explicit (violence) ways: all these are non-negotiable. Thus far, "The production, positioning and consumption of knowledge is far from a neutral, objective and disinterested process" (ibid: 130).

At this point it is important to cite at length Nyamnjoh (citing George, 1992:109) who writes:

Publishers are able to perpetuate their ideologies by ensuring that only people with the 'correct' ideas are published. They know only too well that in order to penetrate the people's heads and acquire their hearts, hands and destinies, they have to make their ideas part of the daily life of people and society, by packaging, conveying and propagating these ideas through books, magazines, journals, conferences, symposia, professional associations, student organisations, university chairs, mass media and various other means (2004:5).

In light of the above assertion, patriotic history is propagated through mass media (newspapers, magazines), radio, television, video clips, songs, books, conferences and pamphlets as the only correct versions of truth. All versions of truth that are not in tandem with meta-narratives are, either censored or deemed to be in contravention of the laws of the land like the Broadcasting Services Act which was passed on 3 April 2001, Public Order and Security Act (POSA)which came into effect on 10 January 2002 and shortly followed by AIPPA. The Broadcasting Services Act gives the government extensive control over licenses issued to private broadcasters, POSA limits public demonstrations whilst AIPPA controls the independent media by giving wide-ranging powers to Media and Information Commission (MISA-Zimbabwe, 2004:2). These measures have, cumulatively, resulted in a high degree of control on the part of the government over the flow of information and a corresponding shrinking of the space for freedom of expression in Zimbabwe (MISA, 2004: 2).

After such a serious blow to its confidence in the year 2000 in the February 2000 Referendum where the 'NO' vote won and in the parliamentary elections when a newly formed political party, Movement for Democratic Change nearly stormed into power, ZANU-PF overtly urged farm invasions. These farm invasions which were orchestrated by the war veterans, who violated property rights as they confiscated land belonging to white commercial farmers, were taken over by ZANU-PF. The 22 February 2000 Constitutional Referendum [and a near defeat in the parliamentary elections of 2000], marked a turning point in the fortunes of the ZANU PF party and was an important milestone in the political history of Zimbabwe (MISA-Zimbabwe, 2004:1). The white farmers' cardinal sin was the alleged support they rendered to MDC and sponsoring the resounding 'NO' vote against the government-sponsored Constitutional Referendum of February 2000. The long and short of it is that official and received historiography was overhauled to meet the goals of the new political dispensation. The new historiography negates any history devoid of the political discourse. It is, therefore, counter to any form of academic historiography. However, as Nyamnjoh (2004) notes, even academic publishers manipulate views before publications are made. It is, therefore, possible that Ranger's views on the new historiography championed by ZANU-PF are both censored and manipulated by the publishers as well as manipulating the public views on ZANU-PF and its Third Chimurenga.

In the light of the above patriotic history is a narrative which thrives on excluding post-independence political players from the ownership of the Zimbabwean liberation struggle as epitomised by the exclusion of decreased oppositional leaders from being the National Heroes Acre. ZANU-PF uses both inclusionary and exclusionary tendencies by conflating the ownership of land and the ownership of history since it can be argued that the Third Chimurenga is read as patriotic history, as much patriotic history is entrenched and concretised as well as fleshed in the concept of the Third Chimurenga. Tendi succinctly asserts that Patriotic History's primary theme is land dispossession. While white farmers excluded black Zimbabweans from owning land (which they monopolised), ZANU PF has also excluded other black Zimbabwean (for instance, those that support opposition parties) from owning history. For instance, it is only ZANU-PF which defines who, in the post-independence era, deserves to be accorded a 'National Hero' status. Fisher, (2002) posits that official documents specify that Heroes Acres represents those who fell in the struggle, the illustrious sons and daughters of the nation who distinguished themselves through profound service and paid the supreme sacrifice for Zimbabwe to be born (Fisher, 2002:81), but it is ZANU-PF Politburo [11]that makes

[11]ZANU-PF Politburo is the highest decision making body that that formulates and decides policy for ZANU PF and members are appointed by the President and

the ultimate decision. While ZANU PF constructs heroines and heroes as those deceased people that contributed to the liberation war project and , white farmers, some scholars, institutions and some civil society organisations also constructed white farmers and white industrialists as heroes and heroines without whom Zimbabweans could not survive. For ZANU-PF, one can only be declared a hero or heroine when dead, yet the concept of heroism is not largely a posthumous issue that one attains posthumously as there are many living heroes in Zimbabwe for example the likes of Strive Masiyiwa (economic hero) who has created a multi-million mobile company, Kirsty Coventry (sporting heroine) who lifted the name of Zimbabwe high at the Beijing 2008 Summer Olympics, and many other who continue to serve Zimbabwe diligently in various sectors of life. Patriotic history makes heroism to be a static concept that cannot be contested as it remains interred in the Zimbabwe's liberation struggle as if it is the only struggle there is in life.

As such any narrative that delves into alternate forms of the past is deemed subversive and counter establishment, that is, it is seen as complicit to regime-change agendas sponsored by Britain and her cronies. Whilst it can be argued that there are alternative narratives about owning history as well as owing land, but by fetishising knowledge through the war-like discourse of patriotic history, ZANU-PF shuts out such alternative forms of ownership. Indeed, it can be said that the underlying logic of reclamation of land in Zimbabwe is that Africans owned and own the land and that colonists foisted their own versions of ownership [which they would not want to be challenged]. This fits into the concept of fundamentalisms which (as noted elsewhere in this chapter) evangelises a form of cardinal truth that is shuts out to other versions

---

the first Secretary of the party.Article 8 section 40 of the ZANU PF constitution, which deals with the appointment of politburo members reads: "Soon after the election of the president and the first secretary and members of the central committee, the president and first secretary of the party shall, during the sitting of congress, appoint from the newly elected central committee, two vice presidents and second secretaries, the national chairperson, the heads of departments of the politburo, the committee members of the politburo and the deputies to the heads of department" (see ZANU-PF Constitution).

of the truth and inclusionary to the versions that seen as politically correct.

Interestingly, Fisher quotes one elderly man who says the government should stop this practice of appointing heroes-a loaded statement that implies that some people who eventually get buried at the Heroes Acre do so due to being merited by government and not by their overt heroic deeds. The term 'appointment' suggests selection done at the discretion of an interested group. Max Weber argued through his concept of value-freedom from value judgements, that is, facts should be presented as they are by separating the causal hypotheses and empirical generalizations of science from value judgments, that is, one's moral, political, and aesthetic preferences. [12] As such groups have to be objective and separate facts from vested interests. However, the fetishisation of knowledge in Zimbabwe is dome at the level of groups which cannot apply Weber's concept of value-freedom. For instance, when a popular soccer player Adam Ndlovu passed on, it raises questions over the issue of 'who is a hero' since ZANU-PF (PF) has vested interests as it still clings to defining heroism in political terms narrowed to 'ZANU-PF*ism*.' Furthermore, citing a joke about Joseph Chinotimba's welcoming speech where he congratulated Kirsty Coventry for winning a gold and three silver medals at the Beijing 2008 Summer Olympics swimming competition by saying 'Forward with unity. Forward with Kirsty. Down with whites. Down with those without knees,' Willems contends that "the joke not only criticises the politicisation of the conferral of 'national hero' status and the appropriation of 'national heroes' for party politics but also comments on the widening of the criteria that determine who qualifies for hero status (Willems, 2010:9). This aptly demonstrates how the notions of historical memory, identity and nation thrive on exclusionary and inclusionary lines, that is, it excludes those that it does not favour and include those it finds favourable. As such ZANU-PF thrives to (re)construct a past that

---

[12] 'Social Science, Value Free.' International Encyclopaedia of the Social Sciences. Retrieved December 23, 2016 from Encyclopedia.com: http://www.encyclopedia.com/social-sciences/applied-and-social-sciences-magazines/social-science-value-free

eclipses counter-narratives. Patriotic history as a form of history is largely patrician.

The received historiography pedalled by the ruling party, ZANU-PF has a penchant for a homogenous past for all Zimbabweans despite the fact that such a past has many versions to it. This stance is evident and manifests in the 2013 ZANU-PF campaign statement, 'Indigenise, Empower, and Employ' (ZANU-PF Campaign pamphlet, 2013). What should not be lost here is that the narratives such as the preceding one seek to equate anything contrary to ZANU-PF's stance as a regime-change agenda sponsored by imagined imperialist forces led by the former colonizer, Britain. Ranger (2005: 220) contends that the post-independence historiography is "[narrower] than old nationalist historiography which celebrated aspiration and modernization as well as resistance." Such an interpretation of Zimbabwean experience is inclined towards negating to the dustbins of history any historiography that competes with official discourse. However, "the production, positioning and consumption of knowledge is far from a neutral, objective and disinterested process" (Nyamnjoh, 2012:130). Put differently, assertions of phrases like "interested parties" presuppose that there is a possibility of neutrality when in fact this is euphemism for subjectivity and in this context, patriotic history. In addition, as early as 1983, Emmerson Mngangwa (then Minister of Rural Housing) said: "Blessed are they who will follow the path of the Government laws, for their days on earth shall be increased. But woe unto those who will choose the path of collaboration with the dissidents for we will certainly shorten their stay on earth" (The Chronicle, 5 April 1983).What can be gleaned from the foregoing citation is the intention by the government of the day to be even with those that choose to tow a different line of thinking. The speech is not only blasphemous, but it is intent on silencing oppositional voices something that has become acute in the twenty-first century as epitomised in the two draconian laws, that is, Access to Information and Privacy Act (AIPPA) and Public Order and Security Act (POSA).As noted elsewhere in this chapter, these two pieces of legislation which echo the colonial laws, have further stifled

215

dissenting voices that try to destabilise the received historiography by offering an alternative voice.

According to Ranger (2005), starting in 2000 and drawing from its important role in Zimbabwe's liberation struggle while facing a strong opposition for the first time, ZANU-PF began to repackage and propagate the country's liberation history in a narrow and authoritarian narrative. It made use of public intellectuals like the late Vimbai Chivaura, Tafataona Mahoso, Isheunesu Mpepereki, Claude Mararike, Ibbo Mandaza and Godrefy Chikowore for the reproduction of a narrative called 'patriotic history' (see Ranger, 2005). It is such instance of monolithic memory that 'patriotic history' pedalled by ZANU-PF seeks to attain. The fetishisation of knowledge is further reflected in the definition of a hero or a heroine by ZANU-PF as the ruling party. I cite two events that can be nuanced as fetishisation, that is, the death of two prominent Zimbabwean public figures from Matabeleland in recent years, that is, Enos Nkala (a former ZANU-PF stalwart) and Adam Ndlovu (a famed soccer player) graphically captured how ZANU-PF literally owns the historical memory, identity and the sense of nationhood in contemporary Zimbabwe (Tendi, 2010). Despite calls from the public for the latter to be declared a national hero for his heroic exploits, in national colours as part of the famous Dream Team, on the soccer field, the ruling party pointed out that Adam Ndlovu, for starters, did not participate in the liberation war (Tshuma, Newsday, December 18 2012). On that ground alone, Adam did not qualify to be buried at the National Heroes Acre, let alone, at the Provincial or District Heroes Acre. The public sentiments were aptly echoed by ZIFA Bulawayo treasurer, Siphambaniso Dube who said: "Truly Adam Ndlovu is a national hero if politics is not the only sphere of influence for one to be declared a national hero, like was done for Jairos Jiri"(Tshuma, Newsday, December 18 2012). This clearly illustrates how the notion of heroism is heavily bigoted to the extent of excluding contemporary version of heroism.

However, the shamed and the controversial Enos Nkala whom many blamed for the Gukurahundi atrocities visited upon parts of Midlands and Matabeleland was declared a national hero. According to Ndlovu-Gatsheni "Gukurahundi (a Shona term for the Storm that

216

sweeps away the chaff, paving way for the normal rainy season) [...] was marked by the massacre of about 20,000 Ndebele-speaking people [by the Korean-trained Fifth Brigade]" (2007:75) According to Dongozi reporting for Zimbabwe Independent "when President Robert Mugabe learnt of the recent death of his comrade-in-arms, Enos Nkala, whom he had visited in hospital the previous night, he immediately declared him a national hero." (Zimbabwe Independent, September 6 2013). Werbner (1998), (cited in Fisher, 2002) succinctly posits that there is politicisation of the memorial complex, in particular the ruling elite's appropriation of the memory and identity of those who died for state ends. In short the National Heroes Acre has become a site of fetishism in defining Zimbabwe's past.

The heroic deeds of the hero are constructed from a selective memory which critically omits some aspects of history. For instance at the burial of Enos Nkala, his participation in the Gukurahundi massacres and his involvement in the Willowvale scandal (the Willowgate scandal) were glaringly omitted from the speech read by President Robert Mugabe at the man's graveside (Zimbabwe Independent, September 6 2013). This makes patriotic history to be a typical example of fundamentalisms.

Conclusion

It is important to conclude this chapter by once again drawing similarities between epistemologies of patriotic history and colonial history, which are the two sides of the same coin. Nyamnjoh writes: It (colonial and colonizing epistemology) tends to limit reality to appearances (the observable, the here and now, the ethnographic present, the quantifiable) which it then seeks to justify (without explaining) with meta-narratives claiming objectivity and a more epistemologically—secure truth status (Nyamnjoh, 2012:131). Patriotic history is also engaged by the ruling party, ZANU-PF to justify its policies without taking the realities of a twenty-first century Zimbabwe, that empty rhetoric is not a substitute to jobs, health, food, education, housing and other needs that ordinary Zimbabweans can do with. Whilst patriotic history about allegiance and fidelity, it negates alternatives forms of the past, and those forms it chooses to remember are bluntly distorted and distilled to propagate a university and not pluriversity (Nyamnjoh, 2012:131) version of the truth. Thus, patriotic history as a form of fundamentalisms becomes problematic when it silences dissenting voices as voices of enemies of the state instead of accepting the multilayered nature of truth and the past as sites of struggle. It can be argued that a different aspect of patriotism in form of allegiance and fidelity was seen when some white farmers expected their employees to rally around them during the times when they were attacked by ZANU-PF youths and war veterans. However, Chikowore (2002) argues that the armed struggle should be the guiding spirit of Zimbabwe's heritage and patriotism because:

> Zimbabwe is the product of a bitter and protracted armed struggle. That armed struggle should serve as the guiding spirit through the presidential elections and even beyond. The right to choose a president of one's own choice should not be considered as a mere exercise of a democratic right. It is the advancement of a historical mission of liberating Zimbabwe from the clutches of neo-colonialism. Any illusion about it constitutes a classic example of self-betrayal and self-condemnation to the ranks of perpetual servitude. The stampede for democracy should not undermine the gains of the liberation war (Chikowore, *The Herald*, February 16 2002). Thus, patriotic history becomes an extension of the two earlier forms of chimurenga since the Third Chimurenga "becomes part of an unbroken thread of resistance, in a discredited nationalist historiography" (Raftopoulos, 2003: 234).

To borrow the title of Raftopoulos' (2003: 217) article, 'the State in Crisis: Authoritarian Nationalism, Selective Citizenship and Distortions of Democracy in Zimbabwe,' patriotic history is all about authoritarian version of truth and the past, selective citizenship since those are seen as 'traitors' are "systematically denied the right to citizenship, freedom of expression, protection under the law, access to land [...]" (Hammar and Raftopoulos, 2003 :11), and patriotic history distorts the ideals of democracy like the right to choose one's own leader. In the above assertion, Chikowore distorts the concept of democracy by narrowing the selection of future presidents to those that measure up the guiding spirit of the liberation war. In short, patriotic history entrenches fundamentalisms in Zimbabwe by presenting a narrower version of truth.

References

Alexander, J. and Tendi, B. 2008. A tale of two elections: Zimbabwe at the polls in 2008. *Concerned African Scholars Bulletin,* 2 (80): 5-17.

Deslandes, A. 2009. 'Activism As Fetishism.' A Pamphlet Essay for Activists. Sydney, December 2009.

Engmann, R A A. 2007.*Under Imperial Eyes, Black Bodies, Buttocks, and Breasts British Colonial Photography and Asante "Fetish Girls"* A Paper presented in honour of Nan Rothschild at the Society for Historical Archaeology.

Fisher, J L. 2002. *Pioneers, Settlers, Aliens, Exiles: The Decolonisation of White Identity in Zimbabwe.* Sydney: ANU E. Press

Hammar, A and Raftopoulos, B. 2003. 'Introduction,' In A Hammar and B Raftopoulos (eds), *Zimbabwe's Unfinished Business: Rethinking Land, State and Nation in the Context of Crisis.* Harare: Weaver Press.

Hove, M. 2016. 'Nonviolent campaigns in Zimbabwe, 1999 to 2013: strategies, methods and effectiveness.' PhD Thesis. Durban University of Technology.

Lan, D. 1985. *Guns and Rain: Guerrillas and Spirit Mediums in Zimbabwe.* Harare: Zimbabwe: Publishing House.

Masunungure, E. V. 2009. 'Voting for change: The 29 March harmonized elections.' In E V Masunungure (ed). *Defying the winds of change.* Harare: Weaver Press, 61-78.

MISA-ZIMBABWE. 2004. 'The Access to Information and Protection of Privacy Act: Two Years On.' ARTICLE 19.Retrieved 21 December 2016 from www.article19.org.

Moyo, S., and Yeros, P. 2004. 'Introduction,' In S Moyo and P Yeros (eds), *Land Occupations and Land reform in Zimbabwe: Towards the National Democratic Revolution.*

Moyo, S. 1995. *The Land question in Zimbabwe.* Harare: SAPES Books

Muponde, R. and Primorac, R. (eds). 2005. *Versions of Zimbabwe-New Approaches to Literature and Culture.* Harare: Weaver Press

Ndlovu-Gatsheni, S J. 2007. 'Fatherhood and nationhood: Joshua Nkomo and the re-imagination of the Zimbabwe nation.' In K Z Muchemwa and R Muponde (eds), *Manning the nation: Father figures in Zimbabwean literature and society*. Harare: weaver Press.

Ndlovu-Gatsheni, S J. 2013. 'Politics behind politics: African Union, SADC and the GPA in Zimbabwe.' In B Raftopoulos. (ed), *The Hard Road to Reform: The Politics of Zimbabwe's Global Political Agreement*. Harare: Weaver Press.

Nyamnjoh, F B. 2012. 'Education in Africa 'Potted Plants in Greenhouses': A Critical Reflection on the Resilience of Colonial.' *Journal of Asian and African Studies*, 47, 129-154.

Nyamnjoh, F., B. 2004. 'From publish or perish to publish and perish: What 'Africa's 100 Best Books' tell us about publishing Africa.' *Journal of Asian and African Studies*, 39(4), 1-23.

Raftopoulos, B. 2009. 'The crisis in Zimbabwe, 1998-2008.' In B Raftopoulos and A S Mlambo (eds), *Becoming Zimbabwe: A History from the Pre-Colonial Period to 2008*. Harare: Weaver Press.

Raftopoulos, B.2003. 'The State in Crisis: Authoritarian Nationalism, Selective Citizenship and Distortions of Democracy in Zimbabwe.' In A Hammar and B Raftopoulos, *Zimbabwe's Unfinished Business: Rethinking Land, State and Nation in the Context of Crisis*. Harare: Weaver Press.

Ranger, T O. 2004. 'Nationalist Historiography, Patriotic History and the Zimbabwean Nation: The Struggle Over the Past,' *Journal of Southern African Studies*.

Ranger, T.O. 2005. 'Rule by Historiography: The struggle in Contemporary Zimbabwe.' In R Muponde and R Primorac (eds), *Versions of Zimbabwe*. Harare: Weaver Press.

Sadomba, Z., W. 2013. 'A decade of Zimbabwe's Land Revolution: The Politics of the War Veteran Vanguard.' In S Moyo and W Chambati (eds), *Land and Agrarian Reform in Zimbabwe: Beyond White Settler Capitalism*. Harare: African Institute of Agrarian Studies.

'Social Science, Value Free.' International Encyclopaedia of the Social Sciences. Retrieved December 23, 2016 from Encyclopedia.com: http://www.encyclopedia.com/social-sciences/applied-and-social-sciences-magazines/social-science-value-free

Tendi, B.-M. 2010. *Making History in Mugabe's Zimbabwe: Politics, Intellectuals and the Media: Nationalisms Across the Globe.* Oxford: Verlag Peter Lang.

Tendi, B-M. 2008. 'Patriotic History and Public Intellectuals Critical Power.' *Journal of Southern African Studies, 34*(2), 379-396.

Tshuma, L. 1997. A *Matter of (In)justice: Law, State and the Agrarian Question in Zimbabwe.* Harare: SAPES Books.

Willems, W. 2010. 'Beyond dramatic revolutions and grand rebellions: everyday forms of resistance during the 'Zimbabwe crisis'.' *Comminicare,* 29, 1-17.

Newspaper Articles

NewsDay, December 18 2012

The Chronicle, 5 April 1983

The Guardian, September 2 2002

The Herald, February 3 2002

Zimbabwe Independent, September 6 2003.

Chapter Nine

History, culture, religion and [under-]development in Africa

Nkwazi Nkuzi Mhango

"... 'romanticism', though it continued through the nineteenth century and very much influenced social and economic theorists and politicians, is tangential to the doctrine which I will call populism" (Kitching 2010: 2).

Introduction

The quote above summarises all three elements this chapter is interrogating *vis-à-vis*, political and socio-economic facets of [under-]development in Africa. As the quote nicely asserts, development has been doctored, romanticised and essentialised not to mention being monopolised by the one side, the West, that superimposes its *diktat* on others as it ignores its unfair trajectory that enabled it to achieve such level of *development*. Such development needs to be deconstructed (Escobar, 2011) apart from being redefined to meet the understanding of others globally. Although the terms "development" and "underdevelopment" seem to largely depend on biased and controversial Eurocentric and materialistic definition[s], however narrow, romanticised and highly propounded and protected, they are now universal phenomena. Despite the weakness of superimposing them to all countries of the so-called world to follow Europe's trajectory (Kitching, *Ibid*, p. 1) without highlighting the importance of manner in which was attained, time and history of the victims of the terms. Epistemologically, it does not make any sense in whatever discipline for Europe that burglarised, they offer us a hunch to start the deconstruction. One would argue that in defining and assessing development or underdevelopment, whoever doing so must make sure that everything dealt with must have some degrees of intersectionality based on multisectoral applicability and neutrality. Africa to think that the duo can be at par in material development or seize is a big false; and whoever thinks that way he or she is not doing ay justice academically. For example, Friedmann (1967) argues that the general underpinnings of the theory of economic development appear to be a fundamental requirement for greater autonomy rather than as an end in itself (p. 40). This means that development is not supposed to be monopolised or superimposed on others. Instead, development needs to be defined clearly as oxygen is defined to suit accommodative understanding globally. So, too, development is not supposed to be narrow, tyrannical and prejudiced. Looking at the type of development under the neoliberal policy and definition, its definition based on theories and practices, there are some missing links. Where is the autonomy, for countries whose development is defined by others? Thanks to populistic academic psyche, there is no way I can avoid scooping from the definitions however academically poisonous they might be. Therefore, I cannot avoid or ignore them for my peril. In this chapter, I will address the history of Africa based on cultural imperialism and religion as the agents of [under] development; mainly from the time colonialism and slavery were introduced to Africa up until now. I will try as much as I can to icepack such humongous history in one chapter, which is very hard to do.

First of all, the term [under] development that is used as standard for defining the term is relatively normative (Waas, Verbruggen and Wright, 2010, p. 631), idiosyncratic; and needs to be qualified; namely to answer the question: Development or underdevelopment in what, by who and for whom? This chapter seeks to address three facets of African continent namely, economically, politically and socially.

Secondly, whatever definition one uses is situational and inferential due to the fact that there is no agreed meaning or definition of the two concepts.

Third, when it comes to development, as an ambiguous, relative and insufficient term, we need to redefine it in order to give the readership the tool to understand what we postulate or propound. For the purpose of this chapter, development means, *inter alia,* the attainment of high standard, quality or level in anything someone does or pursues provided it is legal and acceptable as it revolves around humanity and justice. Philips (1977) maintains that there is no satisfactory definition of development that does not imply capitalism even in the most technological definition (p. 7) not to mention epistemologically and culturally. Phillips goes on arguing that, to the contrary, underdevelopment is wrongly and biasedly viewed as an original state of things simply because it has to be measured based on the lens of the so-called developed countries that appointed the status to themselves in order to bully and exploit others based on utopian straggle to attain it. To do away with murder, such developed countries in bombing others with their definitions of development, do not follow from the premises of historical materialism (Toms, 2010, p. 13) which may expose them and how they attained their development after robbing others. I can argue that what is defined as development is nothing but the ruse of forcing other non-Western countries to replicate the West almost in everything without underscoring the enabling environment that helped the West to outdo others. Refer to enabling environment such as slavery, colonialism, neocolonialism and the monopolisation of the so-called international organisations such as the World Bank, the International Monetary Fund among others.

Fourth, differently from others, my definition of development will revolve around the improvement of human wellbeing but not material attainment geared by greed and enhanced by criminality or injustice as it is in the case of the West. For, this chapter, development is something that is supposed to be universally moral. I live in the so-called developed country, Canada. Whenever I see how animal rights are protected however manipulatively. I suspect the term, chiefly when I remember human beings who are left out of this development paradigm. The Aboriginal Canadians provide an ideal example. Their lives are more miserable than animals. Pets, in Canada, just like any Western country, live better lives than some humans. To wherever store you go to, there is an isle our two special for pet foods from dogs, cats, and birds. Ironically, there are no traditional foods for the Aboriginals. Their white settlers took their land and confined them in reserves. As if this was not enough, their traditional foods and hunting areas either were violated or occupied so as to leave the Aboriginals with nothing to eat except to adopt

225

settlers' food. So, too, the settlers introduced alcohol and drugs to reserves so as to completely destroy the lives of the Aboriginals. Can we call this development really whereby somebody robs another and hijacks him? This reminds me of the civilisation that colonial agents and their masters introduced to Africa to end up alleging that they civilised Africans while they violated them. Mhango (2015) questions the real meaning of civilisation if colonialism and slavery and its total uncivility were civilisation (p. 407) to indicate how some concepts are misconstrued and misrepresented.

As for animals, one would candidly say that if humans are sincerely serious in protecting animals' rights, would stop eating and taming them. I, sometimes, wonder how animals can have more rights and expensive rights than humans in some areas of the world. One day, we were casually talking about animal rights. One Aboriginal boy told me animal rights' activists pretend to protect animal rights while they abuse them by keeping them as pets for their exploitation, gratification and satisfaction without underscoring that they naturally were created to live and wonder in the wild as they abuse and trample on Aboriginal' people's God-given rights as the true owners of this land invaders call theirs. This assertion stimulates the discussion in point based on development or otherwise whether it should hinge on humanity or materiality resulting from quintessential human coloniality and individuality.

Even when it comes to development, sometimes, I feel left out, especially when I remember how children in Africa are taught to care about environment. Here I see in public places where people abuse utilities such as water and paper to indicate that they are either selfish or do not know that doing so causes harm to mother earth. Sometimes, people are too lazy and too ignorant to grasp little things that have huge impacts on the world such as frugality, collectivity of humanity, morality and whatnots. Furthermore, when I consider how people consume stupidly not to mention throwing a lot of food to trash, I doubt the whole concept of development and civilisation. The *Globe and Mail* (1 October, 2012) reports that Canadians waste approximately 40 per cent of food, or $27-billion worth annually, according to the Value Chain Management Centre, an independent think tank based in Guelph, Ont. And just over half (51 per cent) of that gets tossed from households. If a country with small population of approximately 40 million, how many tons of food the so-called developed countries push to the trash annually simply because they do not care about others let alone chronic and unnecessary consumerism? Apart from Canada, Vaughn (2011) notes that when it comes to committing the offence of food destruction American families are among the worst offenders due to the findings that an average family of four throws out $600 worth of good food every year, and that 14% of that is food that hasn't expired or even been packaged, (p. 4). Statistically speaking, the scale of food destruction is sacrilegious by all standards. Lipinski *et al.,* (2013) disclose that the Food and Agriculture Organisation of the United Nations (FAO) estimates that 32 percent of all food produced in the world was lost or wasted in 2009 (p. 5). Despite such criminality and recklessness, those committing this crime still pride themselves to be developed. What type of development is this if we face it? While developed countries are throwing food to the trash, the report by the World Bank issued in 2012 discloses that Africa had as many as 19 million people living with the threat of hunger and malnutrition in West Africa's Sahel region. Good news, the same report said that Africa can feed itself and generate an extra US$20 billion in yearly earnings if African leaders can agree to dismantle trade barriers that blunt more regional dynamism. However, FAOSTAT, (2011 cited in Rakotoarisoa, Iafrate, and Paschali, 2011) notes that in 1980, Africa had an almost balanced agricultural trade when both agricultural exports and imports were at about USD 14 billion, but by 2007 its agricultural imports exceeded agricultural exports by about US$ 22 billion, (p. 1). Again, how could one blame our people in the so-called developed world while neoliberal policies encourage them to consume ravenously as a sign of development simply because businesses can make more dollars. Consider this. Fast foods claim many lives in many Western countries by causing either diseases resulting from consuming many calories, much oil and sugar and overfeeding. Yet, the governments do not ban them simply because the businesses pay taxes.

227

Religion and slavery

Just like any human society, Africa has a very long history of civilisation which has passed through many epochs good and bad. However, much of the history of Africa was biasedly written by colonisers who omitted some facts and added some fabrications in order to justify their criminality of colonising, occupying and robbing Africa. Tamale, (2011, p. 16 cited in Nhemachena, 2016) observes that in the 1960 and 1970, researchers flocked to Africa to study African sexual orientation in relation to fertility whereby images of oversexed, promiscuous, less moral and less brainy Africans were never far from the minds of the demographers and other researchers interested in the study of fertility control (p. 15).

It is clear that they did so in order to prove that their coloniality civilised Africa while it actually sent it back many decades as far as development is concerned. Nhemachena (*Ibid*) argues that before the eyes of colonisers, Africans could not imagine or create institution, history, art, culture or anything except their primitiveness (p. 20) however when you clinically observes the truth you find that the different was the case. I can cite one element that uniquely differentiates humans and beasts. Language is the major element that shaped human genius due to the fact that it enables them to communicate and exchange skills based on their needs, choices and interests. Maintaining that Africans were primitive devoid of imagine is the proof that those making such a statement had some mental problems due to the fact that nobody taught Africans their language. Africans have many more languages and richest culture than any human race on the globe. For the sake of argument, even if we buy into Western conceptualisation of development based on material success as opposed to underdevelopment that is manipulated to be the natural state of thing, I may argue that the history of Africa starts at the time when slavery and thereafter colonialism were introduced to Africa. For, before then, a little is documented (Fage, 2010: ix) despite the fact that the East and North East Africa are historically believed to be the cradle of mankind. This informs us that we do not know our whole history as a species. This being the case, I will start the history at the time the two crimes mentioned herein above were introduced in the in the 8th and 9th (Trans-Saharan as it was introduced by Arabs) and the 15th century (Trans-Atlantic as it was introduced by Arabs and Europeans) due to the fact that recording, however doctored it is, started. Due to the genesis and changing nature of slavery, some scholars either tie it to race or religion (Alexander, 2001, p. 45); due to the fact that the duo fully participated in perpetrating this crime against human, particularly and latterly Africans not to mention how their books of authority namely the Bible (Leviticus 25:44-46 (NLT); (Exodus 21:2-6 (NLT); (Luke 12:47-48 (NLT)); (1 Timothy 6:1-2 (NLT)); (Ephesians 6:5 (NLT); and (Exodus 21:20-21 (NAB)and the Quran (33:50); (23:5-6); (4:24); (8:69); (24:32); (2:178); and (16:75) legalise and validate this inhuman and ungodly phenomenon in the name of God. Wright (2010) maintains that at the time and the ages when the Bible was written slavery was a universal phenomenon and it was part and parcel of the culture and people accepted it as a fact of life; also see Meager, (2006); and Whitford, (2009). For more information about slavery in the Bible, Genesis 16 provides a glimpse in the phenomenon and how it was acceptable before God. Abdullah, (1984) concurs with Alexander noting that despite the fact that the Qur'an did not abolish it [slavery] in clear, direct language, its teachings did attempt to raise the moral and material status of slaves and to encourage their freedom, (p. 34) which seems to be hypocritical, mainly when we consider the fact that Allah who sent the Quran is said to be Omni conscious. This is a bit controversial due to the fact that slavery in Trans-Saharan slavery was practiced many years after the writing of the Quran. Clarence-Smith, (2006) differs from Abdullah citing Clarence-Smith who brings out of a set of synergistic syllogisms on the assumptive plane that the Qur'an failed to eliminate slavery; and that removing this practice would shake the faith itself due to the fact that the Prophet was totally unaware of the concept of abolition as an idea as well as in practice; and the fact that the whole Islamic social structure with its attendant system was based on a type of slavery associated with the organization of the harem, (p. 119).

The recent evidence shows that slavery is still in existence in some Islamic world even presently due to the fact that this practice is cultural and religious to such societies (Oliver, 1991, p. 117 cited in Thompson, 2011) notes that there can be no doubt due to the fact that the slave trade received a great impetus from the rise and spread of Islam (p. 3) just like it was with the rise of Christianity. Again, it depends on who writes what. Pro-Christian and pro-Islamic scholars tend to defend their faiths even where it is impossible and useless to do so. Ironically, some of those doing so are the progenies of the victims of the same phenomenon thanks to being hoodwinked and indoctrinated to believe more in their neo-religions that employed them to abuse and insult their own people and history. However, despite all efforts, the link between Christianity and Islam and slavery has become difficult to erase. Thompson *(Ibid)* notes that when Europeans began to access more areas of the continent, slave traders largely avoided Muslim communities during any type of raiding as a courtesy to their fellow traders, (pp. 23). So, too, religions have always played chameleonic roles based on double standard. For example, when Christianity found that slavery was unviable, it changed tack so as to start fighting the same evil it created and enunciated as it is for Islam. Based on a Latin proverb that *verba volant, scripta manent* literary, words fly away, writings remain chances are that there is no nonbiased written evidence to scientifically link Africa with the genesis of this phenomenon. And if there is, it is doubtful due to the fact that much of the history of Africa was written by the same people who enslaved and colonised it. To the contrary, when it comes to Christianity and Islam, they wrote their own history and purported them to have come from God who seems to discriminate against Africans so as to need to be a coloniser that needed to be preached through propaganda and deception (Ekon, 2014: 193) just as any colonial penetration of any country.

After briefly tracing the genesis of slavery in the world and Africa, many would like to know why Africans were enslaved at such a big scale but not others. Mhango (2015) argues that they were naturally healthier, stronger, hardworking and adapted to an agrarian society. Secondly, slavery was introduced to Africa due to the individualistic drive of those who looked down on others as inferior creatures to them. Essentially, slavery was authored based on racism that has been going on up until now. Loomba, (2015) argues that the British Empire has had a pretty horrible press from a generation of 'postcolonial' historians who were incongruously disrespected by its racism (p. 8) that has been extended up until now under neoliberalism as an extension of colonialism in the world. Loomba goes on and links the International Monetary Fund (IMF) to the exploitation of the so-called third world countries in its neoliberal policies which have a lot of conditions. There is no way one can analyse slavery without touching on racism as Jordan, (1812) argues that when the Africans *were discovered* by Europeans the most arresting characteristic was his colour (p. 1) which is the same reason why other races are now favoured compared to Africans who are discriminated against. It is even sad to note that even Africans themselves have fallen in the same notorious booby trap thanks to the role religions played to hoodwink and dupe them. Look at how foreigners who live in Africa are generously treated while the same maltreat Africans. Mhango (2015) as with Mawere and Mubaya (2016) cites an example of the Jarawa people in Andaman Islands in India, who are treated by Indians like animals while Indians in Africa are being treated like gods and enjoying more opportunities. Whitford, (2009) explores the mythology in the US wherein on the morning of 10 June, 1964, Senator Robert C. Byrd a former Kleagle of the West Virginia Ku Klux Klan spent 14 hours convincing the senate how blacks were ordained to be slaves basing his argument in Genesis 9:18-27 saying that Africa was founded by Ham whose father Noah cursed by becoming black. So, for him, black people were inferior; and thus would be legally enslaved. While Byrd tried as much as he could to portray Africans as the castaways, in 1583 Martin Luther got it right; and decided to do justice saying that the world was filled with black devils and white devils (Carey 2006: 10).Apart from Luther whose rebellion changed the world, what one can expect from people like Byrd who came hundreds of years after Luther and harbour bigotry against Africans when they are in the positions of power of defining development? To be precise, in commenting in chapter 1, verse 4 of his Commentary on the Epistle to the Galatians, Luther cited in Carey (*Ibid*) goes on showing who is dangerous between the black and white devils noting that "the white devil of spiritual sin is far more dangerous than the black devil of carnal sin" (p. 16). All this even figuratively shows how whites decided to belittle Africans either for the purposes of exploiting them or resulting from mere bigotry and ignorance. For, historically, there are no records showing that Africans ever involved in carnal sin or homosexuality. So, we can say that figuratively, Luther was trying to show how wrong perception of colours and the role assign to them sometimes can be misleading. Remember Byrd and the like are the ones under the Church who reached at the apex of blasphemy by contending if Indians had soul. Grosfoguel (2013) notes that the rationale was that "If Indians" did not have a soul, then it is justified in the eyes of God to enslave them and treat them as animals in the labour process" (p. 82). Again, such imbecilic thinkers are the ones who laid the foundation of the current institutions that are defining our development. Can there be any justice based on inherent racism that has gone on even today under the neoliberal policies the West has always espoused and superimposed on others?

Religion and colonialism as two bedfellows

As it is in slavery, religion, particularly Christianity had a very big role to play during the colonisation in many parts of Africa and Islam in the Sudan, Libya, Mauritania and Saharawi. Colonialism is self-explanatory in that it is widely known due to the effects it has in many countries ex-colonies as well as colonisers. In simple parlance, colonialism is a foreign and superimposed government in an occupied entity known as country. Therefore, when I talk of colonialism I simply mean the system under which Africa was occupied and ruled by foreign countries. However, it should be noted that colonialism might be foreign or home depending who is doing the colonising as it currently is in many African countries under illegal governments that have been in power either by tampering with the constitution or lording it over the citizens. This chapter deals with the former though.

If it was not for the role missionaries, explorers and merchants played in Africa, colonialism would not have succeeded. So, missionaries were colonial agents that were sent to penetrate (*penetencia* or spying) Africans so as to get their secrets and sell them to their master back home in Europe. Under the pretext of offering education, missionaries as any agents of colonialism, were able to dupe Africans into obedience and mythology that ended up paving the way to colonialism. Despite that, missionaries were strategically different from other colonial agents such as traders, explores and colonial administrators however this difference does not exempt most, if any, missionaries of colonial times from the crime of colonising (Gallego and Woodberry, 2010: 295). The so-called explorers, merchants and missionaries were nothing but colonial trinity. Every group had the role to play at different times and levels to make sure that Africans were brainwashed for colonial governments to come in. Woodberry (2002, 2004 cited in Gallego and Woodberry, 2010) disclose that some Catholic colonial powers, as Italy, banned the entry of new Protestant missionaries to their colonies (p. 304). Based on racist and colonial ideology, missionaries did not come to Africa to civilise it as they maliciously used to allege. They came to Africa to pave the way to colonialism simply because black people were erroneously considered to be inferior to white ones. You can see this in their dogmatic teachings in which everything white is holy and everything black is satanic. Song of Solomon 1:5 suffices to show us how being black is evil and punishable not to mention the discrimination blacks face. The song reads:

> I am black [*dark*], but comely, O ye daughters of Jerusalem, as the tents of Kedar, as the curtains of Solomon. Look not upon me, because I am black, because the sun hath looked upon me: my mother's children were angry with me; they made me the keeper of the vineyards; but mine own vineyard have I not kept.

When it comes to white, things are holy jolly. All angels appear in white. Jesus has never been portrayed wearing a black garb. He is always in white apart from himself being white, as if he was. White according to the Bible, Leviticus 13:13 means clean. 2 Chronicles 5:12; Psalm 51:7; Song of Solomon 5:10; Daniel 12:10; Daniel 15:35; and Psalm 68:14, among many verses that denote that white is pure. However, deniers may argue that the language used in the Bible and Quran are figurative, the truth will always hauntingly hunt them.

Due to being brainwashed, there are things we do either consciously or otherwise that are purely symbolic and connotative of racism against blacks. For example, during funeral and mourning, people wear black while white is donned as a symbol of purity and cleanliness. Sadly however, even the victims of this systemic and universal racism fall in the same trap. This racism is entrenched in Christianity as well as Islam. For example, during the papal conclave that elect the pope of Catholicism connotes racism. Tobin and Wister (2009) testify that the world can know if a new pontiff has been elected or not by looking at the sfumata, or white smoke signal whereby black smoke from the chimney on the roof of the Sistine Chapel shows that the College of Cardinals did not decide on the new Pontiff. To the contrary, white smoke indicates to those in St Peter's Square that a new Pontiff has been chosen (p. 80; also see Wüst, 2010; Hayes and Hromic 2014; and Manalo, 2015). This is pure racism even if it is committed under the shield of religion.

Racism does not end in the process. Even the product of this process has always produced racist results in that recently, there has never been a black pope to lead the church that prides itself to be universal. Thanks to the effects of Islam and the caste system in India, Vidyarthi (1995) claims that "white is the colour of peace, harmony, goodness and honour, red denotes danger and war, and black is the colour of evil and ignorance." Greek mythology also used colours to interpret some concepts. For example, according to Aslam (2006) the blue denoted heaven, the scarlet charity, the purple martyrdom, and the white chastity, purity, and black darkness (p. 1) or absence of light or the blackness of the grave (Petru, 2006) which is ridiculously a racist interpretations. Moreover, Hall (2010) notes that the colour black symbolizes lust, sin, evil, dirt, faeces, death, and so for to show how racists cannot do justice to anything black including Africans themselves. This means that there is nothing good can come out of Africa except its free labour during slavery and colonialism and currently resources. Therefore, even in defining development such biases are likely to affect those defining it. The just ended US elections provide an ideal example wherein, apart from being a flaw, the racist Donald Trump was voted by many racists that proved to be the majority voters. Remember, this is the leader who accused Africa of corruption as if the US and the West are not corrupt said that Africa needs to be colonised "for another 100" (The Nigerian *Post,* 14 January, 2016 cited in Mhango, *Forthcoming*).I know how provocative such ideologies are, mainly to Africans and some equality lovers among whites. However, I hope it is more provocative for the victims, under whatever ruses, be they religious or political, to embrace the same obnoxious, old-fashioned and toxic ideologies for their own peril. Now, one may ask: what does this have to do with development in Africa. There is a link. How much money and time do our people spend either on studying such garbage not to mention spending money on books and literatures that discriminate against them? How many Africans now kill each other because of religious reasons as it recently happened in the Central African Republic (CAR) where Christians and Muslims killed each other? How much property was destroyed not to mention lives pointlessly lost? How many men and women are still using lighteners to look white? How many white bigots still believe that they are superior to other colours as if they applied for being created the way they are? Don't we have non-white people such as Indians and Arabs who think they are white despite the fact that black was the organically the colour of Indians (Hall, *Ibid*) not to mention some Africans who lack self-confidence and self-worthy?

Religion has many more negative impacts on Africa than positive. However some people argue that religious institutions offer social services such as education and partly health, when you consider permanent impacts they have on the African society, you find that Africa loses much more than it gains. For example, when missionaries came to Africa, they taught people to hate mundane things (wealth) while the same grabbed land. How many thousands of hectares do churches and mosques own in Africa while, in some countries, citizens are landless? Desmond Tutu, retired archbishop of Cape Town, South Africa notes that "when the missionaries came to Africa, they had the Bible and we had the land. They said 'let us close our eyes and pray" (*Guardian*, 19, August 2003). Apart from grabbing land in Africa, to crown it all, such organisations in many unsuspecting African countries enjoy tax holidays under the pretexts of the provision of social services. The story does not end up here.

In some countries, presidents cannot take power without holding either the Bible or the Quran so as to be sworn in as a sign of trustworthiness without underscoring the fact that the same harbingers of these faiths proved to be fickle in dealing with Africans as Tutu, indicates above. Go further. Well, missionaries provided education that has never helped Africans to fully liberate themselves. Does this sort of colonised and toxic education help Africa *vis-à-vis* development? Once such leaders come to power, they misuse public funds funding religious organisations as it recently happened in Tanzania where the government has offered to build the headquarters of the Tanzania Muslim Council (BAKWATA) at the whooping cost of Tshs. 5 billion (*Daily News*, 16 August, 2016) while the same country has many pupils who study under trees not to mention unpaid teachers. The same countries offering such a project still begs for money to top up its budget. Furthermore, the government said that it decided to construct the BAKWATA's headquarters as it's thanks to religious leaders for maintaining peace. Again, you wonder. Is peace in Tanzania maintained by religious leaders or the people? Isn't this a bribe to such organisations if not the sign of partnership in duping the citizens? I see no peace in religious organisations, especially when I consider the enmity they create among our citizens based on denominational ideologies. To me, true and sustainable peace in any country will prevail as long as there is justice but not indoctrination of the *hoi polloi*. I may argue that our leaders tend to cow tow before religious leaders and their organisation simply because they are the products of these religions not to mention using them to hoodwink the citizens in various countries. If the government can build the headquarters of a religious organisation by negating its schools and hospitals, how much money does such a country lose to offering tax holidays to such organisations? Jesus paid tax to the government. Why don't religious organisations, especially Christian ones emulate him? Now you can see why religious organisations are always rich so as to attract many quacks who appoint themselves bishops, apostles and whatnots in order to rob the general population.

[Under] development

Africa sits on immense resources so as to become one of the world's richest and superpower *vis-à-vis* resources yet it has the poorest population. Why? As you can note above in the incident where the government intends to build the headquarters of a religious group, Africa lacks priorities and vision. When it comes to development, Africa is still in the receiving end. The IMF and the World Bank (WB) as colonial agents have made sure that Africa is perpetually bullied and exploited. Loomba (2015) cites Joseph E. Stiglitz, Nobel laureate and once Chief Economist at the WB maintaining that the IMF's methodology in dealing with developing countries has no border with a colonial ruler (p. 14). What else can we add if such words are coming from the horse's mouth? Through their colonial drives the International Financial Institutions (IFIs) as they are referred to despite being purely imperialistic organisations have made sure that Africa remains colonised, especially through using local colonisers and bad policies that have never added up to Africa's progress. Thanks to such neo-economic colonialism, Africa is viewed as underdeveloped either measured by its own standards or neo-imperialistic ones. If you look at corruption, bad governance, bad services, big governments and such things, you sometimes agree with the category of the material underdevelopment. To the contrary, when it comes to humanity, Africa still has something to offer. Mhango (2015) argues that Africans who were enslaved in the Americas contributed a lot in the highly touted industrial revolution due to the fact that they produced surplus that enable colonial Europe to sit down and invent (p. 23) which is obvious if we consider the size of the number of slaves that worked without any payment for many years in the Americas. Mhango goes on to put the number of Africans who were shipped to the Americas at the range of 9 to 12 million without including many more that died at sea on their way to the Americas or those who were shipped to other places. Essentially, slave trade derailed Africa as far as technological and innovation are concerned. Bairoch (1993: 8 cited in Nunn, 2007) concurs with Mhango noting that "there is no doubt that a large number of negative structural features of the process of economic underdevelopment have historical roots going back to European colonization" (p. 139). For, the Africans who were shipped to the Americas were energetic and young people who would have produced more for Africa not to mention resources colonialism robbed Africa for a long time. Nunn goes on arguing that the trans-Atlantic slave trade alone saw approximately 12 million slaves exported from Africa whereas another 6 million were exported in the other three slave trades (p. 142). Such findings expand the number of the victims of slavery. Nunn (2008 cited in Nunn, and Wantchekon, 2011) maintains that the slave trade, which occurred over a period of more than 400 years, had a significant negative effect on long-term economic development (p. 3221) for Africa and Africans. If we consider the dangers slaves faced and ordeals they suffered and went through, chances are that over 50 million Africans perished, mainly if we consider how rudimentary ships, dungeons and the handling of slaves were. Another element that we need to consider is the length of the journey. Remember, boats or ships that ferried slaves had no doctors or medical services. When a slave fell sick, the solution was to throw her or him to the ocean. This was the then slavery. When it comes to the fact that Africa lost energetic and healthy population, the same is repeated in modern slavery whereby African academics go for green pastures in Western countries. Mhango (*forthcoming*) puts the figure of such brains to hundreds of thousands.

Apart from contributing to the industrial revolution, we need to underscore the fact that African commerce, institutions, ways of life and all other ingredients of a free and able society were felled to give room to colonialism. To know how advanced and developed Africa was, try to imagine. Who offered any aid or handout, loans and whatnot before the introduction of colonialism? Who treated Africans so as to become healthier than others and be enslaved? There were institutions and systems that ran Africa swiftly and efficiently. We are talking of institutions; there is evidence all over the place that Africa taught Europe metallurgy, especially iron smelting (Young and Sessine, 2000: 6) which they started many years before Europe which was so ignorant so as to regard the Americas as the "new world" while it actually was not. Again, due to better than thou mentality, what Europe did not know was not known to anybody. However, historical records show that Africa did trade with Far Asia many years before Europe became aware of it. Dussubieux, *et al.,* (2008) maintain that archaeologists share the same certainty that most of the glass beads in sub-Saharan Africa that predate European arrival were imported from India (p. 2; also see Shillington 2012: 154; and Wood 2012: 21). Remember; this is many years before Europe did not know even the way to India. Refer to how Christopher Columbus made a goof calling Americas' Inuit Indians and Caribs West Indies (Malhotra, *et al.,* 2007: 185) after failing to reach India thanks to his ignorance of the place while Africans had already used monsoon winds to conquer the Indian Ocean. Apart from trading with Asia, Africa boasts of being one of the harbingers of iron technology which started many millenniums in Egypt under Nubians before the arrival of Europeans. Furthermore, Bantu speaking people who are believed to have originated from the grasslands of Cameroon are renowned for their iron technology (Childs, 1991: 337). This shows that no society was barren or static. What provokes is the colonial tendency of wanting to discover and own almost everything while the evidence is out there that Europe was the last to join ancient civilisations such as China and Egypt among others.

Now let us delve into development be it cultural, material, moral, social or political and whatnots. As introduced above, development is a relative term that needs qualification in order to functionally make sense. Development in what and who determines it using what criteria and why? Is it development in development or development in underdevelopment? Where does this development take us from and where does it take us; who is included and who is excluded and why? Is it based on time, needs and inclusiveness or individuality and or commonality? Is this development universally achievable? Who gains and who loses and why? These questions are very important but provocative due to the fact that some development like that of Western Europe and the Americas was attained and necessitated by others whose development was destroyed or stagnated and they were exploited and excluded. This is the story many Africans, especially academics need to tell and tell and retell so that the coming generations should know the real truth. It is hard; I know. However, nobody should condemn us to silence while we can still think. Sometimes, that what is referred to as development can turn out to be scam of keeping us hostage thanks to the ever changing goal posts. When I consider different financial and economic policies the IMF and the WB have instructed in Africa without any viable success, I tend to believe that everybody needs to define development depending on possibility but not superimposition that tends to max out without success as it is in the case of economic experiments on Africa which Easterly (2009) maintain that they are based on failed and recycled ideas and old fashioned way of thinking (p. 373) that have always achieved the same. There is consensus that IFIs' neoliberal policies have failed to promote development (Vreeland, 2006: 360), especially in Africa which is why we query and regard it to be an economic scam. Again, such recycled and failed ideas are viewed as nuggets from developed world that can develop Africa while the same authoring such litany are the same who colonised Africa and still do the same. Due to the confusion of the definition of development, even the goons who are subscribing to such a scam are referred to as progressive, democratic, modern and whatnots while the duo is hard at learning. When it comes to learning the trio does not show any sign of development by doing just the same expecting different results which is madness in essence. Redress the guys you colonised and enslaved and see how they will catch up.

When it comes to Africa, I may argue that it was developed in its own way based on its needs and time. For example, when colonisers arrived in Africa, they found that Africa was evergreen thanks to its knowledge of conserving environment. What happened when Europe started to consume timbers at large scale? Isn't Africa facing deforestation due to this massive and careless consumption? Another example can be drawn from Ankole long horned cows in Uganda. This elegant cow is now facing extinction after Western scientists duped Ankoles that they would cure them while they destroyed them in order to give room for their so-called hybrid cows. In the name of bettering their cows, Ankole ended up being duped so as to lose them. Again, if you look at the dangers hybrid cows and their products pose compared to traditional African cow, you can decide by yourself who was developed and how. Look at how Africa is losing its elephants and rhinos due to the greed geared and enhanced by neoliberal policies based on careless consumerism and free market. Aren't Asian emerging economies robbing Africa of its resources simply because the international system sanctifies this greed embedded in capitalism, individualism and materialism? If Africa was able to conserve its resources before the coming of colonial ticks, how can one say it was underdeveloped? Who is developed; the one who decimates everything or the one who conserves everything? Who is developed and underdeveloped between the materialist and moralist? You can judge yourself, particularly when it comes to environmental challenges the world is now facing whereby Africa produces a fraction of the second in global warming, over-consuming and whatnots. Currently, some parts of the world face drought. The list is long. For those who come from the societies where rainmaking was a technology that Western cultural coloniality felled, think there is a solution to this problem. Arguably, this technology in some African societies was a real thing but not a hoax. Berglund, (1976 cited in Huffman, 2000) testifies to this maintaining that "rainmakers are special herbalists, not chiefs, who try to influence supernatural forces through the manipulation of rain medicines and ritual, (p. 15; also see Håland, 2005; Gandure, Walker and Botha, 2013; and Babane and Chauke, 2015). I understand; some detractors will dispute this fact as a myth while at the same time they subscribe to mythologies such as religious protection from evils that are based on beliefs. If it is accepted that God gave manna to Israelites, what is wrong with accepting the fact that Africans had rainmaking technology? Isn't this development in its own right? Risiro, *et al.,* (2012) concur maintaining that "the study found that traditional methods of weather forecasting can be utilised for the purposes of short term and long term seasonal weather predictions by local communities" (p. 565).Looking at many aspects of African traditional societies, one finds that they were more developed in some aspects more than the so-called developed countries. For example, African women have never negated their infants or denied them of their right to breastfeeding. What is the situation in the so-called developed countries where women are denying their infants breast milk? Thanks to their ignorance of the importance of breast milk, economically, psychologically and physiologically, some women in the so-called developed countries under the ignorance of modernity are not breastfeeding for their peril and that of their infants. Even animals know when, why and how long breastfeeding should be carried out. The *US Department of Health and Human Services,* (2011) notes that:

> Although much is known about rates of breastfeeding in the population, mothers' breastfeeding practices have not been well understood until recently. The Infant Feeding Practices Study II, 42 conducted during 2005–2007 by the U.S. Food and Drug Administration (FDA) in collaboration with CDC, was designed to fill in some of the gaps, (p. 6); also see the Office of the Surgeon General (US, and Centres for Disease Control and Prevention (2011); Afshariani (2014); and Byers (2015).

Despite being a basic, natural and simple knowledge in Africa, the same failures will come to Africa to teach breastfeeding based on their ignorance and failures and go away priding themselves of civilising Africans. Geared by ignorance and selfishness, and latching on materiality and individuality devoid of morality, women who deny their infants breast milk care more about their beauties and bodies but not the development and wellbeing of their innocent infants. Apart from such human catastrophe, resulting from ignorance, to infants in the developed world, consider environmental danger mining is now posing in Africa after the introduction of toxic and contaminant chemicals all geared by greed (Bugri, 2008; Keeley and Scoones, 2014). Many mining companies from the so-called developed countries are contaminating African soil pointlessly (Kitula, 2006: 410). Later, once chips are down, they will blame this phenomenon on Africa while they are the ones who largely contributed in creating the problem. Consider long and negative impacts the introduction of Genetically Manipulated Foods (GMF) will cause Africa in the future. Again, why GMF are introduced to Africa? First, it is because of lazy and visionless leadership that has always acted as an agent of colonialism if not an extension in Africa. Secondly, it is because African traditional foods are discouraged in order to give room to GMF the West will use to make money and control Africa in its drive for neocolonialism as espoused in neoliberal policies championed by the IFIs and some gullible and visionless African leaders.

I think we need to agree on one thing that Western development is more materialistic while African development is didactic. This is why Africans did not need or colonised any people due to the fact that they were satisfied with their material wellbeing and they knew how morally wrong doing so is.

When it comes to social development, the story of the religion above suffices to tell it all. Since the introduction of cultural colonialism embedded in religions, Africans have lost their true moralistic culture. They are now the shadows of who they used to be. They have new identities from names, beliefs, fashions, education, languages and whatnots. Africa, if I may say it, needs to invent new uncontaminated Africans who will rebel, redefine and push it to the future. The Africa we have today is problematic, especially when I look at the engines that are supposed to propel it to the future. Young people are now risking their lives to go to Europe and America for "green" pastures. The academics too are perishing under the brain drain dressed as brain gain while it is a brain game. Leaders left so many years ago after they started receiving orders from their former colonial masters. A few Africans left with courage and sanity are discouraged by the black colonial governments that do not need them for fear of awakening their people. So, when it comes to development, Africa needs to turn things around for the better by deconstructing everything renowned to have pulled it back (Mhango, *forthcoming*). Slavery and colonialism destroyed all already-established institutions so as to leave Africa empty handed to end up depending on its former colonial masters to establish alien institutions that have never worked for the interests of Africa since independence. Again, where did these institutions go? Nunn and Puga (2012) answer the question maintaining that "the slave trade had adverse effects on subsequent economic development because they weakened indigenous political structures and institutions, and promoted ethnic and political fragmentation" (p. 2) not to mention socio-political consequences. Consider the suffering and perpetual trauma those born of slaves have endured in foreign lands they were forcibly taken and sold not to mention perpetual degradation and exploitation. This is why the economic development achieved by means of colonising and enslaving others those who pride themselves to be economically developed and dupe others to follow their trajectory is wrong and unattainable without redressing their victims. A thug who burgles my house and robs me of everything so as to become materially rich but morally poor cannot define my development. And if he does so without returning my property, his definition and development will be totally vicious and fickle and misleading. This is why it is hypocritical and a big lie to allow criminals who colonised enslaved and robbed Africa to justly and judiciously define development for their victims, in particular at the time their crimes are still committed by extension under whatever system and doctrine such as neoliberalism, globalism, capitalism you name it. Arguably, true and meaningful development must revolve around humanity but not criminality and duplicity, justice not injustice, morality and not immorality and material aspects of the concept must be the last element to be considered. Humanity and justice should come first. This is where the importance of history as a tool of emancipation becomes evidently imperative, especially for the victims. There is no way development can revolve around things first then around humanity. For the victims, subscribing to such a ploy is to turn humans into things which case is dangerous as Freire cited in Vaught (2015) maintains that the oppressed have been reduced to things (p. 201); and thus they need to fight for their humanity as the cardinal requirement instead of entering the struggle just as mere objects expecting to later become human beings who are not organically accepted as humans with all rights just like any other humans.

Conclusion

With cases and examples adduced herein above, suffice it to say, nobody can exclusively own development in all aspects of life. So, too, nobody is solely entitled to define development for others without asking crucial questions such as to whose interests, why, when, how, and above all, in what the said development is defined and measured. Arguably, defining development for others is one of colonial mentalities based on manipulative *holier than thou*, especially when such definition and measures purposely or otherwise excludes some aspects of some societies as it currently is under the neoliberal policies geared by greed and self-interests as it is espoused by Western countries not to mention being superimposed on others (Mhango, 2015).

Additionally, those whose traditions, religions and policies have always discriminated against Africans because of the pigment of their colour will never do them just when allowed to define them or define any concept that is applied to them as we have seen in development. For Africans to do away with this colonial everything, they need to rebel against all systems that seek to belittle them so as to perpetually exploit them. I would argue that for Africa to survival this conspiracy against it, nothing it needs to do but to seek redress for all evils that was committed against its people. More importantly, whatever development aspect is defined and measured should revolve mainly around humanity but not materiality or coloniality. It should involve material as well as moral aspects of development in order to become meaningful and inclusive. Development that is devoid of inclusivity is nothing but a problem resulting from individuality and academic inequity. Instead of allowing neoliberalism to define, redefine and dictate development as a philosophy, Africans should seek to incorporate their philosophy mainly Ubuntu which is known to cover all aspects of live for a human being based on equity, equality, justice and humanity. If neo-religions are allowed to apply their holier than thou policies on our people, what is wrong for Africans to seek to incorporate their philosophy?

Therefore, it goes without saying that Africa is developed and underdeveloped in some areas the same way, as it has been proved herein above, others are. Therefore, we need to negotiate and agree or disagree about the concept of development. We have shown herein above how developed countries greedily and maliciously waste food while other people on earth are dying of hunger and malnutrition. Using African lenses, when a neighbour goes with an empty stomach, you do not have the right to waste food even if it is yours. Therefore, when I argue and urge that development should revolve around humanity, I invoke such a school of thought which is development towards world's wellbeing based on interdependence and interconnectivity. The same applies to environment, economy, politics and all other aspects of life. Under *Ubuntu* which literary means 'a person is a person through other persons' (Gade, 2011: 303; also see Gade, 2012), meaningful development should be inclusive as it revolves around humanity based on equity. However, such understanding of development based on collectivistic culture is totally different conceptualised from the individualistic culture's perspective. Mapadimeng (2009) argues that "Ubuntu culture could contribute to socio-economic development (p. 78) if it is nicely applied based on its foundations (also see Mhango, 2016). However, when it comes to the individualistic, like animals in the jungle, everybody carries his cross.

In sum, development that is arrested or monopolised by one section of human society, so as to solely define, dictate and superimpose on others is problematic; and it needs to be deconstructed, overhauled and redefined altogether in order to be meaningfully accommodated in the understanding of others not to forget serving the interests of the mankind. Every society has its levels and aspects of development. And there is no human society that is devoid of development be it materialistic or moralistic one. What differ are the lenses and motives used in defining the said development. There is no way a hyena can define development for a deer and do it justice. Essentially, when the goat allows such sacrilege to happen, it will be marking the end of its future and its progenies. It is through this anomaly wherein Africa developed the West ended up being referred to as backward and underdeveloped. Backward and underdeveloped in what, why and how?

Abbreviations

BAKWATA–Baraza la Waislam Tanzania
CAR–Central African Republic
CDC–Centres for Disease Control
FAO– Food and Agriculture Organization
FDA–Food and Drug Administration
GMF–Genetically Manipulated Foods

IFI–International Financial Institution
IMF–International Monetary Fund
NLT–New Living Translation
WB–World Bank

References

Abdallah, Fadl. 1987. Islam, Slavery, and Racism: The Use of Strategy in the Pursuit of Human Rights, *American Journal of Islamic Social Sciences 4(1)*: 31.

Afshariani, Raha. 2014. Maternal Benefits of Breastfeeding, *Women's Health Bulletin 1(3)*.

Alexander, John. 2001. Islam, archaeology and slavery in Africa, *World Archaeology 33(1)*: 44-60.

Aslam, Mubeen M. "Are you selling the right colour? A cross-cultural review of colour as a marketing cue." *Journal of marketing communications 12.1* (2006): 15-30.

Babane, M. T., and M. T. Chauke. 2015. The Preservation of Xitsonga Culture through Rainmaking Ritual: An Interpretative Approach.

Bible (Matthew 8.28-34; 15.22; 10.8). 1999. *Journal for the Study of the New Testament 21(73)*: 33-58.

Brian, *et al*. 2013. Reducing food loss and waste, *Working Paper*, World Resources Institute.

Bugri, John T. 2008. The dynamics of tenure security, agricultural production and environmental degradation in Africa: Evidence from stakeholders in north-east Ghana, *Land Use Policy 25(2)*: 271-285.

Byers, Helen L. "The Benefits of Breastfeeding." (2015).

Carey, Katherine Jeannette Moody. "John Webster's the White Devil: A Literary Artefact of the Jacobean Struggle for Power by King, Pope, and Machiavel." (2006).

Childs, S. Terry. "Style, technology, and iron smelting furnaces in Bantu-speaking Africa." *Journal of Anthropological Archaeology 10.4* (1991): 332-359.

Clarence-Smith, William Gervase. Islam and the Abolition of Slavery. Oxford University Press, USA, 2006.

Daily News. 16 August 2016. "Makonda hands over design for Bakwata headquarters, mosque."

Dave McGinn. 2012. "How much in food do Canadians waste a year? Think billions." *Globe and Mail*, 1 October, 2012.

Dussubieux, Laure, *et al.* 2008. "The trading of ancient glass beads: new analytical data from South Asian and East African soda–alumina glass beads." *Archaeometry 50 (5)*: 797-821.

Easterly, William. "Can the west save Africa?." Journal of economic literature 47.2 (2009): 373-447.

Escobar, Arturo. 2011. *Encountering development: The making and unmaking of the Third World.* Princeton University Press.

Fage, John. 2013. *A history of Africa.* Routledge.

Friedmann, John. "A general theory of polarized development." (1967).

Gade, Christian B. N. 2011. The historical development of the written discourses on Ubuntu. South *African Journal of Philosophy 30 (3)*: 303-329.

Gade, Christian B. N. 2012. What is Ubuntu? Different interpretations among South Africans of African descent. *South African Journal of Philosophy 31(3)*: 484-503.

Gallego, Francisco A., and Robert Woodberry. "Christian missionaries and education in former African colonies: How competition mattered." *Journal of African Economies* (2010): ejq001.

Gandure, S., S. Walker, and J. J. Botha. "Farmers' perceptions of adaptation to climate change and water stress in a South African rural community." *Environmental Development 5* (2013): 39-53.

Gavin. Development and Underdevelopment in Historical Perspective: Populism, Nationalism and Industrialisation. Vol. 103. Routledge, 2010.

George Monbiot. "Poisoned chalice." *Guardian*, 19, August 2003.

Grosfoguel, Ramón. "The structure of knowledge in westernized universities: Epistemic racism/sexism and the four genocides/epistemicides of the long 16th century." *Human Architecture 11.1* (2013): 73.

Håland, Evy Johanne. "Rituals of magical rain-making in modern and ancient Greece: A comparative approach." Cosmos: *The Journal of the Traditional Cosmology Society 17*.2 (2005): 197-251.

Hall, Ronald E. "Introduction." *An Historical Analysis of Skin Colour Discrimination in America*. Springer New York, 2010. 1-10.

Hayes, Conor, and Hugo Hromic. "Constructing Twitter Datasets using Signals for Event Detection Evaluation." 22nd International Conference on Case-Based Reasoning, 2014.

Huffman, Thomas N. "Mapungubwe and the origins of the Zimbabwe culture." *Goodwin Series* (2000): 14-29.

Johnston, Anna. Missionary writing and empire, 1800-1860. Cambridge University Press, 2003.Kitching,

Jordan, Winthrop. "The Simultaneous invention of slavery and racism." White over black: *American attitudes toward the Negro, 1550* (1812): 3-7.

Keeley, James, and Ian Scoones. Understanding environmental policy processes: Cases from Africa. Routledge, 2014.

Kitula, A. G. N. "The environmental and socio-economic impacts of mining on local livelihoods in Tanzania: A case study of Geita District." *Journal of cleaner production 14.3* (2006): 405-414.Lipinski,

Lipinski, Brian, *et al.* "Reducing food loss and waste." World Resources Institute Working Paper, June (2013).

Loomba, Ania. Colonialism/postcolonialism. Routledge, 2015.

Malhotra, Anita, et al. "A report on the status of the herpe to fauna of the Commonwealth of Dominica, West Indies." *Applied Herpetology 4.2* (2007): 177-194.

Manalo, Victor. "My Journey as a Social Work Professor." *Reflections: Narratives of Professional Helping* (Click on Current or Archives; Registration Optional) 20.4 (2015): 52-59.

Mapadimeng, Mokong Simon. "Culture versus religion: A theoretical analysis of the role of indigenous African culture of ubuntu in social change and economic development in the post-apartheid South African society." *Politics and religion 3* (2009): 75-98.

Mawere, M. & Mubaya, R. T. 2016. *African philosophy and thought systems: A search for a culture and philosophy of belonging*, Langaa Publishers: Bamenda.

Meager, David. "Slavery in Bible Times." (2006): 1-3.

249

Mhango, Nkwazi N., *Africa Reunite or Perish*. Langaa RPCIG, 2015.

Mhango, Nkwazi *Nkuzi*. *Africa's Best and Worst Presidents: How Neocolonialism and Imperialism Maintained Venal Rules in Africa*. Langaa RPCIG, 2016.

Mhango, Nkwazi. N. *'Global War on Terrorism' or Global War over Terra Africana? How Imperial Powers Seek to Colonise Africa Militarily*. (Forthcoming).

Nhemachena, Artwell. "The Notion of the "Field" and the Practices of Researching and Writing Africa: Towards Decolonial Praxis." *Africology: The Journal of Pan African Studies, vol.9*, no.7, September 2016.

Nunn, Nathan, and Diego Puga. "Ruggedness: The blessing of bad geography in Africa." *Review of Economics and Statistics 94.1* (2012): 20-36.

Nunn, Nathan, and Leonard Wantchekon. "The slave trade and the origins of mistrust in Africa." *The American Economic Review 101.7* (2011): 3221-3252.

Nunn, Nathan, and Leonard Wantchekon. "The slave trade and the origins of mistrust in Africa." Nunn, Nathan. The long-term effects of Africa's slave trades. No. w13367. National Bureau of Economic Research, 2007. *The American Economic Review 101.7* (2011): 3221-3252.

Office of the Surgeon General (US, and Centres for Disease Control and Prevention. "The Importance of Breastfeeding." (2011).

Petru, Simona. "Red, black or white? The dawn of colour symbolism." *Documenta Praehistorica 33* (2006): 203-208.

Phillips, Anne. "The concept of 'development'." *Review of African Political Economy 4.8* (1977): 7-20.

Rakotoarisoa, Manitra, Massimo Iafrate, and Marianna Paschali. Why has Africa become a net food importer. FAO, 2011.

Risiro, Joshua, et al. "Weather forecasting and indigenous knowledge systems in Chimanimani District of Manicaland, Zimbabwe." *Journal of Emerging Trends in Educational Research and Policy Studies 3.4* (2012): 561.

Shillington, Kevin. *History of Africa*. Palgrave Macmillan, 2012.

Thompson, Breanna. "llah and the A'bda: Islam and Slavery in the Americas" (2011) الإسلام و عبودية في الأمريكي.""

Tobin, Greg, and Robert J. Wister. Selecting the Pope: *Uncovering the mysteries of papal elections*. Sterling Publishing Company, Inc., 2009.

Toms, J. Steven. "Calculating profit: A historical perspective on the development of capitalism." *Accounting, Organizations and Society* 35.2 (2010): 205-221.

US Department of Health and Human Services. "The Surgeon General's call to action to support breastfeeding." (2011).

Vaughn, Rachel Ann. "Talking Trash: Oral Histories of Food In/Security from the Margins of a Dumpster." (2011).

Vaught, Seneca. "Illustrating Pedagogy of the Oppressed: A Freirean Approach to Teaching Marvel's Civil War." *Marvel Comics' Civil War and the Age of Terror: Critical Essays on the Comic Saga* (2015): 200.

Vidyarthi, Maulana Abdul Haq. The philosophy of colours in the Holy Quran. *The Light & Islamic Review: Vol.71; Nos. 4-6*; Jul-Dec 1995; p. 6-10, 4-6, 5-7).

Vreeland, James R. "IMF program compliance: Aggregate index versus policy specific research strategies." *The Review of International Organizations* 1.4 (2006): 359-378.

Waas, Tom, Aviel Verbruggen, and Tarah Wright. "University research for sustainable development: definition and characteristics explored." *Journal of cleaner production* 18.7 (2010): 629-636.

Whitford, David Mark. *The curse of Ham in the early modern era: The Bible and the justifications for slavery*. Ashgate Publishing, Ltd., 2009.

Wood, Marilee. "Interconnections: Glass beads and trade in southern and eastern Africa and the Indian Ocean-7th to 16th centuries AD." (2012).

World Bank. 2012. "Africa Can Feed Itself, Earn Billions, and Avoid Food Crises by Unblocking Regional Food Trade."

Wright, David P. "She Shall Not Go Free as Male Slaves Do": Developing Views About Slavery and Gender in the Laws of the Hebrew Bible." Beyond Slavery. Palgrave Macmillan US, 2010. 125-142.

Wüst, Andreas. "Vatican." *Elections in Europe*. Nomos Verlagsgesellschaft mbH & Co. KG, 2010.

Young, Robyn V., and Suzanne Sessine. 2000. *World of chemistry*. Farmington Hills: Gale Group.

Chapter Ten

Interfacing the Past and the Present: Traditional Leaders, Politics and Materialism in Zimbabwe since the Pre-colonial Period

Fidelis P.T. Duri

Introduction

African indigenous political philosophy in pre-colonial Zimbabwe viewed traditional leaders (chiefs, headmen/women and village heads) as selfless and altruistic community leaders, custodians of societal customs and values, whose primary role was to maintain law and order, and ensure peaceful coexistence within their areas of jurisdiction (Bourdillon, 1982; Crisis in Zimbabwe Coalition, 9 November 2010). While concerns have been raised in 21st century Zimbabwe that many traditional leaders, particularly the chiefs, have abrogated their traditional mandate and become political opportunists for purposes of accumulating material wealth (Crisis in Zimbabwe Coalition, 9 November 2010; Jakes, 10 March 2016; Madhuku, 28 August 2013; Mukwambo, 29 July 2011; Mwando, 4 June 2008; Nyakadzeya, 7 November 2013), this chapter contends that this trend has firm roots in pre-colonial times, persisted during the colonial era, and became entrenched after independence. Since the pre-colonial period, there has always been a nexus between political elevation and monopolistic tendencies such as unfettered access to material resources and accumulation of personal/ individual wealth by the aristocracy.

In pre-colonial Zimbabwe, traditional leaders had royal entitlements that enabled them to accumulate considerable wealth. The perks were higher for those in the upper echelons of power, particularly the chiefs. Traditional leaders owned vast tracts of land, parts of which they parcelled out to incomers in return for a fee (Bourdillon, 1982; Mudenge, 1988). They also obliged their subjects to work in their fields at given times (Beach, 1994; Holleman, 1951;

Lan, 1985). Court fees and fines were also part of their package (Holleman, 1951). They regulated mining and trading activities within their areas of jurisdiction and also extracted tribute and taxes from their subjects and incomers (Bhila, 1982; Garbett, 1966; Proctor and Phimister, 1991; Randles, 1981). Thus, in pre-colonial times, traditional leaders were relatively wealthy individuals who owned vast tracts of land, well-stocked granaries, large numbers of livestock, and reserves of ivory and minerals, among other such valuables (Bhebe, 1977; Mudenge, 1988; Proctor and Phimister, 1991).

The establishment of European colonial rule greatly disempowered African traditional leaders and severely threatened their material support base (Makumbe, 1998; Ranger, 2001). Many traditional leaders, particularly the chiefs, sought to maintain their political positions within the colonial administrative framework in order to exploit any emerging opportunities of accumulating wealth (Holleman, 1969; Kriger, 1992). The colonial package, which was disbursed on condition of loyalty, included allowances, stipulated court fees, and attire for special occasions (Blake, 1977; Bourdillon, 1982; Bratton, 1978; Holleman, 1969; Kriger, 1992). The fact that the incentives were higher depending on the number of taxpayers in one's area of jurisdiction meant that chiefs got much more than their administrative subordinates. Thus, most chiefs cooperated with the colonial administration in an endeavour to safeguard their material and other interests.

When Zimbabwe became independent in 1980, Robert Mugabe's Zimbabwe African National Union Patriotic Front (ZANU-PF) government disempowered traditional leaders after accusing them of collaborating with the colonial regime (Lan, 1985). From the late 1990s, however, the ZANU-PF government began to revive and valorise the institution of traditional leadership as it sought to restore its waning legitimacy owing to nationwide discontentment resulting from socio-economic hardships and the challenge posed by the opposition Movement for Democratic Change (MDC) (Phiri, 29 February 2016). From 2000, the ZANU-PF government privileged traditional leaders, mostly chiefs, with perks which included allowances, farms, houses, electricity, phones and vehicles (*Insider Zimbabwe*, 13 January 2005; Mataire, 15 April 2015; Phiri, 29 February

2016; *Zimbabwe Standard*, 24 November 2002). Many chiefs supported the ZANU-PF government (Jakes, 10 March 2016; Jena, 1 March 2015; Madhuku, 28 August 2013; Mwando, 4 June 2008) while considerable numbers of their administrative subordinates supported opposition parties (Gama, 19 April 2011; Gonda, 25 May 2006; Moyo, 25 October 2013) because of the considerable disparity in the perks they were offered. Thus, the political environment became polarised and unsustainable. While traditional leaders in post-independence Zimbabwe have been accused of abandoning their duties as prescribed by African indigenous political philosophical traditions in favour of political opportunism for purposes of self-aggrandisement, this chapter contends that this trend has a long history spanning back to the pre-colonial period.

The theoretical framework that largely guides this study is Karl Marx's Materialist Conception of History. This is a theory of economic determinism which argues that material/ economic conditions determine social relations and historical developments. Central to this Theory of Historical Materialism is the contention that historical developments evolve in a relatively predictable manner that corresponds to the prevailing material/ economic conditions, needs and demands (Cohen, 2000). In addition, the theory asserts that political power is an avenue sought by the upper classes to gain unfettered access to material/ economic resources (Cohen, 2000; Forster, 1999). Karl Marx's Materialist Conception of History is very relevant to this study in a number of ways. Firstly, it challenges historians and other scholars to investigate the material pursuits and tendencies of self-aggrandisement by various levels of the African traditional leadership since the pre-colonial period and the extent to which these authorities abrogated their roles as prescribed by African indigenous political philosophy. Secondly, the theory helps to account for the nature of relations between various levels of the African traditional political hierarchy and the governments of colonial and post-colonial Zimbabwe, which were indeed predictable depending on the varying amounts of material benefits that were availed to court their loyalty. Thirdly, by illuminating how political power is inextricably linked to the access to material resources, this theory helps to explain why leadership succession disputes continued

255

to occur within many African traditional political institutions even when chiefs, headmen/ women and village heads had been disempowered and relegated to mere figureheads at certain times during the colonial and post-colonial periods.

Material benefits of traditional leaders during the pre-colonial period

In pre-colonial Zimbabwe, where the Shona were the largest ethnic group, the chiefdom, with the chief as the highest political authority, was the biggest political unit. Chiefdoms were subdivided into well-defined territorial units called wards, comprising a number of villages, under the control of ward heads or headmen/women. The ward was subdivided into villages, each under the administration of a village head (Bhila, 1982; Bourdillon, 1982; Holleman, 1951).

Traditional leaders in pre-colonial Zimbabwe had numerous opportunities of accumulating personal wealth. Most chiefs and ward heads possessed expansive stretches of land, parts of which they allocated to their subjects and incomers in return for payment (Bourdillon, 1982). According to Father Conceicao, quoted by Mudenge (1988: 165), the rulers of the Mutapa Chiefdom, for example, had lands that stretched beyond "where eyes cannot see." Shona subjects were also required to work in the fields of chiefs or ward heads at given times during the year (Holleman, 1951). Some subjects who had worked in the fields of traditional leaders were rewarded with additional pieces of land (Lan, 1985). In the Mutapa Chiefdom, for example, the subjects worked in the fields of the chief for seven out of a total of every 23 working days (Beach, 1994).

Court fees provided traditional leaders with considerable income. It was customary in most Shona societies for two or more parties involved in a dispute who approached the chief's court for arbitration to pay a goat or two each for their case to be heard. After the arbitration, a satisfied complainant usually gave the chief one head of cattle (Holleman, 1951).

Traditional leaders in pre-colonial Zimbabwe also accrued considerable wealth from tribute that was paid by their subjects as an expression of loyalty. Game tribute surrendered to most Shona chiefs included elephant tusks, lion skins, pangolins (Holleman, 1951), leopard skins, hearts of lions, and the heads and front legs of certain wild animals (Garbett, 1966). Other forms of tribute given to chiefs included gold and livestock (Bhila, 1982). Ndebele chiefs obtained a broad range of goods through tribute which included firewood, grain (Bhebe, 1973), salt, skins, tobacco (Proctor and Phimister, 1991), iron ore, assegais and ostrich eggs (Storry, 1974). Rulers also accumulated many cattle from raiding neighbouring states. During the 18th century, the cattle belonging to Mutapa rulers were so many that some of them had to be loaned to vassal headmen as far away from the capital as 150 kilometres (Mudenge, 1988). Similarly, during the late 19th century, Ndebele rulers had many cattle, some of which they loaned to their Shona subjects (Bhebe, 1977).Thus, according to Proctor and Phimister (1991), the ruler was the wealthiest person in the Ndebele state.

Traditional political leaders controlled most of the economic activities within their areas of jurisdiction that enabled them to accumulate considerable wealth. Some pre-colonial Shona chiefs owned gold mines (Bhila, 1982). Since the 17th century, Rozvi chiefs had stockpiles of ivory and gold, most of which they obtained from tribute payments. They usually sent messengers to trading posts along the East African coast to market these commodities to foreign traders in return for cloth, beads and other goods (Bhila, 1982). In addition, pre-colonial Shona rulers taxed traders who operated, or passed through, their areas (Beach, 1980). In 1575, for example, Chief Chikanga of the Manyika Chiefdom in eastern Zimbabwe allowed the Portuguese to trade in his area on condition that they gave him 200 roles of cotton cloth per year (Ransford, 1968). During the 16th century, Mutapa rulers charged taxes ranging from 5% to 15% on commodities traded within the state by Muslim and Swahili traders (Beach, 1984). In the Mutapa State, every elephant hunter was required to surrender one tusk to the chief and this amounted to 50% tax on each elephant killed (Beach, 1994). In addition, all miners were obliged to cede to the chief 50% of the gold they had obtained (Beach, 1994; Randles, 1981). From the 1630s, it was common for Manyika rulers to demand one piece of cloth out of every bale of goods that Portuguese traders came to market in the chiefdom (Bhila, 1982). Pfete Goveranyika, the Manyika Chief from 1795, often demanded tribute in the form of clothes, glass and beads from Portuguese traders (Bhila, 1982).

It should be noted, therefore, that there were numerous opportunities of accumulating personal wealth for those who ascended to the high echelons of political power in pre-colonial Zimbabwe. In the pre-colonial dispensation, as noted above, the subjects were obliged to sustain the livelihoods of their rulers in various ways. In return, the rulers were expected to be the custodians of societal customs and values, whose basic mandate was to ensure law, order and mutual interaction among their subjects.

Material pursuits of traditional leaders during the colonial period

The Native Regulations of 1898 and the High Commissioner's Proclamation, Number 55, of 1910 authorised European Native Commissioners (NCs) to administer rural African communities while traditional leaders were relegated to colonial administrative auxiliaries (Holleman, 1969; Murray, 1970; Weinrich, 1971). The number of traditional leaders during the colonial period was not static owing to land annexations and subsequent dispersals of people which resulted in some chiefdoms being merged while new ones were sometimes constituted. In addition, some chiefs were either deposed or pensioned. The number of Shona chiefs who were officially recognised by the government stood at 150 in 1902, 271 in 1911, 323 in 1914, 330 in 1921 (Garbett, 1966) and 217 in 1965 (Palley, 1966).

The colonial government paid traditional leaders some allowances in order to court their loyalty and cooperation in various administrative tasks such as tax collection and labour recruitment. The amounts that they were paid varied according to the number of taxpayers in a given territory and the 'degree of loyalty' to the colonial government. With effect from December 1896, for example, Chief Mutasa was receiving £5 per month while his neighbours, Marange and Zimunya, were getting £3 each (NAZ, NUA2/1/1: NC Umtali to CNC, 21 December 1896; NAZ, S1428/32/5: NC Umtali's Quarterly Report, 14 October 1897). In July 1904, Chief Mutasa requested the colonial government to increase his subsidy on grounds that "his people have always been loyal..." and that "owing to much of the land being taken up by settlers and the natives therein having to pay rent to the landlord, he is now deprived of a great part of the tribute that was paid him in former years." In addition, "owing to the increase in the Hut Tax, his people will not be able to support him in the manner that chiefs have been supported" (NAZ, NUA2/1/5: NC Umtali to CNC, 19 July 1904).

On 23 January 1953, the Secretary of Native Affairs released a grading system that was to be used to pay the 192 substantive chiefs across the country. Grade A had nine chiefs with each receiving £144 per year. Included in this category were Chiefs Makoni and Mutasa. Chief Mangwende received an additional £36. Grade B had 18 chiefs with an annual subsidy of £108. Grade C had only one chief, Ndanga, who was paid an annual subsidy of £96 and an additional £24. Grade D had 37 chiefs who received £84 per year. Grade E had one chief, Mazvihwa of Shabani, who received £72 per annum. The other grades and respective annual subsidies are as follows: F (67 chiefs, £60), G (2 chiefs, £48), H (7 chiefs, £36), I (one chief, £33), J (one chief, £30), K (2 chiefs, £24), L (1 chief, £21), M (7 chiefs, £18), N (one chief, £16), O (4 chiefs, £15), P (13 chiefs, £12), Q (6 chiefs, £9), R (2 chiefs, £7.10.0d), S (7 chiefs, £6) and T (3 chiefs, £4). Grade U was for Acting Chiefs who numbered 15 with their annual subsidies ranging from £7.10.0d to £120. Grade V was for the 10 pensioned chiefs whose subsidies ranged between £3 and £18 per year (NAZ, S2583/542: Secretary of Native Affairs, List and Grades of Chiefs, 23 January 1953).

In 1956, the Secretary of Native Affairs announced a revised schedule of subsidies for the "more influential and progressive" traditional leaders that were to be paid "upon good behaviour and general fitness" (NAZ, S2583/542: Secretary of Native Affairs to NCs, 28 June 1956). A total of £13 312 was to be paid out annually to the 273 chiefs in the country. The amount was to be distributed as follows: 11 chiefs received £144 per year, one chief (£120), 18 chiefs (£108), 44 chiefs (£84), 70 chiefs (£60) and the rest (£12-£48). The colonial government also recognised 370 headmen who were paid a total of £4 884 per year with personal subsidies ranging from £4 to £24 per annum (NAZ, S2583/542: Secretary of Native Affairs to NCs, 28 June 1956).

Table 1: Subsidies for Chiefs, 10 May 1899

Chief	District	Subsidy per month
Gambiza	Charter	£4
Nyashanu	Charter	£3
Chilimanzi	Chilimanzi	£5
Hokonyo	Charter	10 shillings
Zimuto	Victoria	£5
Mutasa	Umtali	£5
Nenguwo	Marandellas	10 shillings
Makoni	Makoni	£5

Source: NAZ, N1/2/1: Chiefs and Tribes in Mashonaland and Salaries, 10 May 1899.

Table 2: Subsidies for Headmen, 26 January 1951

Number of Taxpayers	Headman's Subsidy per annum
Under 200	Up to £12
200-400	£12
401-600	£15
601 upwards	£18

Source: NAZ, S2583/542: Memorandum from Minister of Native Affairs, 26 January 1951.

Table 3: Subsidies for Chiefs, 1 July 1951

Grade	Number of Taxpayers	Annual Basic Pay	Personal Allowances
A	5001 and above	£144	£60
B	3001-5000	£108	£48
C	1501	£84	£36
D	400-1500	£60	£30

Source: NAZ, S2583/542: Executive Council Minute: Subsidies of Chiefs from 1 July 1951.

The statistics for 1963 show that Ndebele chiefs received higher salaries from the colonial government than their Shona counterparts. This was largely because most of the Ndebele chiefs were relatively younger and more educated. In 1963, the monthly mean for Ndebele chiefs was £21 as compared to £17 for their non-Ndebele counterparts (Garbett, 1966).

In addition to these financial benefits, traditional leaders often requested the colonial government to grant them other privileges. In February 1912, for instance, Headmen Saunyama, Mandeya, Chiobvu and Zindi from the Inyanga District applied for permits to carry muzzle-loading guns for their own protection (NAZ, NUC2/3/2: NC Inyanga to Superintendent of Natives, 8 February 1912).

The colonial government also stipulated token fees that traditional leaders could receive from their subjects. According to Section 5 of the Native Law and Courts Act of 1937, if a headman's court was officially registered as a Native Court, he was entitled to receive a hearing fee of five shillings for every case (Southern Rhodesia Government, Government Notice Number 108 of 1938). Prior to 1957, chiefs were allowed to charge African businessmen who intended to set up stores and butcheries in their areas an application fee of 20-30 shillings (Holleman, 1951). In a Government Circular to Native Commissioners dated 8 May 1957, chiefs were prohibited from charging fees to applicants for sites to set up premises such as shops and churches. Chiefs were, however, allowed to charge a maximum token fee of five shillings on an incomer who intended to settle in their areas. In addition, a chief was entitled to a customary fee not exceeding 5 shillings from a person who came to report a case at the traditional court (NAZ, S2583/542: Draft Circular to all NCs, 8 May 1957).

As African nationalism gained ground from the late 1950s, the colonial government sought the support of traditional leaders by providing them with an assortment of perks. In 1958, for example, the government organised an excursion by plane for some chiefs to Lake Kariba and the major cities in the country. During the same year, the chiefs were also invited to attend the opening of parliament after which they were taken on a tour of the University College of Rhodesia and Nyasaland. In 1962, the government also constituted the National Council of Chiefs in an attempt to bolster the image of chiefs. In 1964 and 1966, the government also took some chiefs on a world tour which included a visit to the South African Bantustans (Weinrich, 1971).

The salaries and allowances for chiefs and headmen were also increased in 1965, but backdated to 1 October 1964. The salary for 188 chiefs was pegged at £420 per year. The remaining 29 chiefs with a lesser following received a salary of £240 per annum. In addition, 54 chiefs each received personal allowances ranging from £6 to £240 per year (Palley, 1966).

The 1969 Constitution provided for a parliament made up of 26 members, 8 of whom were chiefs or their representatives, and a senate comprising 23 members, 10 of whom were chiefs or their representatives (Weinrich, 1971). During the period 1962-1972, the government provided chiefs with bodyguards and guns to ensure their security (Bratton, 1978). From 1976, the government also appointed some chiefs such as Jeremiah Chirau to the national cabinet (Kriger, 1992). In addition, the salaries of chiefs and headmen were also increased as shown in Table 4. As Kriger (1992: 74) noted, "...the average chief's salary, though small, exceeded the average earnings of black workers." In addition, chiefs and headmen were also eligible for personal allowances of up to $1 860 and $480 per annum respectively for working beyond the call of duty, and travel and subsistence allowances for attending meetings. From the early 1970s, a chief or a headman was given $3 for attending a meeting. If a traditional leader was elected as a Councillor, he was entitled to an additional $360 per year. If elected as the Chairperson of an African Council, he was also given an additional $600 per annum. From 1973, a chief who was a member of the Council of Chiefs was paid an additional $240 per year while the President of this body received another $480 per year. For taking part in a Provincial Council as elected, ex-officio, or co-opted member, a chief got a monthly allowance of up to $85 and another daily allowance of $6 for attending meetings. These earnings were hiked to $100 and $10 respectively just before Zimbabwe attained independence in April 1980 (Kriger, 1992).

Table 4: Basic Allowances for Chiefs and Headmen, July 1976- February 1980

	July 1976	February 1980
Chiefs with more than 500 followers	$1 620	$2 136
Chiefs with less than 500 followers	$960	$1 272
Headmen with more than 500 followers	$420	$552
Headmen with less than 500 followers	$120	----------

Source: Kriger, 1992

In addition, from the late 1950s, the government provided expensive dress which chiefs put on during special official occasions (Holleman, 1969). Despite the fact they were earning more than truck drivers, some of the most well-paid African workers, some 500 chiefs and senior headmen who assembled for a meeting with the colonial administration in Gwelo in May 1961 demanded that their salaries, allowances and other perks be increased (Holleman, 1969).

Most traditional leaders, particularly the highly-paid chiefs, therefore, supported the Rhodesian colonial administration "on which they depended on income and status" (Blake, 1977: 265). In 1959, for example, a delegation of chiefs petitioned the colonial government to ban meetings by the African National Congress, a nationalist movement, in the rural areas (Bratton, 1978; Kriger, 1992). In October 1964, the Domboshawa Indaba, attended by 622 chiefs and headmen, voted in favour of the colonial Rhodesian government's declaration of independence from Britain (Blake, 1977; Holleman, 1969). In fact, many Shona subjects as well as some headmen/ women and village heads came to believe that "the loyalty of their chiefs was directed away from their people towards their source of income" (Bourdillon (1982: 110). In 1959, in Inyanga District, for instance, Village Head Chekecheke beat up Chief Mupatsi after accusing him of collaborating with the colonial government. For the assault, Chekecheke was arrested and imprisoned by colonial officials (Nyaumwe, Interview, 3 August 1998).

This section has demonstrated that a considerable number of traditional leaders, mostly the chiefs, cooperated with the colonial government in order to salvage sustenance from the allowances and

263

other perks they received. Given that traditional leaders had been greatly disempowered by the colonial government resulting in them losing most of the material benefits they had received during the pre-colonial period, many of them had little option but to comply with the new dispensation in order to survive. This section has also illustrated that a significant number of chiefs cooperated with the colonial government as compared to their administrative subordinates owing to the relatively higher perks they received. To a great extent, such conditions greatly destabilised social relations within African communities, for example, when some traditional leaders were accused by their administrative subordinates and subjects for collaborating with the colonial regime, sometimes resulting in fierce clashes.

The disempowerment of traditional leaders from independence to the late 1990s

When Zimbabwe became independent in 1980, the ZANU-PF government disempowered traditional leaders after accusing them of collaborating with the colonial regime. Among other things, they were stripped of their jurisdiction on extra-judicial and administrative issues. Examples of pieces of legislation that stripped traditional leaders of most of their powers included the District Councils Act of 1980, Communal Lands Act of 1981 and 1982, the Customary and Primary Courts Act of 1981, the Provincial Councils and Administration Act of 1985, the Rural Districts Act of 1988, the Chiefs and Headmen Act of 1988, and the Customary Law and Courts Act of 1990 (Phiri, 29 February 2016).

Having been disempowered by various statutes and deprived of the perks they used to enjoy under the colonial government, some traditional leaders sought to extract material benefits from their subjects, unofficially though. A survey carried out by Edwin Runatsa in Masvingo Province in 1998, for example, noted that some chiefs were becoming too greedy and acquisitive as evidenced by their ruthless fining of poverty-stricken peasants for petty offences. An example of a case of ruthlessness was when, without informing the chief, a peasant cut a tree in the middle of his field that was disturbing his crops. The peasant was summoned to the traditional court and ordered to pay a goat first before approaching the chief after which he was fined another goat for the offence. There were also several instances when villagers were ordered to skin the goats at the court after which they handed over all the meat to the chief while they took away with them only the hides and the trotters (Runatsa, 1998).

From the late 1990s, the ZANU-PF government began to revive and valorise the institution of traditional leadership as it sought to restore its waning legitimacy owing to the nationwide discontentment as a result of the implementation of the Bretton Woods austerity measures since the early 1990s. In addition, the ZANU-PF government faced a considerable challenge from the opposition Movement for Democratic Change (MDC) which had been formed in 1999. Thus, the Traditional Leaders Act of 1998 was crafted with a view to empower traditional leaders and enable them to mobilise the rural electorate on behalf of the ruling ZANU-PF elite (Phiri, 29 February 2016). During the new millennium, as was the case during the colonial period, the ZANU-PF government privileged traditional leaders, particularly the chiefs, with hefty perks in order to court their support and use them to mobilise the rural electorate to fight off the challenge from opposition parties.

Material benefits offered to traditional leaders by the ZANU-PF government

From the year 2000, the ruling ZANU-PF government of President Robert Mugabe bought off many traditional leaders, mostly chiefs, with monthly allowances and wages that were above the minimum wage of an average civil servant employee, farms, farm machinery, generators, electricity, houses, mobile phones, vehicles and fuel, among other things (Phiri, 29 February 2016). As far as post-colonial statistics are concerned, in February 2005, for example, there were 268 chiefs in Zimbabwe, 91 of who were in acting capacities (Mugari, 18 February 2005). In March 2013, there were 227 substantive chiefs in the country (Saunyama, 10 March 2013). By August 2015, Zimbabwe had 277 substantive chiefs, 1 300 headmen (of which 400 were recognised by the government while the rest

265

operated informally), and up to 80 000 village heads (Cross, 24 August 2015).

By November 2002, the government had electrified the homes of 142 chiefs (*Zimbabwe Standard*, 24 November 2002). In November 2002, the government announced that it would increase the monthly allowances of chiefs from Z$18 000 to Z$20 000 while those of their aides would be hiked from Z$2 000 to Z$8 000 (*Zimbabwe Standard*, 24 November 2002).

During early October 2004, the ZANU-PF government bought scotch-carts and ox-drawn ploughs worth millions of dollars for chiefs and headmen (MDC Information and Publicity Department, 29 October 2004). On 25 October 2004, Ignatius Chombo, the Minister of Local Government, handed out luxury double-cab Mazda vehicles to 48 chiefs (MDC Information and Publicity Department, 29 October 2004). In February 2005, President Robert Mugabe launched a scheme to provide 177 chiefs out of the country's total of 268 with Mazda B1800 pick-up trucks in addition to the Z$1.3 million monthly allowance they were receiving (Mugari, 18 February 2005). During the run-up to the 29 March 2008 general and presidential elections, more than 100 chiefs were given all-terrain vehicles by the ZANU-PF government (Mwando, 4 June 2008).

In January 2005, a substantive chief was receiving a monthly allowance of Z$1 million while a headman got Z$40 000 (*Insider Zimbabwe*, 13 January 2005). By July 2007, a chief was getting a monthly allowance of Z$2 million from the government while a headman received Z$1 million (Marwezu, 25 July 2007). During the same month, the ZANU-PF government stopped paying allowances to traditional leaders whom it accused of supporting the MDC. For this reason, the allowances of Headman Ziki of Bikita District, and Headmen Masivamele and Sengwe from Chiredzi District were withdrawn (Marwezu, 25 July 2007).

In October 2010, the ZANU-PF government increased the monthly allowances of substantive chiefs from US$200 to US$300 per month, which far exceeded the monthly salary of most civil servants, in addition to other perks and the fines they levied on their subjects. These increments took place at a time when civil servants had been advised by the government that their salaries would not be increased any time soon due to cash flow challenges (*Zimbabwe Daily*, 10 October 2010). In March 2013, the monthly allowances were US$300 for chiefs, US$140 for headmen and US$20 for village heads (Saunyama, 10 March 2013). In May 2016, the government monthly allowances for chiefs were still pegged at US$300 (Ncube, 17 May 2016).

During a meeting of the Chiefs' Council held in early March 2012, most chiefs declared that the 88-year-old President Robert Mugabe should continue to rule Zimbabwe. They went on to request the government to provide them with firearms as a security measure against attacks by opposition supporters. They also pleaded with the ZANU-PF government for more privileges such as diplomatic passports, new vehicles, and exemptions from paying toll gate fees on the country's highways (Nyathi, 8 March 2012). In April 2015, chiefs were exempted from paying toll gate fees (Mataire, 15 April 2015).

Despite these exorbitant perks in a virtually bankrupt country, pro-ZANU-PF chiefs actually bargained for more. At a Chiefs' Council meeting held in Harare in mid-May 2016, the chiefs demanded some more benefits from the government which included duty-free imports of motor vehicles once every three years, access to land of their own choice ahead of their subjects, an increase in their monthly allowances, new vehicles, and government-funded medical aid cover (Ncube, 17 May 2016).

The substantial material benefits which many traditional leaders, mostly the substantive chiefs, received made a considerable number of them to support the ZANU-PF government for the same reasons that they had supported the colonial administration. During a rally held at Nata Business Centre in Matebeleland South Province in mid-September 2011, for example, the local chief advised villagers to support ZANU-PF. He begged his subjects to vote for ZANU-PF because he did not want to lose the vehicle that the ruling party had given him and other benefits, such as monthly allowances (Sithole, 15 September 2011).

Materialism and political polarisation among traditional leaders in 21ˢᵗ century Zimbabwe

Since independence in 1980, Zimbabwean law forbade traditional leaders from taking part in politics. Chapter 15, Section 281(2) of the Zimbabwean Constitution of 2013, for example, stipulates that traditional leaders should not be members of a political party or participate in partisan politics (Jena, 1 March 2015; *Newsday*, 29 March 2015; Nyakadzeya, 7 November 2013). Section 282 obliges traditional leaders to promote cultural values; preserve culture, tradition, history and heritage of their communities; facilitate development; resolve disputes among their people; administer communal lands; and protect the environment (Nyakadzeya, 7 November 2013).

Many traditional leaders participated in partisan politics despite the practice being forbidden under Zimbabwean law. This is largely because of the desire by traditional leaders to seek sustenance from the material benefits availed by rival political parties. In addition, the rival political parties themselves, including the ruling ZANU-PF party, always dangled a broad range of material benefits as bait to lure traditional leaders in order to win their support and that of their subjects. In such a polarised political landscape, the ruling ZANU-PF party, being in control of state resources, had an advantage since it had more to offer in order to lure traditional leaders. This contestation for political space culminated in an unsustainable political environment in 21ˢᵗ century Zimbabwe as traditional leaders sometimes clashed among themselves and with their subjects because of their different political affiliations. Again, more chiefs, being recipients of substantial government benefits, tended to align with the ruling ZANU-PF party while a significant number of their subordinates, such as headmen and village heads, sided with opposition parties because of the relatively lower perks they received.

In reciprocation to the monthly allowances and other incentives they received from the ruling party, considerable numbers of traditional leaders, chiefs in particular, openly rendered unconditional support for ZANU-PF (Phiri, 29 February 2016). In late February 2015, Chief Fortune Charumbira, the President of the Chiefs'

268

Council, for example, admitted that most chiefs in Zimbabwe supported ZANU-PF because of its "attractiveness." He continued:

> No intelligent person cannot seek traditional and church leaders' support in an election. It is unfortunate or fortunate that the attractiveness of ZANU-PF in politics carries the day…ZANU-PF appeals to most of us because of their fight to bring back what we had lost during the colonial rule, where chiefs were stripped of their power and rendered ordinary citizens (Jena, 1 March 2015: 1).

Addressing thousands of ZANU-PF supporters who attended a rally at Dema Growth Point on 27 May 2015, Stanley Chimanikire, Chief Seke, said:

> Let us support ZANU-PF and its leader, President Mugabe. I know some will say that chiefs must not be political, but with me it is different. Let me tell you the people of Seke that if you do not support Mugabe, living in harmony with me will be difficult (*Newsday*, 29 May 2015: 1).

Some chiefs openly campaigned for ZANU-PF during the run-up to elections. In February 2005, civil organisations such as the Bulawayo Agenda and the Zimbabwe Election Support Network (ZESN) expressed concern at the role of chiefs in perpetrating political violence ahead of the 31 March presidential and parliamentary elections. In the Gwanda and Beitbridge Parliamentary Constituencies, for example, they noted that some traditional leaders were influencing their subjects to vote for the ruling ZANU-PF party and threatening them that the use of translucent ballot boxes would enable the authorities to trace every vote cast (*Irin News*, 22 February 2005).

In October 2006, Chief Nyika, from Mhondoro-Ngezi District, summoned Sylvester Matizanadzo, an MDC-T activist, to his traditional court to answer charges of contesting Ward 6 Rural District Council elections in the area against a ZANU-PF candidate. The chief had directed that Matizanadzo should not contest the elections in order to pave way for the ZANU-PF candidate. When

Matizanadzo refused, the chief summoned him to his traditional court to answer charges of insubordination. With the assistance of MDC-T lawyers, Matizanadzo wrote to the chief advising him that a traditional court had no jurisdiction over political issues (Sibanda, 9 November 2016).

At ZANU-PF's annual conference in December 2008, Chief Fortune Charumbira stated that President Robert Mugabe should die in power as was the case with traditional political leaders. In August 2009, Charumbira called on all chiefs in the Chiredzi District to support ZANU-PF (*Zimbabwe Online Press*, 13 August 2009).

During late November 2010, in the Chimanimani District, Chief Saurombe, a known ZANU-PF supporter, forced his subjects to attend a ZANU-PF rally. He also forced villagers to buy the party's membership cards (*Zimbabwe Daily*, 13 December 2010).

On 25 May 2012, Chief Masunda of Bulilima District expressed open support of the ZANU-PF National Chairman, Simon Khaya Moyo, in his bid to contest the Senate seat in the area. Masunda declared that traditional leaders like him should be identified with ZANU-PF because they shared the same ideology of development (*Newsday*, 29 May 2012). In December 2012, Chief Dotito of Mount Darwin District, together with a group of war veterans, reportedly terrorised villagers to vote for ZANU-PF in the forthcoming 2013 general elections (Chidende, 23 December 2012).

On 25 July 2013, in Hoya Village in Muzarabani District, Chief Kasekete ordered Joe Bumhira, one of his headmen, to summon villagers for a meeting to arrange campaigning for ZANU-PF. The chief threatened to evict all non-ZANU-PF supporters from the area. He went on to give the villagers three days to join ZANU-PF or face eviction (Heal Zimbabwe Trust, 25 July 2013).

In Chipinge District during the national harmonised elections of 31 July 2013, some traditional leaders openly pressured their subjects to vote for ZANU-PF. At Chinyamukwakwa Polling Station in Ward 28, for example, Headman Chinyamukwakwa, a well-known ZANU-PF supporter, spent the whole day at the polling station checking on how many of his subjects had come to vote. At Chitepo Primary School Polling Station, Headmen James Mbendana and Mike Jambaya, both ZANU-PF activists, were caught organising villagers to vote. At Mutandahwe Polling Station, Village Head Vengayi Mushawa divided his subjects into groups of 10 and then made sure that they used that pattern to vote (Madhuku, 28 August 2013). This strategy "convinced the subjects that their vote would be detected and had to vote for ZANU-PF" (Madhuku, 28 August 2013: 1).

Some traditional leaders were reported to be openly campaigning for ZANU-PF by, among other things, intimidating their subjects, ahead of the parliamentary by-elections that were to be held in 14 constituencies on 10 June 2015. On 7 April 2015, in the Tsholotsho Parliamentary Constituency, for example, Chief Mathupula summoned Headmen Mahlaba, Meetshwa and Mlevu and ordered them to ensure that ZANU-PF would emerge victorious. He threatened them with unspecified action if Jonathan Moyo, the ZANU-PF candidate, lost the by-election (Nkala, 13 April 2015).

In February 2016, Gorden Moyo, the Secretary-General of the opposition People's Democratic Party (PDP), accused some traditional leaders of campaigning for the ruling ZANU-PF party in a way that imperilled the credibility of Zimbabwe's electoral landscape. He lamented:

> Traditional authorities such as chiefs, headmen or women and village heads have been deployed to police villagers; campaign for ZANU-PF candidates; shunt villagers to vote according to their village arrangements, thereby violating the sanctity of the ballot; cajole suspected opposition members to pretend to be illiterate so as to be assisted to vote for ZANU-PF; unleash terror to the defiant voters...In this way, chiefs act as auxiliaries of the ruling elite...Just as the colonial governments used the patron-client strategy to corrupt the chiefs, the Mugabe regime bought the loyalty of chiefs through the provisioning of personal benefits...Some of these cultural giants have been punished, some de-stooled and some deprived of chiefly privileges while others have been humiliated for refusing to sell their souls...These are the chiefs with the pedigree required to take Zimbabwe back onto the track (Phiri, 29 February 2016: 1).

Some traditional leaders, mostly chiefs, penalised their subjects for supporting opposition political parties. During the 2000 and 2002 legislative and presidential elections, Reginald Matshaba-Hove, the Chairman of the ZESN, noted that the penalties imposed by most chiefs on their subjects who supported opposition parties included "expulsion from the village, physical violence, withdrawal from the local food aid register, or all of them combined" (*Irin News*, 22 February 2005: 1).

In November 2002, Chief Makumbe of Buhera District in Manicaland Province barred food aid from donor organisations such as Christian Care from being distributed to his starving subjects on grounds that it had been sourced from the friends of Morgan Tsvangirai, the MDC President. He said:

> I do not want any food from the people who are sponsoring Tsvangirai to oust our legitimate leader, Mugabe. Proceed to other districts. Here, in my district, I do not need anything from you. I will assist my people (*Zimbabwe Standard*, 24 November 2002: 1).

On 27 July 2011, seven MDC-T supporters from Mutsamvu Village in Chimanimani District took refuge in the mountains after being expelled from their homes by Timothy Madzianike, a ZANU-PF activist and local chief. The seven had, in March 2016, been assaulted by ZANU-PF activists in the area whom they reported to the police. Chief Madzianike then accused the seven MDC-T activists for insubordination by making a report to the police before approaching his court. For this 'offence', the chief fined each one of them US$30 and ordered them to leave his area immediately (Mukwambo, 29 July 2011). Mary Kuretu, one of the victims, narrated their ordeal at the hands of Chief Madzianike:

> Headman Madzianike summoned us to his court...and accused us of reporting ZANU-PF officials and war veterans to the police without first seeking his permission. As punishment, we have been asked to pay US$30 each and leave the area with immediate effect. The headman said he does not want MDC supporters in the area...We slept in the bush (Mukwambo, 29 July 2011: 1).

Pro-ZANU-PF chiefs sometimes penalised their administrative subordinates such as headmen and village heads for supporting opposition parties, particularly the MDC. On 20 May 2006, for instance, Chief Mutambara of Chimanimani District fined his two village headmen, Vhaisai Munjoma and Fabion Musukutwa, five head of cattle each for supporting the MDC. The two headmen were accused of attending an MDC rally that had been held in the city of Mutare the previous month (Gonda, 25 May 2006).

In mid-December 2010, Chief Saurombe of Chimanimani District summoned Donald Sithole, the head of Zhombeni Village, to his traditional court to answer charges of putting up MDC posters calling for a meeting. During the court proceedings, Chief Saurombe made it clear that the MDC-T was not welcome in his area and anyone found campaigning for the party was going to be punished. Sithole was fined one head of cattle which he was ordered to surrender to Chief Saurombe within two weeks (*Zimbabwe Daily*, 13 December 2010).

Chiefs who were loyal to ZANU-PF often ousted their headmen and village heads for supporting opposition parties. In September 2012, for example, Victor Saunyama, the Acting Chief Saunyama in Nyanga District, deposed three headmen: Chifodya Katerere, Didymus Nyamahomba and Alfred Mukombedzi, for supporting the MDC. He went on to replace them with ZANU-PF supporters (Mambo, 28 September 2012).

In October 2013, Chief Pashu of Binga District in Matebeleland North Province deposed the headmen in charge of the villages of Kabuba, Musazi, Muchuuza, Gwangwa River and Nakaluba for supporting the MDC. In the same district, during the same year, Chief Saba also fired the headmen of the villages of Saba, Pashu and Dubola on similar charges (Moyo, 25 October 2013). During the same month, in Masvingo Province, Chief Matubede Mugabe suspended Headman Rangarirai Magunzwa, of Magunzwa village, for supporting the MDC (Moyo, 25 October 2013). In Mudzi North District, during October 2013, Chief Mkota Manhando ousted Headman Claudious Nyamudandara, an opposition supporter, and replaced him with Pascal Chimbweza, a ZANU-PF youth activist. In the same district, Manhando also deposed Headmen Naison Kurima and Tiki Munyonga and replaced them with ZANU-PF apologists (Moyo, 25 October 2013).

On 10 June 2015, in Manicaland Province, Chief Mutasa fired Romberai Medzani, Headman Mandeya 1, after accusing him of supporting the MDC and immediately replaced him by Philemon Medzani, a ZANU-PF activist (Masekesa, 16 June 2015). On 18 January 2016, at Kebvunde Township in Mashonaland West Province, Chief Nematomborefused to have Samuel Zeburoni installed as a Village Headman on grounds that he was an MDC supporter. When Zeburoni appealed to the District Administrator, he was informed that his installation could only go ahead with the approval of Chief Nematombo (Jakes, 10 March 2016).

Traditional leaders were sometimes used by ZANU-PF as conduits of violence in Zimbabwean politics. According to the Crisis in Zimbabwe Coalition (9 November 2010: 1), many traditional leaders in Zimbabwe became "political party activists." In several instances, chiefs became "affiliates and at times touts of the ruling (ZANU-PF) party" (Nyakadzeya, 7 November 2013: 1). In early 2008, Chief Kasekete of Muzarabani District in Mashonaland Central Province called for the murder of villagers who did not support ZANU-PF. By 6 May 2008, eight villagers had been killed, reportedly as a result of the instruction. In June 2008, 22 people were murdered in Muzarabani District while 125 were displaced (Crisis in Zimbabwe Coalition, 9 November 2010). In November 2010, Chief Rukweza from Makoni District in Manicaland Province sent a gang of thugs to beat up Enia Chiwara, an MDC activist, for refusing to buy a ZANU-PF membership card (Sibanda, 4 November 2010).

While many chiefs supported the ruling ZANU-PF party because of the high perks they received, several disgruntled headmen/women and village heads supported opposition parties. In February 2008, Headman Joseph Rimbi, under Chief Musikavanhu, in Chipinge District became "the first traditional (leader) to (openly) break ranks with ZANU-PF" when he successfully filed his nomination papers to contest as an MDC senatorial candidate for Chipinge in the elections that were to be held later during the year (Sibanda, 21 February 2008: 1). Headman Rimbi went on to win the senatorial seat which he held until 24 September 2012 when he died of diabetes at the age of 73 years (*Newsday*, 25 September 2012).

During the run-up to the 2008 presidential and parliamentary elections, Phineas Makore, the heir apparent to the Makore headmanship in Gutu District, openly supported the MDC and distributed the party's regalia throughout the district. He was admitted to hospital after being severely flogged by a group of ZANU-PF war veterans (*All Africa*, 5 November 2015). In November 2015, Makore, declared that he was an MDC supporter but stated that he was living in fear as a result of threats from ZANU-PF supporters. Since the year 2000, Makore had been an MDC activist who provided food and shelter to the party's supporters in Gutu District who had been displaced by politically-motivated violence (*All Africa*, 5 November 2015). He openly declared his support for the MDC when he said: "I am not afraid. I have been working for the party (MDC) for years now. This is a free country and every individual- a chief or no chief- has a right to support any political party of his choice" (*All Africa*, 5 November 2015: 1).

In 2011, Rwisai Nyakauru, an 82-year-old Village Head from Nyamaropa Communal Land in Nyanga District, openly declared his support for the opposition MDC party. On 14 February 2011, he was arrested, imprisoned and tortured by ZANU-PF militia and war veterans for supporting the MDC (*Nehanda Radio*, 24 March 2011). He was incarcerated for 25 days and died on 16 April 2011 as a result of the injuries he sustained from being tortured while in detention (Gama, 19 April 2011; *Newsday*, 25 May 2011).

In March 2015, some headmen in Hurungwe West Parliamentary Constituency openly declared their support for Themba Mliswa, an independent candidate and former ZANU-PF Member of Parliament, ahead of the by-elections that were to be held on 10 June during the same year. In late April 2015, six headmen who were known to be supporters of Mliswa were beaten up by ZANU-PF youths at a campaign rally held in the constituency (Jena, 10 May 2015).

This section has illuminated how, from the year 2000, Zimbabwe's political landscape became highly polarised and tension-ridden with traditional leaders aggravating the situation by siding with rival political parties in order to salvage material benefits, among other things. Political instability is one of the major stumbling blocks to sustainable development. Political violence, for instance, derails community and national development programmes in a number of ways. These include destroying the unity of purpose that is vital for development, erosion of investor confidence and the flight of skilled manpower. As the next section demonstrates, traditional leaders should desist from participating in partisan politics and ensure peace and harmony among their subjects in order to create a conducive environment for development in various aspects of life.

The way forward: Traditional leaders as agents of development and mediators in political violence

Traditional leaders in Zimbabwe should desist from political opportunism driven by selfish desires to accumulate personal wealth. They need to preach peace in their areas of jurisdiction and impartially mediate in cases of political disputes involving their subjects. In addition, as the Zimbabwean Constitution emphasises, traditional leaders should spearhead development in their communities. As a few examples below illustrate, some traditional leaders contributed significantly in this regard.

In July 2009, for example, a headman in Chipinge District mediated in a case of political violence involving his subjects. The case involved Maurice Mazungunye, a war veteran and ZANU-PF supporter, who had confiscated three goats and two buckets of maize from Pedzisai Chitiyo, an MDC activist. The headman convened a court hearing at his village during which he ordered Mazungunye to return the goats and the maize to Chitiyo. Mazungunye reported the headman to ZANU-PF officials in the town of Chipinge. The ZANU-PF officials instructed the headman to stop handling cases involving politics and threatened him with unspecified action. These threats forced the headman to flee to the city of Bulawayo in August 2009 (*Zimbabwe Online Press*, 13 August 2009). This case illustrates how some traditional leaders were criminalised by the ruling party for their efforts to be apolitical.

Some traditional leaders openly condemned political violence and urged their subjects to unite in order to develop their communities. Addressing more than 500 villagers who had gathered at Muwoni Business Centre on 14 November 2010 to mark the International Day of Peace, Chief Chaka of Chirumanzu District said:

> I am not aligned to any political party. I want to unite people to live in peace, exchange ideas on what to do to stir development forward. Let us be in the papers for good reasons not violence...People should be free to live in harmony. I have said to people, particularly the youths in my area, if I hear that you have burnt a house or that you have beaten other people because of politics, then you have to depart from my area. As leaders of constituencies, we urge people to live in peace so that there could be development. Without peace, there is no development (Marevererwi, 18 November 2010: 1).

In February 2011, Henry Chidzivo, the Chireya Paramount Chief of Gokwe District, convened a meeting of his subjects at his homestead at Madzivadondo Village, which was attended by 300 men and 400 women, to advise people against political violence. The meeting was also attended by Chief Chireya's headmen such as Mashomi, Nembudziya, Goredema, Makore and Gumunyu. Part of Chief Chireya's speech read:

> Peace begins with me, peace begins with you and peace ends with us...Lives were lost here in Madzivadondo and blood was spilled that angered our spirit mediums and that should never be repeated. We say this because we are chiefs and chiefs have a duty to protect their people... (Musodza, 17 February 2011: 1).

Headman Nembudziya, who was also part of the gathering, reiterated:

> Be warned, politics does not mean violence. Even those politicians who send you to beat each other will never admit telling you to kill each other...If you kill someone, you will face the wrath of the law and probably go to jail. That will not stop chiefs from charging you or your

relatives for that offence. If you think it will not happen, take part in violence next time and you will see...Taking part in violence next time will mean you have plenty of cattle and goats to pay the price. If you are poor and do not have any livestock, do not dare participate in violence (Musodza, 17 February 2011: 1).

In June 2013, Joel Nyarume, Chief Musana of Mashonaland Central Province, urged his subjects to desist from political violence ahead of the 31 July harmonised elections. His appeal followed the burning down of a homestead belonging to Anatolia Ruondoka, the ZANU-PF Chairperson for Rutope District on 17 June 2013, reportedly by MDC activists. He said, "I want to urge all political parties to shun violence. Parties should encourage their supporters to campaign peacefully" (Matambanadzo, 24 June 2013: 1).

In early November 2013, Chief Gilbert Marange of Mutare District in Manicaland Province emphasised the role of chiefs in ensuring unity, peace and development among their people: "Partisanship serves to create disharmony and if I, as a chief, practise that, then my people will not unite, yet I need them to unite for progress and development to occur" (Nyakadzeya, 7 November 2013: 1).

Traditional leaders can indeed be instrumental in mediating cases of political violence, promoting peace, and spearheading development in their areas of jurisdiction. For them to achieve this end, they should condemn political opportunism motivated by self-aggrandisement and avoid getting involved in partisan politics. As the few examples given in this section illustrate, they need to be advocates of peace and proponents of development in their communities. Lamentably, as shown in this section, those traditional leaders who condemned political violence and sought to impartially arbitrate in political conflicts involving their subjects were often victimised by the ruling ZANU-PF party.

Conclusion

This chapter has presented a materialist analysis of politics and political dynamics in history. It has articulated how political power was closely linked to economic determinism and material wealth since the pre-colonial period. The chapter has identified the pursuit of material wealth as a continuous thread that links the aspirations and operations of traditional leaders in Zimbabwean history since pre-colonial times.

In pre-colonial Zimbabwe, as this chapter has shown, traditional leaders had numerous entitlements that enabled them to accumulate considerable personal wealth. They owned large pieces of land, parts of which they sold out to their subjects and incomers. They also obliged their subjects to work in their fields on a regular basis. In addition, they possessed many cattle, some of which they loaned out to their people. Traditional leaders also controlled various commercial activities in their areas of jurisdiction and extracted tribute and taxes from their subjects and incomers. Thus, material possession by traditional leaders symbolised political power in pre-colonial Zimbabwe. It should be noted, however, that pre-colonial traditional leaders had an ethical responsibility to redistribute or loan out part of their wealth, particularly grain, livestock and land, to their disadvantaged subjects.

With the establishment of colonial rule from the late 19ᵗʰ century, the disempowerment of African traditional leaders severely eroded their opportunities of accumulating personal wealth to the extent of jeopardising their livelihoods. Given this predicament, considerable numbers of traditional leaders, particularly the chiefs, cooperated with the colonial government in order to salvage sustenance from the material benefits they were given on condition of loyalty. The fact that the colonial government paid out material benefits to loyal traditional leaders depending on the number of taxpayers in their areas meant that chiefs earned much more than their administrative subordinates. As a result, many chiefs cooperated with the colonial administration than several of their headmen/ women and village heads. These varied responses demonstrate that economic/ material considerations can be powerful variables that determine the political decisions that people make.

The collaboration of many traditional leaders, mostly the chiefs, with the colonial government illustrates their agency, determination and contingency to exploit prevailing and emerging political dispensations to their advantage in order to eke livelihoods. These developments, however, created tension between many chiefs on one hand, and some of their subjects and administrative subordinates, as well as African nationalists on the other. Social relations were severely compromised as many quarters questioned whether their chiefs were genuine community leaders or colonial government functionaries (Garbett, 1966).

As this chapter has shown, political opportunism by many traditional leaders for purposes of self-aggrandisement, among other things, continued into the post-colonial period. From the year 2000, many traditional leaders, particularly the chiefs, supported ZANU-PF because it had begun empowering them through the Traditional Leaders' Act of 1998 and that, as the ruling party that controlled state finances, it afforded to splash substantial perks for them. Several chiefs were therefore labelled as ZANU-PF trump cards (Mwando, 4 June 2008) and auxiliaries (Phiri, 29 February 2016). As many chiefs were castigated for supporting ZANU-PF because of the substantial benefits they received, several of their disgruntled headmen/ women and village heads sought material and other fortunes by aligning themselves with opposition political parties. Thus, some analysts regarded many traditional leaders in 21st century Zimbabwe as hypocrites who had abrogated their traditional mandate for political expediency in order to accumulate personal wealth (Crisis in Zimbabwe Coalition, 9 November 2010).

This chapter has demonstrated that, during the colonial and post-independence periods, traditional leaders were not stooges of prevailing political dispensations. Their taking sides with certain political institutions or structures, whether covert or overt, at given times during the colonial and post-colonial periods should be understood in the context of agential participation in order to earn livelihoods. It therefore becomes apparent that, in Zimbabwean history since the pre-colonial period, politics has been a theatre of economic pursuits and material contestations. Regrettably, political opportunism by some traditional leaders for purposes of meeting their personal material and other needs greatly contributed in creating an unsustainable environment for development in various ways. As many traditional leaders and some of their subjects became polarised along political lines, tension and violence often characterised relations within communities and the unity of purpose that is one of the cornerstones of development was severely undermined. Among other things, political violence played a significant role in chasing away investors and skilled manpower. There is no doubt that traditional leaders can be important stakeholders in development if, as the Zimbabwean Constitution stipulates, they desist from participating in partisan politics and ensure peace and harmony among their subjects.

References

All Africa, 5 November 2015. 'Zimbabwe: War veterans harass MDC-T supporting chief, demand his eviction from farm,' Available at: www.allafrica.com, Accessed 8 June 2016.

Bhebe, N. 1973. 'Some aspects of Ndebele relations with the Shona in the 19th century,' in: *Rhodesian History*, Volume 4, pp.31-39.

Bhebe, N. 1977. *Lobengula*, Harare: Zimbabwe Educational Books.

Beach, D. N. 1980. *The Shona and Zimbabwe, 900-1850: An outline of Shona history*, London: Heinemann.

Beach, D.N. 1984, *Zimbabwe before 1900*, Gweru: Mambo Press.

Beach, D.N. 1994. *The Shona and their neighbours*, Oxford: Blackwell.

Bhila, H. H. K. 1982. *Trade and politics in a Shona kingdom: The Manyika and their Portuguese and African neighbours, 1575-1902*, Essex: Longman.

Blake, R. 1977. *A history of Rhodesia*, London: Eyre Methuen.

Bourdillon, M.F.C. 1982. *The Shona peoples: An ethnography of the contemporary Shona, with particular reference to their religion*, Gweru: Mambo Press.

Bratton, M. 1978. *From Rhodesia to Zimbabwe: Beyond community development: The political economy of rural administration in Zimbabwe*, Gwelo: Mambo Press.

Chidende, D. 23 October 2012. 'Mount Darwin villagers terrorised,' in: *The Daily News*, Harare: Zimbabwe.

Cohen, G.A. 2000. *Karl Marx's theory of history: A defence*, Princeton: Princeton University Press.

Crisis in Zimbabwe Coalition, 9 November 2010. 'Zimbabwe chiefs must stop the hypocrisy,' Available at: www.nehandaradio.com, Accessed 7 June 2016.

Cross, E. 25 August 2015. 'Traditional leaders,' Available at: www.thezimbabwean.co, Accessed 8 June 2016.

Forster, J.B. 1999. *Marx's ecology: Materialism and nature*, London: Monthly Review Press.

Gama, L. 19 April 2011. '82-year-old headman dies after ZANU-PF torture,' Available at www.nehandaradio.com, Accessed 17 June 2016.

Garbett, G.K. 1966. 'The Rhodesian chief's dilemma: Government officer or tribal leader?' in: *Race*, Number 2, pp.113-129.

Gonda, V. 25 May 2006. 'Headman fined for supporting the MDC,' Available at: www.thezimbabwean.co, Accessed 8 June 2016.

Heal Zimbabwe Trust, 25 July 2013. 'Community updates on the general political environment: Muzarabani South,' Available at: www.archive.kubatana.net, Accessed 8 June 2016.

Holleman, J.F. 1951. 'Some Shona tribes in Southern Rhodesia,' in: E. Colson and M. Gluckman (eds.) *Seven tribes of British Central Africa*, London: Oxford University Press.

Holleman, J.F. 1969. *Chief, council and commissioner: Some problems of government in Rhodesia*, London: Oxford University Press.

Insider Zimbabwe, 13 January 2005. 'Headmen grumble over allowances,' Available at: www.insiderzimbabwe.com, Accessed 9 June 2016.

Irin News, 22 February 2005. 'Zimbabwe: Political violence could keep voters away, say rights groups,' Available at: www.reliefweb.int, Accessed 8 June 2016.

Jakes, S. 10 March 2016. 'Chief stops installation of headman because he is MDC-T supporter,' Available at: www.bulawayo24.com, Accessed 17 June 2016.

Jena, N. 1 March 2015. 'We do not regret supporting ZANU-PF: Charumbira,' Available at: www.thestandard.co.zw, Accessed 8 June 2016.

Jena, N. 10 May 2015. 'Chief Charumbira moves to protect traditional leaders,' in: *The Standard*, Harare: Zimbabwe.

Kriger, N. 1992. *Zimbabwe's guerrilla war: Peasant voices*, Cambridge: Cambridge University Press.

Lan, D. 1985. *Guns and rain: Guerrillas and spirit mediums in Zimbabwe*, Harare: Zimbabwe Publishing House.

Madhuku, T. 28 August 2013. 'Traditional leaders implicated in ZANU-PF rigging scheme,' Available at: www.nehandaradio.com, Accessed 17 June 2016.

Makumbe, J. 1998. *Democracy and development in Zimbabwe: Constraints of decentralisation*, Harare: SAPES Trust.

Mambo, E. 28 September 2012. 'Fear as army invades Nyanga,' in: *The Independent*, Harare: Zimbabwe.

Marwezu, R. 25 July 2007. 'Mugabe withdraws allowances from chiefs backing MDC,' Available at: www.zimonline.com, Accessed 8 June 2016.

Masekesa, C. 16 June 2015. Headman ousted for supporting MDC-T,' in: *The Newsday*, Harare: Zimbabwe.

Mataire, L. 15 April 2016. 'Chiefs exempted from paying toll-gate fees,' Available at: www.zimbabwetoday.org, Accessed 9 June 2016.

Matambanadzo, P. 24 June 2013. 'Zimbabwe: Chiefs condemn political violence,' Available at: www.allafrica.com, Accessed 8 June 2016.

MDC Information and Publicity Department, 24 October 2004. 'ZANU-PF bribes traditional chiefs,' in: *The Standard*, Harare: Zimbabwe.

Moyo, N. 25 October 2013. 'Five more Binga village heads fired over alleged MDC-T links,' Available at: www.thezimbabwean.com, Accessed 8 June 2016.

Mudenge, S.I.G. 1988. *A political history of Munhumutapa*, Harare: Zimbabwe Publishing House.

Mugari, S. 18 February 2005. 'Chiefs' benefits to gobble $27.5 billion,' in: *The Zimbabwe Independent*, Harare: Zimbabwe.

Mukwambo, C. 29 July 2011. 'Chimanimani headman expels MDC supporters,' Available at: www.nzcn.wordpress.com, Accessed 17 June 2016.

Murray, D.J. 1970. *The governmental system in Southern Rhodesia*, Oxford: Clarendon Press.

Murevererwi, R. 18 November 2010. 'Zimbabwe: Chief Chaka makes a peace declaration for Chirumhanzu,' Available at: www.shout-africa.com, Accessed 7 June 2016.

Musodza, C. 17 February 2011. 'Chiefs spearhead national healing process,' Available at: www.mediacentrezim.com, Accessed 8 June 2016.

Mwando, Y. 4 June 2008. 'Zimbabwe: Traditional leaders Mugabe's trump card,' Available at: www.reliefweb.int, Accessed 8 June 2016.

NAZ, N1/2/1: 10 May 1899. Chiefs and Tribes in Mashonaland and Salaries.

NAZ, NUA2/1/1: 21 December 1896. NC Umtali to CNC.

NAZ, NUA2/1/5: 19 July 1904. NC Umtali to CNC.

NAZ, NUC2/3/2: 8 February 1912. NC Inyanga to Superintendent of Natives.

NAZ, S1428/32/5: 14 October 1897. NC Umtali's Quarterly Report.

NAZ, S2583/542: 26 January 1951. Memorandum from Minister of Native Affairs.

NAZ, S2583/542: 1 July 1951. Executive Council Minute 1278/52: Subsidies of Chiefs.

NAZ, S2583/542: 23 January 1953. Secretary of Native Affairs, List and Grades of Chiefs in the Colony.

NAZ, S2583/542: 28 June 1956. Circular from Secretary of Native Affairs to NCs.

NAZ, S2583/542: 8 May 1957. Draft Circular to all NCs.

Ncube, X. 17 May 2016. 'Chiefs demand more from government,' in: *The Newsday*, Harare: Zimbabwe.

Nehanda Radio, 24 March 2011. 'The 82-year-old headman tortured by ZANU-PF,' Available at: www.nehandaradio.com, Accessed 17 June 2016.

Newsday, 25 May 2011. 'Mwonzora case referred to Supreme Court,' Harare: Zimbabwe.

Newsday, 29 May 2012. 'Bulilima-Mangwe chiefs under fire,' Harare: Zimbabwe.

Newsday, 25 September 2012. 'MDC-T Senator Rimbi dies,' Harare: Zimbabwe.

Newsday, 29 May 2015. 'Chief Seke publicly pledges allegiance to Mugabe, ZANU-PF,' Available at: www.newsday.co.zw, Accessed 8 June 2016.

Nkala, S. 13 April 2015. 'Tsholotsho campaign raises stink,' Available at: www.southerneye.co.zw, Accessed 9 June 2016.

Nyaumwe, S. 3 August 1998. Interview at Sherukuru Business Centre, Mutasa District, Zimbabwe.

Nyakadzeya, P. 7 November 2013. 'Political role of chiefs undermines democracy,' Available at: www.financialgazette.co.zw, Accessed 7 June 2016.

Palley, C. 1966. *The constitutional history and law of Southern Rhodesia, 1888-1965, with special reference to imperial control*, Oxford: Clarendon Press.

Proctor, A. and Phimister, I. 1991. *People and power*, Harare: Academic Books.

Nyathi, K. 8 March 2012. 'Zimbabwean chiefs demand guns ahead of polls,' Available at: www.nation.co.ke, Accessed 7 June 2016.

Phiri, G. 29 February 2016. 'Chiefs now Mugabe's auxiliaries,' Available at: www.zimbabweelection.com, Accessed 7 June 2016.

Randles, W.G.L. 1981. *The empire of Monomotapa from the 15ᵗʰ to the 19ᵗʰ century*, Gwelo: Mambo Press.

Ranger, T. O. 2001. 'Democracy and traditional political structures in Zimbabwe 1890 – 1999,' in: N. Bhebe and T. Ranger (eds.) *The historical dimensions of democracy and human rights in Zimbabwe, Volume One: Pre-colonial and colonial legacies*, Harare: University of Zimbabwe Publications, pp. 31-52.

Ransford, O. 1968. *The rulers of Rhodesia from earliest times to the referendum*, London: Camelot Press.

Runatsa, E. 12 April 1998. 'Government must redefine the role of chiefs,' in: *The Sunday Mail*, Harare: Zimbabwe.

Saunyama, J. 10 March 2013. 'Headmen demand perks rise,' in: *The Standard*, Harare: Zimbabwe.

Sibanda, T. 9 November 2006. 'Chief has no power to summon MDC candidate to court,' Available at: www.swradioafrica.com, Accessed 17 June 2016.

Sibanda, T. 21 February 2008. 'Chief Rimbi of Chipinge contesting elections as MDC candidate,' Available at:

www.swradioafrica.com, Accessed 8 June 2016.

Sibanda, T. 4 November 2010. 'MDC official beaten up for refusing to buy ZANU-PF card,' Available at: www.swradioafrica.com, Accessed 17 June 2016.

Sithole, Z. 15 September 2011. 'Vote ZANU, I need transport- chief,' Available at: www.nzon.wordpress.com, Accessed 9 June 2016.

Southern Rhodesia Government, 1938. 'Government Notice Number 108,' Salisbury: Southern Rhodesia Government.

Standard, 24 November 2002. 'Leave with your food, chief tells donors,' Harare: Zimbabwe.

Storry, J.E.G. 1974. *The shattered nation*, Cape Town: Howard Timmins.

Weinrich, A.K.H. 1971. *Chiefs and councils in Rhodesia: Transition from patriarchal to bureaucratic power*, London: Heinemann.

Zimbabwe Daily, 10 October 2010. 'Chiefs get top-of-the-range cars, salary hike,' Available at: www.thezimbabwedaily.com, Accessed 9 June 2016.

Zimbabwe Daily, 13 December 2010. 'MDC activist fined, Deputy Minister Faces arrest,' Available at: www.thezimbabwedaily.com, Accessed 17 June 2016.

Zimbabwe Online Press, 13 August 2009. 'Headman in hot soup for presiding over cases,' Available at:
www.zimbabweonlinepress.com, Accessed 8 June 2016.

Chapter Eleven

A Constitutional 'Gamble': Re-visiting the COPAC Driven Constitutional Making Process in Zimbabwe

Tasara Muguti, Benias Tirivaviri, & Kudakwashe Mapetere

Introduction

The present chapter advances the thesis that Zimbabwe has not yet reached a stage in which a truly people driven and democratic constitution can be crafted due to multi-party vested political interests as demonstrated by the political leadership in the Global Political Agreement (GPA).This claim is premised on a critical estimation of the way the COPAC driven constitutional making process was carried out. Indeed, the major political protagonists were always trying to dominate and manipulate the process at every stage for political expediency which in the end resulted in a 'constitution without constitutionalism'. This as Magaisa, (2009) notes literally meant that when those in power just come up with a set of rules that validate and legitimise their actions with very little input from the ordinary citizens. As a result, the views that were advanced by the people at the outreach meetings ended up not being the people but those of the dominant political parties. The generality of the people were not afforded an opportunity to express their views parsimoniously. There was too much politicisation of the constitutional making process to the extent that people were cowed into submission through manipulation, intimidation and in extreme cases even violence perpetrated by the dominant political parties (Eppel, 2010; Makumbe, 2012; Makuhlani, 2014; ZZZZICOMP, 2010; Sachikonye, 2012).

This chapter largely focuses on the circumstances which led to the drafting of a new constitution since 2009, the way the Constitution Parliamentary Select Committee (COPAC) led process was carried forward, the major impediments to a successful initiative and proffer the way forward in order to come up with a constitution that truly represents the people's aspirations and expectations for the sake of posterity. Article VI of the Global Political Agreement (GPA) of 15th September, 2008, focused on the constitution making process. It also institutionalised the Constitution Parliamentary Select Committee (COPAC) and mandated it to coordinate the constitution making process. The disparities in this process were that the dominant representatives in COPAC were from the three dominant political parties then; ZANU-PF, MDC-T and the MDC-M who had their own political agenda and interests. The aims of the parties involved became that of system manipulation instead of national development. Then the question for many was whether the process was truly people driven or political party posturing by the major political protagonists. The constitutional making process indeed failed to transform itself into real political and economic benefit to the people of Zimbabwe as a result of the context in which it was carried out.

A constitution is a critical document in the lives of a people as it is a fundamental point of all development issues and one of the pivotal tenets of the democratisation process. In the words of the late South African Chief Justice, Ismail Mohammed:

> The Constitution of a nation is not simply a structure which mechanically defines the structures of government and the relation between the government and the relation between the government and the governed, it is a "mirror of the national soul", the identification of the ideals and aspirations of a nation, the articulation of the values binding its people and disciplining its government...a super imposed constitutional arrangements that.... Do not address the real causes of the discontent, are sure to generate their own legitimacy crisis' (http://bulawayoyouthcouncil.wordpress.com//NYDT/Desktop/Consttutional in Final.doc, Retrieved 10/09/11).

A constitution is a set of laws and principles which direct how a country is to be governed and thus, directs development for the country. It contains a social contract between people and their leaders determining their relations. It should be viewed as a supreme document which governs the lives of a people; the leadership and the led (Alex Magaisa, 'Zim: Constitution without constitutionalism', http://www.newzim.proboards86.com, Retrieved 26 August13). A good constitution does not only promote good governance but it is also the cornerstone of development. It should provide the means for every citizen who is willing to work to prosper. The constitution should ensure that the legitimacy of the government is regularly established requiring that its powers are not assumed or exercised without the mandate of the people. This can be achieved through periodic, regular, free and fair elections administered under well-defined electoral laws enshrined in a nation's constitution. A good constitution ensures the protection of fundamental rights of a nation's citizens, impartiality and independent conduct of the major pillars of the state namely; the judiciary, the legislature and the executive and above all, security of all citizens and the rule of law. Indeed, the main objective of any nation should be to achieve a constitutional order that is legitimate, credible, enduring and structurally accepted by its people without compromising the integrity and effectiveness of good governance.

However, in many post-colonial African countries in general and in Zimbabwe in particular, the leadership has been facing daunting challenges in their endeavour to achieve constitutional order. Constitutions have been crafted, trampled upon with impunity and revised countless times to suit the whims of the political leadership and not the people (Olivier, 2007). It is disturbing to note that in most circumstances in which constitutional amendments have been effected, they have been instigated to come up with retrogressive clauses which stifle the people's freedom and provide immunity to the leadership and those closest to them. In Zimbabwe, for instance, the Constitution crafted in 1979 under the Lancaster House Agreement succumbed to a record of 19 amendments before it was replaced by a new constitution in 2014.Prior to 2014, the Zimbabwean constitution has had little positive impact shaping the socio-economic and political evolution of the country. There was no clear separation of powers since the executive was able to consolidate its political dominance over the legislature and the judiciary (Olivier, 2007).

The qualitative research paradigm was used to gather data with a preponderance of the narrative approach meant to understand, convey and create meaning from people's experiences in the constitution making process. The researchers were the chief instruments and their immersion into proceedings of the constitution making process enabled them to elicit data as the principal research instruments.

Background to the COPAC process

Though Zimbabwe's constitutional history dates back to 1888 when the British South Africa Company (BSAC) gained exclusive mining rights over the country from Lobengula, the constitutional history and development will be limited to the decolonisation and independence phase marked by the Lancaster House Agreement of 1979.At independence in Zimbabwe (1980), the country inherited a heavily compromised Lancaster House Constitution which was meant to protect and perpetuate minority "white" Rhodesian interests. Like most transitional constitutions, the constitution was designed to give majority rule to the "black" people but at the same time maintaining Rhodesian white minority interests. The justification was that the constitution would facilitate a smooth transition of power from the white minority to the black majority. Indeed, relations between the blacks and whites had been heavily strained by the Second *Chimurenga* (war of liberation) which had dragged on for almost two decades since the 1960s.A lot of lives had been lost both within and outside the country. Hence, there was the obvious danger of retribution against the whites by the blacks who had been subjugated to colonial rule and its excessive abuses for almost a century.

The new constitution at independence was very defective as it inherited most of the previous regime's oppressive pieces of legislation like The Law and Order Maintenance Act (1960) and Miscellaneous Offences Act lock, stock and barrel (Raftopoulus and Savage, 2004). This legislation had been used by the illegal Smith regime to oppress black people's freedoms and liberties. The majority of the people had thought that these oppressive pieces of legislation and above all, the clause on land ownership were to be scrapped off once the transitional constitutional arrangements had expired after the stipulated first ten years of independence. However, this was not to be. If anything, these Acts were kept lock, stock and barrel and in some instances, they were even further reinforced when the new government began to experience growing political resentment by its citizens. To make matters even worse, some new oppressive pieces of legislation were also instituted to complement the existing ones. These included Public Order and Security Act (POSA 2002), Access to Information and Protection of Privacy Act (AIPPA 2002) and other media reforms which stifled people's freedom of expression, association and assembly (Raftopoulus and Savage, 2004).This was despite the fact that in the early days of independence, the state had enjoyed excellent relations with the workers, students, civic organisations, peasants and the general populace at large.

Undeniably, as the economy began to show signs of distress from the late 80's onwards, the state became heavy-handed and authoritarian towards its citizenry which was becoming more and more restless. The Zimbabwe Congress of Trade Unions (ZCTU) which was an umbrella body for private sector workers, students and civic organisations was beginning to show open signs of resentment and defiance towards the way the government was running the state affairs. Among other concerns, they were beginning to question why the leadership was failing to survive within the confines of the Marxist–Leninist philosophy which had guided Zimbabwean politics during the first decade of independence. This was reflected in the failure by the leadership to adhere to its own Leadership Code. The ZANU-PF leadership was amassing property contrary to the dictates of the Leadership Code. The ZCTU was also beginning to express resentment to corruption and mismanagement among the leadership at different levels. Cases in point were the Willowgate and the Grain Marketing Board scandals which sucked a number of high profile government ministers such Maurice Nyagumbo, Fredick Shava, Enos Nkala, Dzingai Mutumbuka and Kumbirai Kangaiat the time (Makumbe, 1994). Even the Zimbabwean President, Robert Mugabe bemoaned the lack of discipline and corruption among the leadership by noting that:

We must now admit ... that we are reaping the bitter fruits of our unwholesome and negative behaviour. Our image as leaders of the party and government has never been so badly tarnished. Our people are crying for our blood and they certainly are entitled to do so after watching our actions and conduct over the nine years of our government' (Judith Todd 2007: 289).

While commissions of inquiry were instituted to investigate the scandal at the time, there were no individuals who were prosecuted and convicted though some ministers like Maurice Nyagumbo, Frederick Shava, Dzingai Mutumbuka and Enos Nkala resigned on their own volition out of shame (Makumbe, 1994). By the beginning of the 1990's, the Zimbabwean economy was beginning to show signs of serious economic distress. The government was eventually forced to introduce the Economic Structural Adjustment Programme (ESAP) in order to revive the ailing economy. The reforms that were prescribed by the International Monetary Fund and the World Bank resulted in the liberalisation of the economy which greatly undermined the economic productivity of the country triggering widespread retrenchment and joblessness. According to Raftopoulus and Mlambo, (2009:188) the implementation of ESAP in Zimbabwe witnessed an average economic decline of 4 per cent, recovering to only 2.9 per cent in 1998 and 1999. By 1999, statistics provided by the government revealed that 20,710 workers had lost their jobs since the inception of the economic liberalization programme. However, the ZCTU estimated the figure to be over 30,000 (Raftopoulus and Mlambo, 2009). The urban retrenchments had ripple effects in rural areas as retrenched workers either sent their families home or went with them. This increased pressure on land and natural resources leading to a flare up of social tensions that had failed to be resolved in the first decade of independence. These include racial inequalities and land ownership.

The resultant suffering that emanated from the negative effects of ESAP forced Zimbabweans from all walks of life to mobilise and unite against the government. Opposition political parties, students, workers, non-governmental organisations, war veterans, the emerging indigenous black business people and the landless people teamed up to fight for redistribution of land which remained in the hands of the whites well after the expiry of the Lancaster House provisions (Raftopoulus and Mlambo, 2009). The people were now awakening to the fact that the Zimbabwe crisis was to some extent emanating from a constitutional crisis that had plunged the country into a serious socio-economic and political quagmire. The ZCTU under the leadership of Morgan Tsvangirai, the churches and other stakeholders formed the National Constitutional Assembly (NCA) and began to mobilize the people for a holistic amendment of the constitution. The NCA was founded in 1997, and officially launched in 1998 at the University of Zimbabwe, by Zimbabwean individual citizens and civic organizations, amongst which were trade unions, opposition parties, student groups, women's groups, representatives of the informal sector and church groups (Todd, 2007:408). The NCA was inspired by the popular uprisings of the 1990s, and came to see the present constitution as an ideal umbrella cause in pursuing an array of political, social and economical causes. The constitution was seen by the NCA, then led by Lovemore Madhuku, as particularly problematic in that it allowed too much power to be vested in the hands of the president and that it was heavily compromised as it continued to maintain certain clauses which had outlived their usefulness. The NCA was advocating for a people – driven constitution in which all the people had a right to express their views freely on governance issues. In Madhuku's words:

> The content of a Constitution must be determined by the political experiences of the people in that country. People must have a sense of meaning of what they are putting in there. So you can't just get a Constitution from the library. The Constitution must come from the spirit and hearts of the people
> (http://www.kubatana,net/html/archive).

The formation of the Movement for Democratic Change (MDC) in 1999 added more weight to the cries for an indigenous/ home grown constitution. Faced with the NCA initiative, the government was quick to hijack the constitution initiative and constituted the Constitutional Commission (1999) which was tasked to come up with a new constitution for the country. However, attempts to craft a new constitution in the year 2000 were rejected by the people in a referendum due to a number of interlocking factors. The "no vote" was due to the fact that the government initiative was dominated by views of the ruling party ZANU-PF which was determined to maintain the status quo. Since people realized that their views were heavily diluted in the proposed constitutional document they overwhelmingly voted against it and as a result the Lancaster House document inherited at independence prevailed. The no vote was the first democratic process which was also a litmus test for ZANU-PF to see if people still supported it. The Hansard (2001) observed that the Constitutional Commission lacked wider consultation as it was purely elitist (500 members comprising of mostly Members of Parliament) from the ruling ZANU-PF party. The people's perception was that it was an attempt by ZANU-PF to smuggle a constitution of its liking. In her comparison of the 2000 Constitutional Commission initiative with the Rhodesian regime's attempts in the Pearce Commission (1971 and 1972) to compel the African people to say 'yes' to a deal that would have led to independence under the Ian Smith's.

Rhodesian Front without majority rule, Todd (2007: 410) aptly noted that "the deal then was about the retention of power by Ian Smith and the Rhodesian Front. The deal today is about the retention of power by Robert Mugabe and ZANU-PF". After the people resoundingly voted against the 2000 constitutional initiative, the search for a viable, acceptable and credible constitution continued thereafter. In September 2007, Zimbabwe's three main political parties, ZANU-PF, MDC-T and MDC negotiated in secret The Kariba Draft Constitution, a document which was later referenced in Article 6 of the Global Political Agreement (GPA). ZANU-PF wanted to smuggle the document into the COPAC driven process so that it would become a reference point to the constitution making process.

The institution of Constitutional Amendment No. 19 resulted in the Global Political Agreement (GPA) of 2008. The Agreement gave birth to the Government of National Unity (GNU) between ZANU-PF and the two MDC formations led by Morgan Tsvangirai and

Arthur Mutambara, respectively. Among a host of other things, the GPA reiterated the need for a people driven and people oriented constitution in Zimbabwe. Article VI of the Global Political Agreement (GPA) explicitly states that 'the fundamental right and duty of the Zimbabwean people to make a constitution by themselves and for themselves' and provides for the people of Zimbabwe 'to hold such public hearings and such consultations as it may deem necessary in the process of public consultation over the making of a new constitution for Zimbabwe' (Global Political Agreement 2008: 6-7). As such, since June 2010, Zimbabwe embarked on a new drive towards the crafting of a new 'people' driven constitution. The justification was that it was imperative for Zimbabwe to come up with a new constitution before any meaningful and credible elections could be held. This was based on the fact that the rule of law had been under constant attack in Zimbabwe and that central to this was the negation of the following: the independence of the judiciary; the independence of the Attorney- General's office, the prosecution service and the need for security sector reforms. Therefore, it is in the light of the above historical background that the COPAC constitutional process should be examined. Other countries that had embarked on participatory constitution-making processes before were Albania, Eritrea, South Africa, Uganda and to a lesser degree, India, Iraq and Nigeria (http://www.sokwanale.com, August 2012).

The unfolding of the COPAC led constitutional initiative

The process to draw a new constitution in Zimbabwe started in earnest in mid-2010 after a lot of bickering. The wrangling emanated from the fact that there was lack of unanimity among the different interested stakeholders on the way the constitutional process was to unfold. Towards the launching of the constitutional process, Amnesty International, (2014) acknowledged rampant reports of intimidation in rural areas where villagers were threatened with violence if they did not support the ZANU-PF's position that the new constitution was to be premised on the heavily compromised Kariba Draft. Initially, the threats were meant to intimidate villagers into endorsing the heavily compromised Kariba Draft constitution

(*The Financial Gazette*, 25/03/10), Shumba, 2010). The Kariba Draft constitution, which was agreed to in 2007 by the then former ruling party, ZANU-PF and the two formations of the MDC without public consultation, was vehemently criticised by civil society organisations as an attempt by the parties to impose a constitution on the people (http://www.kubatanablogs.net/kubatana/p=3222, posted 10/10/10). Once the initial hitches were overcome the constitutional outreach programme was launched on the 16th June 2010 at the Harare International Conference Centre (HICC) by the three Principals to the GPA, Robert Mugabe, Morgan Tsvangirai and Arthur Mutambara. Though the Principals preached the gospel of inclusivity and non-violence at the launch, the First Stakeholders Conference had an inauspicious beginning as it was not without incident. There was sloganeering and singing by supporters of the main political parties, ZANU-PF and the MDC, and the pandemonium that ensued made it impossible for the speakers of parliament to commence the proceedings. There was selective violence at the launch in which MDC delegates including the Speaker of Parliament were allegedly attacked by ZANU-PF militia and war veterans who advocated that the new constitution be crafted around the Kariba Draft (Interview with Stanford Chiondegwa, Masvingo, 07/04/2012).However, the conference was only able to proceed the following day after the intervention of the 'Principals'. The nationwide public outreach commenced on 23 June 2010 and the outreach meetings were concluded within 90 days as stipulated by the GPA. The COPAC process involved: the appointment of the Constitution Select Committee, the First All Stakeholders' Conference, outreach consultations, data upholding, setting of thematic committees, the drafting stage, the Second All Stakeholders' Conference, Draft Constitution Debate in Parliament and the referendum. The closure to the COPAC process came down with the holding of the constitutional referendum on 16 and 17 March 2013 in which 94.5% voted in its favour (Mukuhlani, 2014). While the authors in no way attempt to critique all the COPAC stages, a critical analysis of how the outreach programmes were largely carried forward will leave one in no doubt that the constitutional making process which was a product of the GPA was not 'people driven' but driven to the people by the dominant political players.

A critical reflection of the process

Judging the way the process was carried forward, one is left in no doubt that Zimbabwe has not yet reached the stage in which a truly people driven and democratic constitution can be crafted. Indeed, one did not have to wait for the finalisation of the process to reach that conclusion. A flawed and defective process could never ever have delivered a perfect document. Most respondents noted that the constitutional making process was as critical as the final content of the constitution itself to the extent that a defective constitution making process led to a defective outcome. As observed by Blessing Vava, an NCA information officer 'if the people participate fully and effectively in a proper people driven constitution reform process there is assurance that the outcome will be a document that enshrines fundamental liberties and lays the foundation of a free and democratic nation' (The zimbabweanmail.com/opinion/8181-consttutionnalism-zimbabwe.htmlposted10/10/11).

Nevertheless, the COPAC driven constitutional making process was marred by a lot of errors, inconsistencies and controversies which obviously had serious implications for the final outcome. Among other constraints, the process was affected by logistical problems, an inhibiting environment, political party influence and coaching, political intolerance and loss of life, lack of political will and racial discrimination. The process was also characterised by intimidation and violence perpetuated by the supporters of the main political parties in Zimbabwe and above all, the security sector which remained highly politicised even in the new political dispensation brought about by the GPA. This was anticipated since the interests of the political protagonists seemed to overshadow national interests in the Zimbabwean political landscape. Thomas Deve, a policy analyst commented that 'in the prevailing political environment, the political stakes were so high that to think of a people driven constitution remained a pipe dream' (Interview with Thomas Deve, 15/03/12). Mugabe and his party ZANU-PF were determined to maintain the status quo which undoubtedly gave them unlimited access to state power. The two MDC formations did not only want to deal with the Mugabe regime but with their own contestations over future electoral rivalry and positioning over possible state power (Raftopoulos, 2010, Muguti, *et al*, 2013). As noted by Terence:

> it was very treacherous of the MDC, especially the formation led by the PM to vilify and victimize its civic friends and strategic partners for trying to knock sense to the party and its leadership that they were playing their cards wrong in allowing themselves to fall for the ZANU-PF trap by making it a preserve of the politicians alone to author a constitution on behalf of the people' (*The Dailynews on Sunday*, May 20-26, 2012).

Logistical challenges

On the first day of the commencement of the outreach programme, there was confusion as COPAC had allegedly failed to provide adequate resources to outreach teams. The outreach programme was marred by a myriad of challenges after its launch as members of the teams were failing to get food at hotels with authorities having backtracked on prior arrangements. COPAC delayed the disbursement of the Shona version booklets for the talking points and recording equipment (Annual Review of The Performance of the Inclusive Government of Zimbabwe, February 2010- February 2010). Many respondents in Chivi District (Masvingo Province) noted that most COPAC outreach teams arrived at venues late or never turned up at all. As a result, the meetings were generally characterized by low attendance levels as people would leave the meeting venues dejected after having waited in vain. In some instances, consultative meetings failed to take place because the people were not advised in time for the meetings. Some interviewees felt that this was sometimes deliberately so as to disadvantage supporters of other political parties. Some residents of Masvingo opined that a consultative meeting held at Masvingo Teachers' College was only known to ZANU-PF supporters and hence, selected views were produced. In Mashonaland East, for instance, outreach teams failed to conduct meetings as teams were evicted from hotels as a result of non-payment or late payment of hotel bills by COPAC. At one stage, the Midlands outreach teams had to travel back to Harare for accommodation after failing to secure accommodation in the Midlands Province (Annual Review of the Performance of the Inclusive Government of Zimbabwe, February 2010- February 2010). Some residents of Masvingo testified to the fact that outreach teams were ejected from Lees Inn, the Chevron and Flamboyant hotels for the same reason. COPAC blamed its shortcomings on the fact that it had difficulties in accessing the requisite funds from donors and government on time.

However, while COPAC admitted that it faced daunting financial challenges, some of the administrative and implementation challenges could have been avoided and it could have achieved a lot more with fewer resources if direct consultation with or even direct involvement of the civic society (CSOs) had been allowed. It is a truism that a number of these organizations have functional structures in rural areas which they use in their work with specific interest groups which COPAC could have taken advantage of by consulting or including in the process. Some of the organisations that could have been made use of include Zimrights, Care International and Red Cross International, among others. The other challenge was that COPAC's work was shrouded in secrecy to the extent that the public outreach programme was dogged by controversy. In January 2010, COPAC was temporarily forced to suspend the outreach programme due to political party differences over secondment and impartiality of the outreach rapporteurs. The resultant effect of such cancellation meant that COPAC continued to miss stipulated deadlines to the extent that the Referendum once slated for July 2010 was not met (Civil Society Magazine, 2010 volume1). Indeed, almost two months beyond its initial set deadline, the COPAC driven process tottered from one crisis to the other.

An inhibiting environment

Contrary to Article 18(e) of the GPA which unmistakably affirmed that parties to the agreement should 'take all measures necessary to ensure that structures and institutions they control are not engaged in the perpetration of violence', evidence on the ground demonstrated beyond doubt that the ZANU-PF machinery was still intact. This proved that the Inclusive Government was not successful in dismantling the infrastructure that was used by political parties to maintain the status quo. Violence by pseudo war veterans and youth militia was witnessed in many parts of the country prior to the unveiling of the constitutional making process (Annual Review of The Performance of the Inclusive Government of Zimbabwe, February 2010- February 2010). Shumba, (2010) observed that the process was hijacked by ZANU-PF sympathisers and functionaries such as the army and militia who were intimidating villagers to support the Kariba Draft. A Short Wave (SW) Radio report stated that:

> The Joint Operations Command (JOC), a state security organisation only accountable to Robert Mugabe, is spearheading ZANU-PF campaign to foist the Kariba draft on the people of Zimbabwe...Armed and uniformed soldiers have been threatening and intimidating villagers to support ZANU-PF's views in many districts of Manicaland and Masvingo provinces (Amnesty International, 29/06/2010).

ZANU-PF supporters also attacked human right activists. Erwin van der Borght, Amnesty International's Africa director indicated that '...intimidation and harassment of activists undermines Zimbabwe's efforts to a new constitution with public consultation and is a worrying reminder of the organised violence that took place in 2008' (Amnesty International, 29/06/2010).Amnesty international further observed that in the six months leading to the commencement of the COPAC process it had received reports '...of intimidation in rural areas with villagers threatened with violence ahead of the formal start of the constitutional process' (Ibid).

This obviously militated against full citizen participation. It was further disturbing to note that individuals and CSOs organisations intending to do civic organisation work were arrested for allegedly contravening draconian pieces of legislation like POSA and AIPPA.

Thus, the fear of repression perceived or real, had a negative impact on the extent to which people were eager to take part in the outreach constitutional process. This then gives credence to the argument that Zimbabwe has not yet reached a stage where a people driven constitution can be genuinely embarked upon since the ground is not even. The constitution making process had emerged in conditions that were generally inhibitive to good constitution making. Short term bargains by the elites and powerful interests groups militated against the working for an everlasting constitution for the country. Restrictions of fundamental freedoms such as freedom of association, freedom of speech and expression definitely undermined the credibility of the constitutional making process and this was witnessed on countless occasions during the outreach programmes throughout the country. It is telling to note that on the 24th of June 2009, hardly two days into the inception of the outreach programme, three Zimbabwe Peace Project (ZPP), Zimbabwe Election Support Network (ZESN), Zimbabwe Lawyers for Human Rights (ZLHR) Independent Constitutional Monitoring Project (ZZZICOMP) observers, Tapera Maveherevhedze, Godfrey Nyarota and Cornelius Chengu were arrested at Makunu Primary School, Mutare North, Manicaland Province where they were monitoring the constitution making process. They were accused of practicing journalism without accreditation (Annual Review of The Performance of the Inclusive Government of Zimbabwe, February 2010 - February 2010). This was viewed as a contravention to Section 81 (3) of AIPPA. Reports indicated the three monitors were arrested at the instigation of a well-known ZANU-PF activist and a member of the Zimbabwe War Veteran Association. Another activist in Mutare, Eddy Ziyera, and the political coordinator of an independent monitoring project was detained for many hours and later on discharged without charge for having brought food for the detained monitors (Amnesty International, http://wwwkubatanablogs,not/Kubatana/?p=3222, posted 10/10/11). In Marondera (Mashonaland East) on the 25th June, three MDC-T activities, Rodrick Shamu, Themba Musimara and Mkanyaidze were abducted by unidentified state security agents and were later found detained at Marondera Police Station. In another incident a few days later, Amnesty International alleged that three other civil society monitors, Paul Nechishanu, Artwell Katandika and Shingairayi Garira were abducted by ZANU- PF supporters to Scarffel Farm in Kaonde District in Mashonaland West and assaulted with logs. The three sustained serious bodily injuries as a result of the attacks (Amnesty International, http://wwwkubatanablogs,not/Kubatana/?p=3222, posted 10/10/11). The above incidents demonstrate that the environment in which the COPAC driven process was carried out was politically charged making it impossible for people to air their views and opinions without restraint.

Some people even lost their lives during the outreach programmes which further reinforce the fact that the time for a people driven constitution is not yet ripe. ZANU-PF was accused of having initiated an operation code named *'Vhara Muromo'*(shut your mouth) in the rural areas to suppress dissenting voices during the outreach meetings (Annual Review of The Performance of the Inclusive Government of Zimbabwe, February 2010- February 2010, Makumbe, 2011). Reports by CSOs and the independent media collaborate that Manicaland and Masvingo recorded the largest number of violent attacks and cases of intimidation. In January 2010 alone, about eight (8) cases of torture, assault and various forms of intimidation attributed to ZANU-PF youths, the Zimbabwe Republic Police (ZRP) and the Zimbabwe National Army (ZNA) personnel were reported in Mudzi, Kuwadzana, Domboshava, Mhondoro, Chiramwiwa and Harare (Civil Society Magazine 2010, volume 1). These developments rendered the operating environment risky and unconducive for people to freely contribute during the consultative and outreach processes. Public consultations were intermittently cancelled in some areas following the outbreak of violence. On 11 August 2010two MDC activists Pedzisai and Muzambi were attacked by ZANU PF activists when they tried to attend a COPAC outreach meeting in Chipinge Central Constituency (A ZZZICOMP review of 11 to 22 August 2010).In Zaka District, Masvingo Province, Chiredzi and Hwange the violence against MDC supporters was perpetrated by then war veterans' leader Jabulani Sibanda. Sibanda was accused of intimidating, harassing and forcing people to air out ZANU-PF positions. Chiefs in Gutu District, among them, Chief Pius Mapetere Mawere, actually told Jabulani Sibanda in his face to stop dividing their people and interfering with their constitution making rights (Interview with Kudakwashe Mapetere, 26/04/2014). Many people were alleged to have been assaulted, displaced or went into hiding after having been accused of having expressed views that were regarded as sympathetic to the MDC and at variance with ZANU-PF expectations. The above position was serialized in several editions of *The Masvingo Mirror*, a Zimbabwean weekly newspaper.

The worst forms of chaos, intimidation, harassment and violence were experienced in Bulawayo and Harare towards the finalisation of the outreach process. As a result, some people in these areas failed to exercise their legitimate right to participate in the outreach constitutional process contrary to what had been articulated in the GPA. Violence erupted on 19 September 2010 at Mai Musodzi Hall in Mbare, Harare where there were clashes between ZANU-PF and MDC supporters resulting in the death of an MDC activist, Chrispen Mandizvidza (Interview with Chamunorwa 13/09/13). According to independent sources, most of the violent disruptions and disturbances were as a result of intolerance and allegedly perpetrated by ZANU-PF supporters. It was consistently reported in the *Zimbabwe Standard* and other independent newspapers that the constitution-making process constantly faced fresh setbacks as ZANU-PF would always step up efforts to disrupt the writing of a new constitution using war veterans and war collaborators who were using a combination of force and legal means to stop the process.

Political party influence and coaching

While Article vi of the GPA unequivocally stipulated that, 'it is the fundamental right and duty of the Zimbabwean people to make a constitution by themselves and for themselves' (GPA, 2008: 6), political parties undoubtedly hijacked the process and played a dominant role in the constitution making process. This was evidenced by the fact that rapporteurs were appointed on the basis of political affiliation. Furthermore, political party liaison committees were set up with representatives of ZANU-PF and the two MDC formations at community level (Annual Review of The Performance of the Inclusive Government of Zimbabwe, February 2010 - February 2010). A close examination of the above clearly reveals that the constitution making process was not all inclusive and eventually became the preserve of the dominant political parties, ZANU-PF and the two MDC formations in contravention of the letter and spirit of the GPA. Smaller political parties complained of exclusion in participating in the outreach programmes during the COPAC-led process (http://www.thezimbabwean.co.uk/news/32375/opposition-parties-threaten-constitution.html, Assessed 25 September 2014). As a result, this evidently undermined the people's right to craft a constitution of their own choice. The political parties, ZANU-PF and the MDC- formations stand accused of coaching people on what to say during the outreach meetings. This was collaborated by various reports which highlight that some people did not express their views freely as they were forced to adopt party positions. It is noted that 70 per cent (196) of the recorded coaching violations were in Mashonaland Central, Mashonaland West and Masvingo provinces which traditionally have always been ZANU-PF strongholds (ZZZICOMP Report Showing the outreach process, 11-22 August 2010). Even the MDC-T could not be absolved from coaching either. At one occasion the MDC-T national chairman, Lovemore Moyo urged supporters to wait for the party's guidance at the referendum. He uttered 'referendum is coming and we will come as a party to tell you how you should vote. We should be united when we go for the referendum. If we say it's okay, you have to support us, even if we say it's not good you have to support us as well' (*The Herald*, July 25, 2011). Indeed, the talking points to guide the public outreach process have been modelled along political party interests. Anoziva Muguti (Co-coordinator, Masvingo Residents and Ratepayers Association) acknowledged that he had the privilege of having sight of the drafts on the talking points distributed to the supporters of the GPA political parties (Interview with Anoziva Muguti 07/04/2012). He concluded that the "talking points" were very partisan, very prescriptive and suggestive with a high probability that the outreach programme was unlikely to adequately represent the views of the people. At a coaching session he attended organised by the MDC-T he discovered that people were left with very little option or none at all to air their own views other than those proffered by their political parties. This then gives credibility to the assertion by Trevor Maisiri (2010), executive director and co-founder of the African Reform Institute that Zimbabwe needs to project the voice of the people in the new constitution. He noted that 'the deception has always been to amplify the voices of the politicians in the GNU as that of the total heartbeat of Zimbabwe. Some if not all the leaders in the GNU have actually been extrapolating their own political voices laced in their political ambitions and desires and these have mistakenly been taken to be the national notion and desire' (Civil Society Magazine, 2010, volume 1). Welshman Ncube, then Secretary-General of the smaller MDC formation and an outstanding and reputable professor of constitutional law, hinted on countless times that some sticking points of the constitution would be negotiated by the political leaders and thus nullifying whatever input ordinary people would make.

Citizen attendance and participation

While COPAC was viewed as a public institution, the Committee stands accused of having operated clandestinely and in secrecy in some instances. Central to this accusation was COPAC's failure to furnish citizens with schedule meetings on time and progress of the process through both electronic and print media. In situations where COPAC publicized the meeting points and dates, it failed to comply with the publicized schedules. For instance, it was advertised in *The Sunday Mail* of 28th June 2010 that public consultations were scheduled to be held in Guruve District, Mashonaland Central Province but COPAC later decided to cover Shamva District without any prior notifications (Annual Review of The Performance of the Inclusive Government of Zimbabwe, February 2010- February 2011). Furthermore, while it was an acclaimed fact that it was a fundamental right of each and every Zimbabwean to take part in the constitution making process irrespective of their geographical location, there was no serious attempt by COPAC to engage the more than three million Zimbabweans living in the Diaspora.

Indeed, it should have been imperative for COPAC to incorporate these in its planning due to the uniqueness of the Zimbabwean historiography in which a large number of people have left the country due to economic and political instability, among other factors. Despite the fact that COPAC made promises to hold outreach programmes in the Diaspora through the establishment of a website, very little was accomplished since in most cases the line chart was inactive, hence many Zimbabweans failed to make their input to this all important process. This further reinforces the argument that Zimbabwe has not yet reached the stage in which a people driven constitution can be honestly crafted. Tatenda Chinoda, the Chairperson of the Community Based Organisations (CBOs) attributed limited people's participation to 'the fear of the known and unknown' (Tatenda Chinoda, 2010). He posits that many people could not make it to the outreach consultations centres because the meeting schedules were posted too late and that the schedules were deferred more often than not. He concluded by noting that 'the mere sight of men and women in dark suits and dark glasses sent shivers down the cognitive spines of civil society. Hitherto, there has not been any meaningful security sector reforms that allay their fears and assure them that these security organs have been depoliticised' (Tatenda Chinoda, 2010). The conduct of the COPAC teams also left a lot to be desired. There were instances in which COPAC teams lacked professionalism and failed to facilitate discussions that would allow participants to express their views freely. The speed with which some of the critical issues were expected to be responded to was astonishing. Only the party coached participants would quickly stand up and regurgitate coached material before independent thinkers made decisions. Translation of language from vernacular to English in some instances was a challenge to the rapporteurs. In a rigid style, the rapporteurs would move to the next issue and before some participants made head or tail of proceedings, the session would be closed.

Special interest groups

During the COPAC outreach programmes; there was little consultation with special interests groups like the youths and the differently-abled. The visually and hearing impaired were marginalised due to communication barriers as they used different media of communication (Braille and sign language) which were not being used during the outreach meetings. COPAC reports revealed only 22, 58% of outreach meeting participants nationwide were youths (http://www.copacgva,org, posted 21/10/11). By all standards this figure was incredibly low considering that the youth constitute about 66% of the Zimbabwean total population. The skewed youth participation was ascertained by statistics from some provinces in the country. Out of a total of 11 556 participants in Bulawayo, only 2 611 constituted youths. In Matabeleland South province only 7 000 youths took part in the process out of a total of 48 000 participants. The above statistics reflect that in each province less than 10% of the youth were able to cast their opinion during the collation stage (http://www.bulawayoyouthcouncil).

Furthermore, the above statistics just confirm the presence of the youths at the meetings and not necessarily their meaningful or positive contribution to the constitutional making process. This should be evaluated in the context of Zimbabwean historiography in which the political parties have permeated the youths and use them as political pawns to advance party interests. The youth driven violence in the elections of 2000, 2005, and 2008 authenticates this view. Furthermore, several media reports confirmed that ZANU-PF youth militia attempted to influence the way people responded at outreach meetings (http://www.financialgazette.com and http://www.sokwanele.com.thesis,Zimbabwe/archives.5442).

Critics of the COPAC process argue that in comparative terms, the 2000 constitutional process was much better because there was a deliberate attempt to include the participation of youths as evidenced by consultations in schools, colleges, universities, churches and some youth centres. The timing of the COPAC outreach stage was criticised as it resulted in the exclusion of students. The outreach meetings were carried out when universities and colleges were in session as well as during times when most school going pupils were in school. Consequently, these interest groups' views were not factored into the envisioned "supreme law of the land". Even in instances when COPAC made veiled attempts to reach out at tertiary institutions, the efforts were not always successful due to interference by political parties. We bear testimony to what transpired at Great Zimbabwe University when lecturers and students from both the University and the Teachers' College walked out in protest at an outreach meeting when ZANU-PF youths and women disrupted the process by singing revolutionary songs and chanted the slogan *'Va-Mugabe chete'* literally meaning Mugabe is the only one who should lead the country which was completely out of context and contrary to the proceedings.

Racial discrimination

While racism is outlawed under Zimbabwean law it reared its ugly face at some of the outreach meetings when "non-black" citizens were harassed and even ejected from COPAC meetings. Some Zimbabwean "white" citizens were barred from making contributions at the outreach meetings. This was done in the full glare of COPAC officials and the law enforcing agents. Indeed, high levels of intolerance and racial discrimination manifested themselves in Harare during the outreach meetings from 18th to 20th September 2010.At an outreach meeting at Queen Elizabeth High School, white residents and diplomats were chased away on the basis of their race. The COPAC team members and police did nothing to contain the situation (Annual Review of The Performance of the Inclusive Government of Zimbabwe, February 2010- February 2010, by the Civil Society Monitoring Mechanism (CISOMM). This obviously impacted on race relations and had the potential to marginalise the minority white population in particular in the country's socio-economic and political development.

The timing of the constitution making process

As already alluded to earlier on, a constitution is a critical document in the lives of a people as the supreme law of the country. It should be a document for posterity and sustainability. As such, it is prudent that the crafting of a constitution should be done in a conducive environment, one which is free of undue political influence. Unfortunately this was not the case with the process in Zimbabwe due its short-termism as it was mooted with the idea of elections in mind. Thomas Deve observed that the process was carried out in an environment in which the political stakes were very high between the major political parties and the heat of polarisation was on and this tended to cloud better judgment (Interview with Thomas Deve, 20/03/2012).There were divergent political viewpoints between the dominant political parties and they all wanted their party positions to prevail in the final document. Furthermore, the process was carried out by the major belligerence with elections in mind. Both ZANU-PF and the two MDC formations wanted the promulgation of a constitution that would guarantee them victory in the forthcoming election. The vested political interests by the different parties made the whole exercise a fast track process that paid scant regard to the views, aspirations and interests of the ordinary men and women, youth and the elderly which the new constitution, sought to protect. As noted by Viva:

It is grossly erroneous for ZANU-PF to use the constitution reform agenda as a yardstick to destroy the opposition MDC and buttress its hold to power. It is equally erroneous and wrong for the MDC to attempt to manipulate the new constitution making agenda as a shortcut to removing Mugabe. It should be taken into cognizant that writing a new constitution is one thing and political endeavours are other things. The arguments by the MDC that after the constitution making process the nation will go to the polls which will remove Mugabe and herald the advent of democracy should be dismissed as nonsensical and unrealistic' (The zimbabweanmail.com/opinion/8181-constitutionalism-zimbabwe.html posted 10/10/11).

According to Tichaona Zindoga, both ZANU-PF and MDC officials acceded to the fact that the COPAC process had a number of grey areas (*The Herald*, 27 July, 2011).At a discussion in Harare, Professor Ncube, a constitutional law expert and leader of the MDC-N observed that critical issues had not been captured because the outreach programme had been hurried, which led to core issues being overlooked. He further noted that only a fifth of the things that were supposed to be in the constitution were asked and that the time frame for making the constitution tentatively put at 18 months was inadequate (*The Herald*, 27 July, 2011).The fact that the process ran into all kinds of problems logistically and politically does not need a rocket scientist to ascertain. That it was likely to become a document for political expediency of the views of the dominant force is also a matter of fact, for better or worse. Then Prime Minister Tsvangirai even buttressed this view when he once revealed that his party would discard the product of the COPAC process if his party got into power. In this sense, one may argue that the Prime Minister in essence viewed the COPAC process as a conflict transformer. This was because the process was rushed and papered over as it was mooted with elections in mind. The dominant political parties were just hastening the process so that they could still use the currency of their marginal political popularity to win the impending elections. This has persuaded critics of the process to dismiss the COPAC initiative as antithetical to a people driven process. They perceived the process as a political tool aimed at capturing the needs and wants of the three parties to the GPA. This, they argued would culminate in a 'constitution without constitutionalism'.

Media reforms

It is paramount to underline that the right of freedom of expression is the bedrock of democracy and development. In a truly democratic dispensation, the media should play an important role in the enjoyment of the right to receive and disseminate information (Civil Society Position on the New Constitution of Zimbabwe 15/11/11). However, during the COPAC process, a restrictive media framework remained in place with repressive legislation very much unbroken, notwithstanding the appointment of the Zimbabwe Media Commission. The public media and broadcaster were steadfast in their support for ZANU-PF denigrating everything that appears to be pro-MDC. Reportage on the constitution making process unfortunately reflected that editorial slant. The biggest victim of that partisan approach was undoubtedly the reform process itself in that the input from the people reflected opinions from the political divide – as opposed to the views and aspirations of Zimbabweans (Civil Society Magazine, 2010 volume 1). It's interesting to note that the first draft was leaked to the press even before the document was made public. Thereafter, ZANU-PF apologists and propagandists Tafataona Mahoso, Vimbai Chiwaura and Christopher Mutsvangwa were screened live on Zimbabwe Television on countless times castigating the drafters and accusing them of all sorts of things including smuggling entirely new items into the document and ignoring the people's input. They were given vast acres of space in the public electronic and print media something that was not extended to the two MDC formations.

Challenges in resolving sticking issues

This was definitely an area of concern to all patriotic and progressive Zimbabweans. During the outreach programme, Zimbabweans had loudly and clearly made their views on issues like dual citizenship, death penalty, devolution of power, presidential powers and term of office, among others, known in spite of the intimidation and manipulation of the people by their political parties. However, the so-called 'parked' issues were shifted from the people to the Principals to the GPA who were to make a decision on these issues. This was in direct contravention to Section 6 of the GPA which unreservedly mandated the people to come up with a constitution of their choice. The process was also wrecked by what seemed to be an internal ZANU-PF plot unfolding within COPAC which appeared to involve the other two parties the MDC-T and the MDC-N designed to deliver a "technical knock-out blow" against Mugabe through term and age limits (*Zimbabwe Independent*, 2012). Observers posited that Mugabe feared that there was a faction linked to the then Defence Minister Emmerson Mnangagwa that included

311

ZANU-PF COPAC co-chairperson Paul Mangwana which intended to manipulate the process to its advantage. Obviously this did not augur well for the successful completion of the process as a constitutional making process should not be targeted at specific individuals but issues. George Charamba, Secretary for Media, Information and Publicity adumbrated that:

> It is sad that the constitution-making process has been surrounded by many people pushing for their own interests and the document is full of ugly fingerprints from external forces, embassies and political parties. We have 26 people working on the process and COPAC within its ranks is working against the same process with contentious meddling. This will be lifted from the management committee and taken straight to the principals who are signatories to the GPA and are now taking full control of the process (*Zimbabwe Independent*, 2012).

How disgusting! Indeed, COPAC and the Principals were not supposed or expected to negotiate for the people but just to collate their views.

In spite of the numerous challenges that confronted the COPAC process, the final draft of the Zimbabwean constitution was eventually signed by the Principals to the GPA on 31 January 2013. Since then, even some of the modest changes that were brought about by the new constitution have remained unimplemented. If anything, recent development in Zimbabwe indicate that the ruling ZANU-PF lacks the commitment and stamina to uphold the new constitutional provisions. Instead, three years into the new constitution, the ZANU-PF government, which 'resoundingly' won the 2013 general elections, leading to the demise of the GNU, is making several frantic efforts to amend the constitution in order to curtail people's fundamental democratic rights and freedoms. This is in response to mounting resentment by the majority of the people to ZANU-PF's misrule through massive countrywide demonstrations by Zimbabweans across the political, religious and civic divide. Thus, what we have is a leadership which is more concerned with constitutionality rather than constitutionalism. In the words of Magaisa, in Zimbabwe, 'instead of the constitution being the supreme legal document regulating the exercise of state power, it has become an instrument for control and attempts to legitimise arbitrary actions' (http://www.newzim.proboards86.com).

Concluding Remarks

Deducing from the foregoing argument it is discernible that Zimbabwe has not yet reached the stage in which a truly people driven constitution can be crafted. Thus, one thing that Zimbabwe needs in relation to its constitution is sobriety since a constitution is the soul of nation and the foundation upon which good governance should be anchored. Ideally, being sacrosanct, a constitution should safeguard the rights and protect the interests of the people in the exercise of state power. As Magaisa remarks 'As in South Africa in the early 1990s, a people-driven, more inclusive and home-grown constitution is what Zimbabwe desperately needs at this stage…that could be the most convenient forum to address the critical problems currently facing the country' (http://www.newzim.proboards86.com, Assessed 26/08/2013). Nevertheless, like in the previous constitutional making endeavours during the colonial and post-colonial periods, Zimbabwe once again took the wrong turn during the COPAC-led initiative. Zimbabweans dream of a new Zimbabwe which guarantees freedom for its entire people and which ensures a democratic government which enjoys legitimacy and the support of all patriotic Zimbabweans. A constitution should reflect the aspirations of the people, a country's history and the people's experiences. A constitution should be a timeless document which must not be reversed when there is change of leadership. The COPAC-led process was Parliamentary-driven and not people-driven hence it was a constitution to the people and not by the people. As it stands today, the meaning of a people driven constitution is interpreted differently by different people. Indeed, the meaning is heavily diluted and influenced by one's political persuasion. As correctly observed by Brian Raftopoulos:

> the complexity of this task must be set against the many challenges facing such a process, including the continued recalcitrance of a former

liberation movement determined to defy a plebiscite rejecting its continued rule, the impediments in implementing the regional body's protocols on democratic accountability, and the perplexing task of navigating a path between demands of the 'good governance' agenda of the international community and a still resonant anti-imperialist messaging of resurgent nationalist politics' (Raftopoulos 2010:710).

Perhaps, the best way forward in this heated, poisoned and polarised political environment is to have the process spearheaded by an independent committee to be nominated by all stakeholders; government, civil society and the business community. Indeed, the process should be inclusive and should be put forward to the public for robust debate and analysis. Responses from the public must then be collated, analysed and given a legal framework. Furthermore, Zimbabwe needs a united and vibrant civil society which is prepared to stand against the political leadership, since politics no matter how dumb, can get the better of reason. What we have now is a fractured and fragmented civil society which resultantly cannot provide a checking mechanism to the leadership. Indeed, during the COPAC process, civic society took three distinct positions. Some like the NCA decided to completely snub the process and adopt a 'Take Charge' stance, effectively condemning it and intending to campaign for a 'NO VOTE' come referendum time. Others decided to be active participants through strategic and meaningful engagement whilst others again resolved to monitor the process against established benchmarks and standards of constitutionalism and constitution making: openness, inclusiveness, transparency, legitimacy, accessibility, receptiveness, among others.

References

'Attack on activists sparks fears of a new wave of Zimbabwe violence', 29 June 2010, http://www.amnesty.org.en/news-and-updates, Retrieved 16 September 2014.
'JOC sends soldiers to enforce ZANU-PF views in outreach programme', 25 June 2010,

http://www.swradioafrica.com/news250610/joc250610.htm, Retrieved 16 September 2014.

Alex Magaisa, 'Zim: Constitution without constitutionalism', http://www.newzim.proboards86.com, Retrieved 26 August2013.

Amnesty International, 'Challenges facing the Constitutional Parliamentary Committee (COPAC) Outreach process since inception' http://wwwkubatanablogs,not/Kubatana/?p=3222, Retrieved 19 August 2014.

Annual Review of the Performance of the Inclusive Government of Zimbabwe, February 2010- February 2010, by the Civil Society Monitoring Mechanism (CISOMM).

Civil Society Position on the New Constitution of Zimbabwe, Commissioned by the Non- Governmental Organisations (NANGO)and the Crisis in Zimbabwe Coalition (CZC) on behalf of the Civil Society Constitutional Coordinating Mechanism (CSCCM), 15/11/11

Deals with way forward for constitution (http://www.zimbabwesituation.com.jun26a_2009.httl, Retrieved 16 July 2014.

Eppel, S., 'Initial Thoughts on the Matabeleland Constitutional Outreach Experience', *Solidarity*

Peace Trust, 1st Nov. 2010, http:/www.solidaritypeacetrust.org/870, Retrieved 10 October 2014.

Faith Zaba, 'Mugabe fights knockout plot', *Zimbabwe Independent*, April 5 to 12, 2012.

Gabriel Shumba, 'Zimbabwe in 2010: A Short Guide to the Future', http://www.irinnews.org/Reportaxpx?Reportld=85200, Retrieved 18 November 2014.

Global Political Agreement, 15 September 2008.

Haberson, J.W, (ed), 1987. *The Military in African Politics*, Praeger Publishers, New York.

Hansard, J. 2001. *Some lessons of Constitutional Making from Zimbabwe*, The Journal of African Law, No. 45(2), hhtp://www.zimbabwesituation.com.jun26a_2009.httl, Retrieved 19 October 11.

http://bulawayoyouthcouncil.wordpress.com//NYDT/Desktop/C onsttutional in Final.doc, Retrieved 10/09/11.

http://ww.financialgazette.com...91060/constitution_making_proc ess_hits_snag.html, Retrieved 15 May 2013.

http://www.bulawayoyouthcouncil, wordpress.com/2011/07/19/constitution-making-process-in-Zimbabwe- avenues-for-effective-youth-participation, Retrieved 10 May 2012).

http://www.kubatana.net/html/archive/demgg/100311inzwa.asp? specode=090707constdex&sector=DEMGG&year=2010&rang estart=271&intMain=2010&intTodayYear=2012, Retrieved 18 October 2014.

http://www.kubatanablogs.net/kubatana/p=3222, Retrieved 10 October 2013.

http://www.sokwanale.com, Retrieved 27 August 2014.

http://www.sokwanele.com.thesis,Zimbabwe/archives.5442, Retrieved 21 June 2013.

http://www.thezimbabwean.co.uk/news/32375/opposition-parties-threaten-constitution.html, Retrieved 25 September 2014.

http://www.Thezimbabweanmail.com/opinion/8181-constitutionalism-zimbabwe.html, Retrieved 10 October 2014.

Interview with Anoziva. Muguti (Co-coordinator, Masvingo Residents and Ratepayers Association), Masvingo, 07/04/2012.

Interview with Johnson Chamunorwa, Harare, 13/09/13.

Interview with Kudakwashe Mapetere, Masvingo, 26 April 2014.

Interview with Stanford Chiondegwa, Masvingo, 07/04/2012.

Interview with Thomas Deve, Senior Policy Analyst, SEATINI, Masvingo, 15/03/12.

Kersting, N., 2009. (Ed), Constitution in Transition: Academic Inputs for a New Constitution in Zimbabwe, Friedrich Ebert Stiftung, Harare.

Makumbe, J. 1994. 'Bureaucratic Corruption in Zimbabwe: Causes and Magnitude of the Problem', *Africa Development*, XIX: 3.

Makumbe, J. 2012. '*Zimbabwe: Political Context Study*', in Andreassen, B.A and Crawford, G. Eds, *Human Rights, Power and Civil Action: Comparative Analysis of Struggle for Rights in Developing Societies*, Routledge, Spring.

Moto, November 2001.

Magaisa, A., 'Constitutionality versus Constitutionalism: Lessons for Zimbabwe's Constitutional

Reform Process', *Open Society Initiative for Southern Africa*, 2011, http://www.osisa.org/openspace/zimbabwe/constitutionality-versus-constitutionalism

Muguti, T. Hlongwana, J. and Tavuyanago, B. 2013. '*Untenable Marriages: Situating Governments of National Unity in Africa's Political Landscape since 2000*', *Journal of Developing Communities* 1(4):149-157.

Mukuhlani, T, 2014. 'Zimbabwe's *Government of National Unity: Successes and Challenges in Restoring Peace and Order*', Journal of Power, Politics and Governance, vol 2(2):169-180.Olivier, L, 2007. *Constitutional Review and Reform and the Adherence to Democratic Principles in the Constitutions in Southern Africa*, OSISA.

Raftopoulos, B, 2010. '*The Global Political Agreement as a Passive Revolution*': Notes on Contemporary Politics in Zimbabwe', The Round Table: The Commonwealth Journal of International Affairs, 99:411, 705-718.

Raftopoulus, B and Savage, T. (eds), 2004.*Zimbabwe: Injustice and Reconciliation*, Institute of Justice and Reconciliation, Cape Town.

Raftopoulus. B and Mlambo. A, (eds), 2009. *Becoming Zimbabwe*, Harare, Weaver Press. Sachikonye, L., 2011. 'Zimbabwe's Constitution-Making and Electoral Reform Processes: challenges and opportunities', Draft paper prepared for the Conference on 'Legitimacy of Power – Possibilities of Opposition' organised by Department of Political Science and Public Administration, Makerere University and Chr. Michelsen Institute.

See media report from COPAC; http://www.copacgva,org, Retrieved 21 October 2013.

Sithole, N, 1988. *The Secret of American Success. Africa's Great Hope*, Gazaland Publishers, Washington DC.

Tatenda Chinoda, 'Zimbabwe National Constitutional Outreach Programme: Perspective of a Civil Society Observer – A Stream Of Consciousness'. Paper presented at A Building Local Democracy Workshop, Flamboyant Hotel, Masvingo, 13/10/10.

Terence, 'New constitution won't guarantee freedom', *The Dailynews on Sunday*, May 20-26, 2012.

The Financial Gazette, 25 March 2010.

The Herald, 25 July, 2011.

The Herald, 27 July, 2011.

Todd, J.G, 2007. *Through the Darkness, A Life in Zimbabwe*, Zebra Press, Cape Town.

Trevor Maisiri, "Civil Society – A Neglected Role" in Civil Society Magazine 2010, volume 1.

ZZZICOMP Report Showing the outreach process, 11-22 August 2010.

www.ingramcontent.com/pod-product-compliance
Lightning Source LLC
Chambersburg PA
CBHW022137020426
42334CB00015B/936